The Giant's Rival

THE GIANT'S RIVAL

The USSR and Latin America

Cole Blasier

Revised Edition

UNIVERSITY OF PITTSBURGH PRESS

Published by the University of Pittsburgh Press, Pittsburgh, Pa. 15260
Copyright © 1987, Cole Blasier
All rights reserved
Feffer and Simons, Inc., London
Manufactured in the United States of America

Library of Congress Cataloging in Publication Data

Blasier, Cole, 1925–
    The giant's rival : the USSR and Latin America / Cole Blasier. —
Rev. ed.
       p.   cm.—(Pitt Latin American series)
    Bibliography: p. 191
    Includes index.
    ISBN 0–8229–3576–7.   ISBN 0–8229–5400–1 (pbk.)
    1. Latin America—Relations—Soviet Union. 2. Soviet Union—
Relations—Latin America. I. Title. II. Series.
    F1416.S65B57   1986
    327.4708—dc 19   87–25174
                                            CIP

Chapter 6 is adapted from "The Soviet Union," in *Confronting Revolution: Security Through Diplomacy in Central America,* edited by Morris J. Blachman, William M. LeoGrande, and Kenneth Sharpe (New York, 1986). Assistance from William LeoGrande and Harold Sims is gratefully acknowledged.

*Dedicated
to the memory of
Philip E. Mosely
scholar, teacher, diplomat,
who befriended a generation of students
and led the development of
Soviet studies in the United States*

Contents

Tables

Preface

In what important ways have Soviet relations with Latin America changed since 1982 when the text of the first edition of *The Giant's Rival* was written? Most notable is that the USSR has developed much closer political and economic relations with Nicaragua. Relations with Cuba are about the same, although there appears to be a toughening of the stance of both governments on economic matters, and Cuban intervention in Africa has become old hat. In general there was an increase in Soviet trade with Latin America in the early 1980s due to Soviet purchases, especially in Argentina. By 1986, however, there was a decline in turnover, including Soviet exports.

Pro-Soviet Communist parties have continued to consolidate their pursuit of the peaceful road in countries like Argentina, Brazil, and Costa Rica, and of the armed road in countries such as El Salvador and Chile.

In Cuba, the most important country for Moscow, the pressing needs of the economy have continued to plague the Soviet budget, but Moscow has faithfully maintained its economic and military assistance. As in the past, Soviet unwillingness to satisfy all of Cuba's requests has put strains on the relationship. In 1986 the total of Soviet exports to and imports from Cuba, which had been rising steadily in the 1980s, appears to have declined for the first time since 1972. Soviet exports were about the same as the previous year, but imports fell off noticeably. One must approach such comparisons with caution, however, since Soviet price subsidies distort value figures as evidence of material exchanges.

Soviet ties with Nicaragua have increased steadily since 1982 as U.S. economic and military sanctions against the Sandinistas mounted. At that time it was already clear that Soviet economic aid would continue and that the Soviet government approved transfers of Soviet arms from Cuba. After 1982 Soviet economic and military assistance grew substantially, although it is still far less than that granted Cuba in the early years of the

Castro regime. Perhaps most noteworthy is that the USSR has become almost the sole supplier of petroleum to Nicaragua, probably under highly concessionary terms. Trade with Europe and other capitalist-oriented partners represents a declining share of Nicaragua's global commerce. Thus, the Sandinistas are far more dependent economically and militarily on the USSR and the socialist countries than in 1982. Soviet influence in Nicaragua probably has risen accordingly.

Soviet interference in El Salvador, which was so widely discussed in the early years of the Reagan administration, now receives less attention. The armed threat to the incumbent government continues, but probably more from the anti-Duarte military or the heavily armed Marxist-led opposition than from the Communist Party, one of its backers. The Communists have consolidated their armed supporters into a guerrilla group, one of five fighting the Duarte government.

By 1982 it was already clear that the USSR had more cordial relations with Grenada than with any other governments in the Americas except Cuba and Nicaragua. But the Soviet and Czech deliveries of arms to Grenada had not yet become public knowledge. Soviet arms agreements with the Bishop government were disclosed after U.S. forces occupied the island.

The guarded approach taken in the first edition to the prospects for Soviet trade has been supported by Soviet performance since 1980. Imports from Argentina, especially grain, zoomed in the early 1980s but fell off sharply in 1986, to about 15 percent of the previous year. Imports from Brazil also fell in 1986, but then stood somewhat above Argentina's. Except for Cuba and Nicaragua, Soviet trade with other countries was numerically insignificant. Most noticeable was the low level of Soviet exports.

In this edition, Soviet relations with Central America to 1987 are treated in a new chapter 6, the section on Grenada has been updated to the time of the U.S. landing, and the conclusions, chapter 8, have been rewritten in light of recent events. Many trends reflected in the original tables have continued into 1987; I have noted major new departures here and in the text.

The literature on Soviet relations with Latin America has grown since 1982. Some new titles are W. R. Duncan, *The Soviet Union and Cuba: Interests and Influence* (New York, 1985); William H. Richardson,

Mexico Through Russian Eyes, 1806–1940 (Pittsburgh, 1987); Aldo C. Vacs, *Discreet Partners: Argentina and the USSR Since 1917* (Pittsburgh 1984); Jiri Valenta and Herbert J. Ellison, eds., *Grenada and Soviet-Cuban Policy: Internal Crisis and U.S./OECS Intervention* (Boulder, 1986); and Augusto Varas, ed., *Soviet Latin American Relations in the 1980s* (Boulder, 1987). Eusebio Mujal Leon is also editing *The USSR and Latin America* scheduled for publication in 1988.

My thanks, as always, to Frederick A. Hetzel, Catherine Marshall, and others on the staff of the University of Pittsburgh Press for their high standards and forebearance.

Pittsburgh
1987

Preface to the First Edition

My professional life has been divided down the middle, half concerned with Eastern Europe and half with Latin America. I have lived and traveled about as much in one region as the other and know their languages equally badly. Even now, some friends who know me as a Sovietologist are astonished about my work in Latin America, and vice versa. Philip Mosely, to whom this book is dedicated, advised me in 1947 not to take up my Rotary Fellowship in Chile—sound advice then—but, if followed, would have spared you reading this preface. Some strange coincidences led me down this curious path.

Marking time between the Pacific War and returning to college in the summer of 1946, I stumbled on an article in *U.S. News and World Report* on the growing influence of the Communist party in Chile. Bernard Redmont was the responsible editor. His article ignited my interest in Latin America and the Soviet Union, a subject which has occupied me intermittently ever since. Early in 1979, I attended a party in Moscow where I met Redmont, then a CBS correspondent, for the first time, closing that circle thirty-three years later.

The genesis of this book happened in between. With Redmont's article in mind, I went to Chile for one year in 1947 and wrote a history of the Communist party. My interest in the USSR aroused by this research, I returned to New York in 1948 and entered and later completed graduate work in international relations and Soviet studies at the Russian Institute of Columbia University. During most of the 1950s, I was a Foreign Service officer in Belgrade, Bonn, Oberammergau (advanced Soviet studies), Washington (Soviet research), and Moscow. Leaving the service in 1960, I returned to the Latin American field at universities in Cali, Colombia, and Pittsburgh. By the middle 1970s, I was able to return again to Eastern Europe, first as an exchange scholar in Poland. In 1979, I became the first American scholar to undertake resident research on contemporary Latin America at the Institute of Latin America in Moscow. I have had frequent visits to the Soviet Union since as the U.S. representative for the U.S./USSR exchange in Latin American Studies.

The title of this book, *The Giant's Rival: The USSR and Latin America,* accurately and, in my view, regrettably, reflects the reality of Soviet-American rivalry in the region. As self-conscious competitors of the United States, Soviet leaders have always been preoccupied with discrediting imperialism and U.S. influence in the hemisphere. In their own way, U.S. officials have done no better, too often more concerned with Soviet or Communist threats in the region than with the Latin American countries themselves. I believe each corner of this troubled triangle would benefit, as would the world, if each dealt with the other two separately, allowing bilateral relationships to stand on their own merits. In the long run, both the Soviet Union and the United States will hurt their relations with Latin American countries if their policies are determined by super-power rivalries. Latin Americans do not want to become victims of Soviet-American political struggles. My title points up a lamentable reality, but one I do not seek to perpetuate.

My first debt for help in preparing this study is to Soviet scholars and administrators dedicated to the study of Latin America. If I had not had the benefit of their company and advice, I should never have gained such confidence as I now possess about the nature and origins of Soviet policy. Scholars from the Institute of Latin America are foremost among these: Victor Volsky, Director; Lev L. Klochkovsky and Anatoli N. Glinkin, chiefs of the departments of economics and international relations; A. D. Maevsky and Anatoli N. Borovkov of the international liason department; and Piotr Iakolev, who accompanied me on most of my appointments. Sergo Mikoyan and his staff of the journal *Latinskaia Amerika* were most helpful. I also appreciate the time that scholars took for me at the Institute of World Economy and International Relations, the Institute of the USA and Canada, the Institute of the International Workers' Movement, the Institute of Economics of the World Socialist System, the Ministry of Foreign Trade, the State Committee for Foreign Economic Ties, and the Chamber of Commerce. Most particularly, I appreciated the unfailing courtesy and helpfulness of the various librarians at the Institute of Latin America. I should like to go beyond this formal list to acknowledge the many instances of kindness by other scholars but will not do so out of respect for their privacy in the still sensitive state of U.S.-Soviet relations.

The most important things I have learned about Latin America came from residence in Mexico, Chile, and Colombia, my friends and associates in these countries being far too numerous to mention. With respect to my Latin American acquaintance in Moscow, I owe a special debt of gratitude to former Ambassador Carlos Serrate Reich of Bolivia and to Carlos Muñiz Ortega of Peru, the author of the first book on Soviet–Latin American relations, both of whom contributed so much to my research stay in Moscow. Other diplomats who received or entertained me include Horacio Adolfo Basabe and Carlos Rodolfo Rivas of Argentina, Obertal Mantovanelli Netto of Brazil, Hernando Pedrahita of Colombia, Elvin B. F. McDavid of Guyana, Benjamin A. L. Clare of Jamaica, Rogelio Martinez Aguilar of Mexico, Juan José Calle y Calle of Peru, and Ignacio Sucre of Venezuela. I have also had the pleasure both in the USSR and abroad of meeting many young Latin Americans who have studied in the USSR and whose views have proved most helpful. Ladun Anise of Nigeria and Pittsburgh gave invaluable advice on the Cuban role in Afica.

The Kennan Institute of the Woodrow Wilson Center in Washington, D.C., financed preparatory work for this book. Its secretary, S. Frederick Starr, gave me much appreciated assistance. My travel and residence in Moscow was financed by the International Research and Exchanges Board (IREX) in New York, whose president, Allen Kassof, took his valuable time to persuade an unbelieving veteran of the cold war that field research in the Soviet Union was feasible. I am also grateful to Wesley Fisher of IREX for his help and advice since my return. The National Council for Soviet and East European Research financed the bulk of the research and writing. The Department of Political Science and the Center for Latin American Studies of the University of Pittsburgh has supported me in innumerable ways. I am also most grateful to Eduardo Lozano and Dale Winkels, the Latin American and Slavic bibliographers of the University of Pittsburgh Hillman Library.

My research assistants, most particularly Silvia Borzutsky, Aldo Isuani, and Aldo Vacs, have helped gather material and given valuable criticism. Gerard Fichet of the Economic Commission for Latin America provided a masterful critique of the economic chapter, as did Carmelo Mesa-Lago the chapter on Cuba. James Malloy and Martha Blasier, my severest and most sympathetic critic, provided the impetus necessary to pull together what I hope is a coherent set of conclusions and recommendations.

Pittsburgh
1982

The Giant's Rival

1 The New Soviet Presence

Before 1970 the USSR and Latin America were, literally and figuratively, worlds apart and, except for Cuba, had few and fitful relations with one another. Since 1970 the Soviet Union has established a presence in the Western Hemisphere unique in history.

The USSR now has diplomatic, commercial, and cultural relations with many nations in the region. Cuba used to be the only country with which the USSR had significant economic relations; now Argentina and Brazil have important trade ties too. Soviet naval, air, commercial, and scientific craft visit the Caribbean, Atlantic, and Pacific waters regularly. Peru has Soviet arms, and military attachés have been exchanged with several countries. The international Communist movement in the region has attracted fresh attention as a result of Cuban military operations in Africa, powerful revolutionary movements in Central America, and Grenada's wooing of the Soviet camp.

What are the major questions that this new situation poses and which this study will attempt to answer? First, what are the purposes of the USSR in its much expanded relations with Latin America, the benefits and costs of those relations, and the Soviet impact on the region? Second, what is the nature and political significance of Soviet trade with the area? Will it ever become significant for the continent as a whole? Third, what are Soviet tactics and strategy in promoting national liberation movements and revolutionary change in the area, particularly as these relate to local Communist parties? What is the Soviet position with respect to peaceful and armed revolutionary strategies? Finally, what are the major converging and diverging interests in the Soviet-Cuban relationship? Is Cuba a Soviet pawn or partner?

I will attempt to answer these questions in the chapters that follow. In the meantime, it will be instructive to examine the significance of the new Soviet presence from a global perspective and that of the major actors:

the United States, Latin America, and the Soviet Union. The great powers now have less freedom of action in their spheres. The small countries in each sphere stand up more to their patron superpower than they used to.

From a global perspective, the Soviet presence in the Western Hemisphere symbolizes a trend from bipolarity to multipolarity in the world as a whole. Latin America used to be in the almost exclusive sphere of the United States, Eastern Europe in that of the USSR. Now both dependent regions offer increasing access to the rival great power.

Soviet trade with Latin America increased tenfold in the 1970s, and U.S. trade with Eastern Europe multiplied six times. Closer Soviet relations not only with Cuba but with Nicaragua, Guyana, Grenada, and Chile (1970–1973) have been paralleled by closer U.S. ties with Rumania, Poland, and Hungary. The two patterns of penetration are, of course, different. Soviet trade with Latin America (except Cuba) has consisted mainly of Soviet purchases. American economic relations with Eastern Europe have emphasized U.S. exports and large credits. Soviet ties with Cuba have been far closer than U.S. ties with any Eastern European country. The efforts of each superpower to exclude or restrict the access of the other to its sphere have failed to overcome the forces of attraction in the new, developing relationships.

Growing ties with Latin America, particularly Cuba, have bolstered Soviet influence in Angola and Ethiopia and made Soviet policies better known in the Third World generally. Whether these ties bring the USSR other concrete benefits in the Third World remains to be seen.

American authorities have found the new Soviet presence unsettling and sometimes threatening. Growing Soviet–Latin-American ties have proven awkward to live with. On the one hand, U.S. leaders, usually standard bearers of trade expansion, can hardly deny Latin American countries Soviet markets. Nor can the administration logically stand in the way of Latin American diplomatic ties with Moscow, with whom the United States has developed a sometimes intimate if stormy relationship.

Yet the new Soviet presence does put at risk what has been viewed as one of the nation's longest-standing vital interests: preventing any hostile great power from establishing a military-strategic foothold in the hemisphere. One of the difficulties is defining such a foothold. Recent administrations, for example, have chosen not to consider the presence of Soviet military advisers or visiting Soviet air or naval craft in Cuba as breach of a vital U.S. interest. But the establishment of a Soviet air or naval base anywhere in the hemisphere would be interpreted as breaching that interest.

In practice, Soviet activities in the hemisphere have evoked dismay and fear not because they represent a present threat but because they might threaten vital U.S. interests in the future. The revolutionary situations in Nicaragua, El Salvador, and Grenada fell in that category. The new Soviet presence in the hemisphere is the challenge of a rival hegemonic power for influence in the region.

Latin American governments see the new Soviet presence differently, depending on their own characters. Many view it primarily as a means of strengthening their negotiating position vis-à-vis the United States and other developed countries. This applies primarily to political ties for countries like Mexico and Venezuela, and to trade ties for countries like Argentina and Brazil. The USSR and Eastern Europe are independent of Western control and thus always alternative negotiating partners. Such alternatives can be immensely important to Latin Americans. The fact that many Latin American nations will rarely choose to deal with the East over the West does not eliminate the continuing value to them of Eastern options. And a growing number of countries like Argentina and Brazil are finding the USSR a profitable customer. Huge Argentine grain sales to the USSR are a dramatic example.

For Cuba, Soviet economic and military assistance has been essential to survival. The post-Somoza government in Nicaragua has welcomed Soviet moral and material support, especially in the face of hostility from some Western nations. Allende of Chile, too, had moral and some economic support from the USSR. But Latin American dictatorships, fearful of domestic opposition, may also feel threatened by the new Soviet presence. Such governments have included that of Pinochet in Chile, Stroessner in Paraguay, and the military government in Guatemala.

From the perspective of the Soviet Union, which was treated as a pariah in so many parts of the world during the interwar and early cold war periods, the normalization of relations with many Latin American nations constitutes a kind of legitimization of claims to great power status. The new Soviet access to the region opens up channels of bilateral influence and strengthens the Soviet position in multilateral forums of the United Nations, the nonaligned countries, and the Third World. The USSR also needs many of the consumer products and nonferrous metals that Latin America exports.

The Soviets probably do not regard their diplomatic ties with Latin American nations as a major means of achieving their revolutionary objectives in the area. Indeed, such ties can be an obstacle to revolutionary action. The best political opportunities are generally in countries where the USSR does not have such ties. And it is mainly the Party, not the state network, that promotes revolution.

From the Soviet perspective, greater ties with Latin America have brought other gains and opportunities, accompanied by costs and risks. Trade has zoomed ahead, but mostly because of Soviet purchases in hard and scarce currencies. Except for Cuba, the Latin Americans have not purchased much in return. Cuba has been a political bonanza but a severe drain on the Soviet economy for years with no economic solution in sight.

With its limited resources and its problems at home, the USSR must constantly keep its priorities straight. One is that Latin America is the most distant and strategically least important area of the world. The USSR needs to harmonize its interests in Latin America with its interests in the United States, a difficult balancing act. The Soviet Union has to be careful about expenditures in Latin America which might be better made at home or nearer its own borders. And of course it must avoid strategic commitments to Cuba and other Latin American nations which it is not prepared to fulfill.

• The Need for Political Discrimination

The Communist protagonists in this drama in Latin America fall into three categories: Soviet Party and government leaders, Cuban Party and government leaders, and leading Latin American Communists. Many uninformed observers in the United States and distant countries lump them together. That is partly because all three categories accept

Marxist-Leninist doctrine, seek or have achieved similar political and social systems, and often act along parallel lines. In fact, they sometimes have conflicting interests and policies. Knowing and understanding the interests, actions, and objectives of different groups of Communist actors is important to Western interests. Yet ignorance and an absence of discrimination have often prevailed in the West, settling down like a fog that obscures reality and cripples policy responses.

An even more serious error is lumping together the international Communist movement led by Moscow with most other radical and revolutionary movements in the area. That would include, for example, Allende's non-Communist supporters, the Nicaraguan Sandinistas, and the non-Communist opposition in El Salvador and Guatemala. As will be shown later, other leftist groups differ from and with the Communists in many ways.

Readers need to be familiar with Soviet political categories. The Soviet and Cuban leaders represent "ruling" Communist parties. The Latin American Communists, other than the Cuban, are members of "nonruling" Parties. The ruling and nonruling Parties are coordinated under different sections of the Soviet Central Committee Secretariat and have a markedly differing relationship with Soviet institutions. Members of a third category, non-Communist revolutionary leaders in the Third World, are classified as belonging to national liberation movements. Conflicts between actors in these three categories show how fallacious it is to consider them one and the same.

Soviet conflicts with Castro and his associates are long a matter of record. Chapter 5 describes differences over management and priorities in the Cuban economy as well as revolutionary strategy in the Americas. The repudiation of Ché Guevara by the pro-Moscow Bolivian Communist leader Mario Monje is the classic example of the latter. The USSR has economic interests at home, affected by its large aid to Cuba, as well as global interests, including relations with the United States, that sometimes take precedence over interests in Cuba. For example, the United States and the USSR settled the missile crisis without consulting Castro, thus infuriating him.

Soviet economic and global political interests also shape the policy of local Communist parties. The Parties tend to take moderate stands toward governments which the USSR finds it useful to cultivate. The Argentine military dictatorship, from which the USSR has made huge grain purchases, is a case in point. The USSR has also limited its strategic exposure in some cases, as in distant Chile, where it gave Allende only cautious and limited support.

Castro has been dependent so long on the USSR as a customer for Cuban exports and a source for oil and arms that he must be adept at defending Cuban interests and preventing the USSR from taking charge. What is remarkable is the extent to which Castro appears to remain in command in spite of his own material dependence. In his foreign relations, he has retained such a romantic image of himself as a modern-day liberator—whether in Africa or the Americas—that the Castro cult of personality has sometimes clashed with the more measured and institutionalized Soviet brand of "proletarian internationalism."

Castro's efforts to compete with, in fact, to have pro-Castro forces take over, the leadership of revolutionary movements from the orthodox Parties are well known. In recent years he has supported a variety of radical movements, a strategy welcomed by the Latin American non-Communist Left.

Most of the nonruling Parties in Latin America have followed the Soviet line from top to bottom, a course that has alienated revolutionary nationalists. Such adherence is partly responsible for keeping the Communists' following small, and it has led to splinter groups in many countries. The larger and more powerful the Parties become, the greater the pressures and the capacities for independence of Moscow. Conflict between the local Parties and Moscow is always potential if not actual. The harmony that appears to exist is more a function of the Parties' weaknesses and dependence than their basic interests. That is because most citizens in Latin America, including the Communists, ultimately put the interests of their own countries ahead of those of the USSR.

In order to understand Soviet–Latin American relations better, let us look briefly at the Latin American impact on the USSR, and then at the far more important subject, the Soviet impact on Latin America. Emphasis will be placed on how and where influence is exerted.

• The Latin American Impact

Cuba is the Latin American country that has had by far the greatest impact on the USSR, including superficial signs of Cuba in Moscow. Cuban performing arts groups have been heavily and frequently featured in the capital and elsewhere in the Soviet Union, a kind of reverse lend-lease. Cuban paintings at Soviet museums, such as the Tretyakov Gallery, have brought blazes of color and creativity in contrast to more somber Soviet works.

The Moscow diplomatic list suggests that the Cuban embassy is as large or larger than all but the largest Western embassies, and far larger than any others from Latin America. The Cubans airline office in Moscow, Cubana de Aviación, has been the only one from Latin America. Cuba has maintained consulates general in Leningrad and Odessa, no doubt to facilitate shipments between the two countries. The Cuban embassy maintains its own school so that Spanish has taken its place beside other major Eastern and Western languages in the foreign colony's schools. Students of Latin American nations other than Cuba typically attend other schools such as the American, French, or Italian.

The large Cuban presence in Moscow also helps justify the publication of the daily *Novedades de Moscú*, the Spanish-language edition of the *Moscow News*, a heavily edited news and feature newspaper. The Cuban news agency Prensa Latina also distributes news reports in Spanish in the capital, a service highly valued by Latin Americans from the smaller embassies who lack direct access to world news in their own language.

Cuba's greatest impact by far is through the massive interlocking of the Soviet and Cuban bureaucracies. Almost every phase of Cuban life— agriculture, industry, energy, transport, communications, science, education, research, culture—is intimately associated with Soviet institutions.

Latin Americans are developing a growing understanding of the Soviet Union. There are about thirteen Latin American embassies (other than Cuba's) in Moscow, with staffs ranging from one to sixteen diplomatic officers, many of whom travel not only in the USSR but in

Eastern Europe as well. My own impression, based on brief acquaintance, is that the diplomats quickly gain realistic impressions of the USSR, and seldom become proponents of the Soviet cause.

Perhaps an important yet unremarked result of the growing Soviet interest in Latin America is the integration of Latin American interests and specialists into the Soviet bureaucracy. An increased number of Soviet officials with Latin American experience and/or specialization are now in the Ministry of Foreign Affairs, the Ministry of Foreign Trade, state committees, other agencies, and, of course, the Party.

In the past the member of the Politburo responsible for the Party's international relations, such as Boris Ponomarev, was about the only person with Latin American affairs of any consequence within his or her jurisdiction. More recently, the diplomatic missions under Politburo member and Foreign Minister A. A. Gromyko and all the various government operations under Politburo member and Chairman of the Council of Ministers N. A. Tikhonov gave them legitimate interests in the area. As a result Gromyko and Tikhonov can fully justify speaking out in the few cases when Latin America comes up at Politburo meetings. Latin America is no longer just a concern of the Party; there are vested interests of the government as well.

• The Soviet Impact

The Soviet impact on Latin America (except Cuba) has been limited, partly because few Russians and other Soviet citizens have lived in the area compared to citizens of other large industrial countries. Only a handful of diplomats lived briefly in Mexico and Montevideo before World War II. The new Soviet embassies of small to moderate size have now added a sprinkling of diplomats in many of the capital cities. Following the Soviet pattern elsewhere in the world, most tend to keep to themselves, maintaining a fairly low profile in the local societies. Ambassadors with the glamour of Mikhail Menshikov and Anatoli Dobrynin, who served in Washington, are rare. None, for example, appears to have matched the attention that Alexandra Kollontai attracted briefly as the Soviet ambassador in Mexico City in the late 1920s.

The fact that most Latin American countries did not have Soviet diplomatic representation from 1917 to the late 1960s has tended to limit contacts far more than it would with most Western nations. Almost all Soviet citizens living abroad are under official or quasi-official sponsorship while Europeans abroad usually are in private capacities.

The Soviet Union now has official ties and diplomatic missions in all the major Latin American countries and in most of the smaller ones. If Grenada is included, the Soviets have fifteen embassies in Latin America, other than Cuba. This adds up to a substantial diplomatic contingent. In addition to regular diplomatic officers, there are also representatives from the Ministry of Foreign Trade, officials of binational cultural institutes, and technical assistance personnel, the last-named sometimes found in large numbers at project sites. The USSR also has agreements for the exchange of military attachés with Peru, Argentina, and Mexico.[1]

Cultural relations are systematically encouraged with athletic teams, performing arts groups, films, and exhibitions visiting Latin American countries. The Soviet Union maintains binational cultural institutes in nine of the countries with which it has diplomatic relations. The list of Party, parliamentary, trade, educational, scientific, and cultural delegations to Latin America on visits of two or three weeks is long and impressive until one considers how thinly they are spread over more than twenty countries. Leonid Brezhnev was the only Soviet general secretary to visit Latin America when he came to Cuba in 1974. Politburo members have frequently visited Cuba, Anastas Mikoyan traveled to Mexico, and Sh. R. Rashidov and A. P. Kirilenko went to Chile when Allende was president. Some of the most popular visitors have been in the performing arts, such as the Bolshoi Ballet and the Moscow Circus. Such contacts the ice but do not give Latin Americans understanding of the USSR.

The expansion of Aeroflot the Soviet airline, with service scheduled weekly or more often to Kingston, Lima, Managua, and Mexico City as well as Havana, has greatly facilitated Soviet activities in Latin America. Many seats are reserved for diplomatic and trade officials, but the flights also permit visits by scientists, scholars, and artists who could not come to the Americas if payment were required in hard currencies. There are now regular trips by carefully selected tourists who fan out to other countries from Lima and Mexico City.

An important result of the enlarged Soviet presence in Latin America is rapidly growing Soviet sophistication about the area. I first started reading Soviet sources on Latin America about thirty years ago; these were naive and often based on English-language sources.[2] Today Soviet scholars are better informed and use the same sources as scholars in the West. Because there is a constant need for specialists to work in and on the area, training continues and studying Spanish makes sense. Soviet policy can now be made on the basis of better information than in the past.

Perhaps the most enduring Soviet impact is on the Latin American students who spend five years in university-level training in Soviet institutions of higher learning.[3] Students live and study in Moscow, Leningrad, Kiev, and other Soviet cities. Usually they take one year of intensive Russian and then enter an academic or professional course of study. Many speak excellent Russian, develop close associations with Soviet citizens, and gain first-hand and authoritative knowledge of Soviet society which they take home with them.

Most of the students are recruited in one of two tracks. The first group is selected by Latin American Communist and trade union leaders, and the fellowships are a form of political patronage. They are also designed to produce a pool of knowledgeable, pro-Soviet young people who will eventually occupy positions of leadership at home. The other track is governmental. The Latin American governments select able students, usually from poor families, to study in the USSR as a form of cultural exchange. Students from the second track would be only coincidentally pro-Communist and pro-Soviet. Both groups see the same Soviet reality, almost none wish to remain in the USSR if they have an opportunity to return to a normal life at home, and very few could be easily misled about the nature of Soviet society. Most are sincerely grateful to the USSR for the opportunity to receive a university or professional school education, an opportunity they would probably never have had at home. Many will return home to a nonpolitical role in society neither as pro-Soviet as their benefactors would like nor as anti-Soviet as the radical Right in their own countries might desire.

About one thousand Latin Americans are being trained at the Friendship University Patrice Lumumba in Moscow, and perhaps up to an additional two thousand are in other institutions around the country. Peru, Colombia, Costa Rica, Ecuador, Bolivia, and Nicaragua have sent relatively large numbers of students. Argentina, Mexico, and Brazil have been underrepresented.

Soviet-sponsored organizations flood Latin America with hundreds of thousands of copies of periodicals. Most of these are translations of Soviet journals published worldwide, some in more than thirty languages. At least sixteen Soviet journals are translated and published in Spanish, and of these six are also in Portuguese (see appendix 3). The journals are edited primarily in Moscow, although two come from Prague. The distribution is mainly in the countries with a relatively free press: Mexico City, San José, and Panama in Central America, and Bogotá, Caracas, Guyaquil, and Lima in South America. The *World Marxist Review*, also called *Peace and Socialism*, the organ of the Communist and Workers' parties is published in Prague in both Spanish and Portuguese. Its supplement, the *Information Bulletin*, appears in Spanish but not Portuguese.

Spanish-language translations of the well-known journal of international affairs, *New Times (Tiempos nuevos, Tempos novos)* and *Soviet Union (Unión Soviética, União Sovietica)* are of the most general interest. There are six cultural journals including *Cultura y vida, Teatro*, and *Literatura soviética*. The Academy of Sciences sponsors *Ciéncias sociales (Social Sciences)* and *América Latina*, the only journal devoted exclusively to Latin American affairs. It is curious that the regional journal on Asia, *Problemas del extremo Oriente*, is also translated into Spanish. More specialized journals include *Socialismo: Teoría y práctica, Revista militar soviética, Comercio exterior*, and *Sputnik*. The majority of these publications come out monthly, but a few are quarterly.

Progress Books, which is the translator and publisher of Soviet books in Russian into foreign languages, also publishes selected works of Soviet scholars for distribution in the Americas. The Soviet Press Agency, Novosti, concerned with the dissemination abroad of information and propaganda, also distributes to a select mailing list the mimeographed "Panorama Latinoamericana," termed a "reflection of the economic, political, cultural, and social situation of Latin America in the Soviet Press."

These Soviet propaganda publications and the associated local Communist party's publications perhaps represent a single, cohesive point of view. In countries where their circulation is permitted, they exert substantial influence. The USSR has nurtured anticapitalist, antiimperialist, and anti-American ideas in Latin America for six decades. With access to a variety of Marxist sources, most Latin American students and intellectuals are familiar with the ideas of Marx and Lenin, often more than their counterparts in the United States. This familiarity is partly due to Soviet propaganda, whose singleness of purpose and continuity of argument is unmatched in the region. Many ordinary people never read Communist literature, but most have read authors influenced by the publications of the international Communist movement.

Communist ideas have appeal in Latin America for pragmatic and self-serving reasons. They alienate people from the class-based status quo, which Lenin criticized so harshly. Government becomes an instrument for righting wrongs and changing society. The Soviet-style Communist party is also an entity which helps a small group, unchecked by genuine popular control, concentrate supreme power in its own hands. And it provides a ready-made program for political organization of social and economic development.

In the 1920s and early 1930s, a few Latin American converts to the Communist party looked worshipfully to Moscow. Their attitudes were based mostly on revulsion against the evils of capitalism and foreign domination, idealism, and wishful thinking. Luís Emilio Recabarren, the founder of the Chilean Party, was one such leader. He returned from the USSR disillusioned with what he saw.

Since Stalin's crimes and the shortcomings of Soviet society have become better known, even fewer Latin Americans regard the USSR as a model for their own countries. Since the local Parties zigged with the USSR during the popular front period and then zagged over the Hitler-Stalin Pact, most Latin Americans concluded the local Communists were more consistently loyal to the interests of Moscow than to those of the nation. As a result of this and later subservience, the non-Communist Left regards Moscow more critically and with greater detachment than it used to. As chapter 4 shows, membership in Communist parties is relatively small, and with important exceptions, the Parties have not been influential.

One finds in Latin America an incongruity. There is extensive Soviet influence over the thinking of many Latin Americans, particularly because aspects of the Soviet program, with adaptations, appeal to the needs and interests of some groups, but the Soviet model as a whole rarely dominates, and it is attractive only to a very few. A non-Soviet position, however, is not necessarily accompanied by any enthusiasm for U.S. institutions or policies. Certainly the incessant anti-American propaganda in the region has taken its toll. But U.S. behavior in the area—postwar interventions in Guatemala, Cuba, and the Dominican Republic, interference in Chile, clumsy maneuvering in Central America in the 1980s—has probably done the American image far more harm than the USSR ever could: the Soviet apparatus is experienced in capitalizing on these errors.

Now attention will be turned to principal aspects of Soviet dealings with Latin America: governmental, economic, and Party relations. By *Latin America* is meant here, purely for convenience, all countries except Cuba. Cuba is dealt with separately in chapter 5.

II Building Diplomatic Networks: Political Relations

In spite of its efforts, the Soviet government did not achieve normal diplomatic and commercial relations with most Latin American states until the late 1960s. Before World War II, the USSR had relations with only two Latin American governments, Mexico (1924–1930) and Uruguay (1934–1935). Many Latin American countries established relations with Moscow by the end of World War II, but most broke ties by the early 1950s. Only Mexico, Uruguay, and Argentina sustained relations with Moscow throughout the post–World War II period (see table 1).

In the 1980s the Soviet Union has diplomatic and commercial relations with all the leading countries of Latin America and with most of the smaller ones. Besides Castro, the presidents of Chile, Mexico, Venezuela, Jamaica, and Guyana have visited the USSR, and there is a steady stream of visitors on economic, cultural, and political business in both directions. The Soviet navy has made many visits in the Caribbean, and Aeroflot makes many flights weekly to the region. The Soviet Union has established a greater presence in Latin America than at any previous time in history. Here is how this state of affairs came about.

• From Ostracism to Acceptance

The USSR had relatively little contact with most of Latin America for more than forty years, from 1917 until the 1960s. Why was it excluded from the area for so long? The Soviet and Latin American Communists charge that U.S. imperialism blocked the establishment of Soviet ties. What they mean is that U.S. leaders working through dependent governments in Latin America were able to prevent the establishment of diplomatic ties.

The Latin American governments that did not recognize the USSR had little to say on the subject. The few governments that established

Table 1
Soviet Diplomatic Relations with Latin America, 1917–1982

Note: The symbol ★ indicates recognition without the exchange of representatives.

relations early with Moscow broke them after a relatively short time. Mexico and Uruguay broke diplomatic relations in 1930 and 1935 respectively, citing subversive activities of the local Parties; the offices of Iuzhamtorg, the Soviet trading agency in Buenos Aires, were closed in 1931 in part due to charges of involvement in Communist activities in South America. After World War II, several governments, such as the Colombian and Chilean, ended ties with Moscow alleging its involvement in subversion. Their main targets were the local Communists; charges against Soviet officials were sometimes hazy.[1]

During the interwar and cold war periods, many Latin American governments were controlled by military and civilian leaders who perceived Communists and other leftists as threats. Although the Communists were too weak to pose a danger, the suppression of the Left served as a pretext for concentrating more power in the existing government. Since the Communists freely admitted their political ties with the USSR, the government's charges of Soviet complicity with local Communists were widely accepted, true or not. The classic Soviet defense that its government had no responsibility for the international Communist movement fell on incredulous ears in the West.

The Communists' charge that Washington discouraged Latin American governments from maintaining relations with the USSR may have been true, at least in part. The global, regional, and national power structures in the West opposed communism and the socialist countries generally. Strictly speaking, U.S. official involvement would need to be proved in each case, and it seldom was. In my view domestic politics, in which entrenched leaders used the Communists and the USSR as whipping boys, were more persuasive reasons for the long-time Soviet isolation than U.S. and other foreign pressures.

Finally, it might be argued that the USSR did not have closer relations with Latin America because the Soviet Union had little to offer economically. Although the Soviets were not then able to carry on a brisk trade with all Latin American countries simultaneously, even in the 1920s they probably could have traded far more with Argentina and Uruguay than local politics permitted. In fact, the USSR was charged with dumping oil in Argentina at the time the Soviet trading agency's offices in Buenos Aires were shut down. The impetus to the commercial break was provided by influential domestic and foreign interests whose business would have been hurt by continuing Soviet oil sales to Argentina.

After 1945 the USSR became a superpower with global interests and responsibilities which it gradually began to exercise. Latin America, where the Soviet Union was ostracized, was an area largely beyond the reach of Soviet political and economic influence. The absence of diplomatic relations with many countries was more than just a formality. In the West private organizations or individuals deal directly with foreign countries. In the USSR political, economic, and cultural ties are almost impossible without formal intergovernmental agreements. Such agreements are essential to activate the Soviet bureaucracies, which have exclusive competence within their fields of responsibility in international relations.

The 1960s were the turning point in Soviet ties with Latin America. Castro established diplomatic relations with the USSR in 1960 as an important means of countering U.S. measures to overthrow him. The Goulart government in Brazil established relations in 1961. Eduardo Frei of Chile exchanged diplomatic representatives with Moscow in 1964 for reasons of domestic and foreign policy. In the meantime, however, there were important developments discouraging such actions. The Cuban missile crisis of 1962 was one; guerrilla operations in the hemisphere were another.

By the late 1960s, tensions over many of these issues had subsided. Cuba was more secure in the Caribbean and Castro had stopped supporting guerrilla operations in the Americas. The pro-Soviet Parties appeared rather clearly to prefer electoral participation and the formation of popular fronts to armed struggle.

Global trends also facilitated rapprochment: détente, SALT, and the Helsinki agreements were their symbols. Finally, and perhaps most important, U.S. officials and private interests have been disengaging in Latin America, and Latin American governments are taking more aggressive and independent steps to promote their own interests. Not only are they seeking to diversify their political and economic relations with Western Europe and Japan, but they also wish to open new economic opportunities with the socialist countries of Eastern Europe.

Between 1968 and 1970, the Soviet Union exchanged diplomatic representatives with five Andean countries: Bolivia, Colombia, Ecuador,

Peru, and Venezuela. In the 1970s relations were established in and around the Caribbean with Costa Rica, Grenada, Guyana, Jamaica, and Nicaragua. The USSR probably was not interested in establishing relations with the dictatorships in Guatemala, El Salvador, and Honduras nor with those in Haiti and Paraguay. The USSR broke with the military dictatorship in Chile a few days after Allende's fall in 1973.

The Soviet Union favored relations with the Dominican Republic but required a very clear signal from the Dominican end. The one country with which the USSR particularly wanted relations was Panama under Torrijos because of the political complexion of the government, its strong antiimperialist stance, and its strategic situation.[2] General Torrijos was reluctant to establish relations with the USSR during the canal crisis.

In most of the established bilateral relationships, the USSR played the role of suitor. First, it secured recognition of the Soviet state; second, it exchanged diplomatic representatives; and finally, it established economic and cultural as well as political relations. The USSR did not ordinarily make ideological or political criteria conditions of diplomatic and commercial relations but sought links between states irrespective of differences in social systems.

Cuba and Grenada may have been the exceptions where the USSR was more the wooed than the wooer. Castro desperately needed to sell Cuban sugar to the USSR and to receive Soviet oil and arms. In other cases the Soviet Union made known its interest in relations without seeming too eager, expecting the Latin American government to speak first. The USSR appears to have been happy to exchange diplomatic representatives with almost any Latin American government that would do so. Only Trujillo, on his last legs, was discouraged.[3] This is not to say that the USSR would establish ties with dictatorships of the likes of Somoza's or Stroessner's, but such governments were not interested either. And it is significant that the USSR put such a high value on its relations with Brazil and Bolivia that when repressive anti-Communist dictators took over in 1964 and 1971 respectively, relations were not broken.

· Soviet State Interests

What then are Soviet state interests in Latin America as distinct from the interests of the international Communist movement? For one thing, the Soviet Union needs and wants an official presence in the hemisphere, particularly in important countries like Mexico, Brazil, Argentina, and Venezuela. That presence is necessary for gathering information, establishing channels of communication, and influencing developments in the area. And it also provides a firmer basis for Soviet participation in Third World, United Nations, and other forums. Diplomatic relations with most of the nations of the world, including those in Latin America, have been essential to legitimize the Soviet role as a great power.

The Soviet Union's most immediate interest in Latin America is trade. The USSR needs many of the region's agricultural products and has a huge annual deficit there. That means that it must increase Soviet exports to the area to pay for these imports. Argentina is the prime market because it has so much of what the USSR wants and also has the capacity to absorb Soviet manufactures. Uruguay and Brazil are other favored candidates, but political tensions with these countries have sometimes hampered trade.

Economies at the level of the Andean and Central American countries present opportunities to the USSR to demonstrate its capacities for promoting economic development. Soviet technology should be adequate for these countries, and Soviet assistance could have greater impact than in the larger, richer, and less malleable countries like Argentina and Brazil. Jamaica and Guyana also need foreign assistance, particularly in refining and selling alumina. Government leaders in Guyana and Jamaica under Manley favored socialism and had more in common politically and ideologically with the USSR than most other Latin American governments. Yet one sensed a certain Soviet caution, particularly with respect to large credits. This may have been due partly to a Soviet desire not to cause American concern about Soviet involvement in two small countries near the United States.

The Soviet Union has sold hundreds of millions of dollars of military equipment to Peru, and it seems likely that such equipment has also been offered, if only informally, to Argentina and Mexico. The most immediate gain from such sale would be hard currency, which the USSR can surely use. In the case of Peru, however, the government was forced to request a moratorium on payments to the USSR, which deprives the sale of its balance-of-payments advantages. The extent to which the sale of even that much equipment provides the USSR with important political benefits is questionable. Most Peruvian military equipment is from the United States and Western Europe.

The USSR has also attributed much political importance to its long and friendly ties with Mexico. Close relations with a large and important Latin American country sharing such a long border with the United States provide continuing benefits in the present and insurance for the future. No doubt the USSR prizes its relations with Mexico as the United States does its relations with Poland. The USSR also has much to gain by maintaining easy communications with Mexico and Venezuela as two leading Third World countries. The Soviets have done little business with either Mexico or Venezuela, and the prospects are limited. Nonetheless, Soviet officials work hard to strengthen economic relations with both countries as a means of reinforcing political relations.

Diplomatic relations with governments in South America, Central America, and the Caribbean legitimize and facilitate Soviet naval visits throughout hemispheric waters. The Soviet Union has cooperated with local fishing fleets in Chile, Peru, and Mexico, and cooperation is underway or planned in many other countries. Fishing is among the economic sectors in which Soviet specialists can provide the best technical assistance. Obviously, collaboration in fishing and naval visits serves intelligence and strategic purposes in distant waters.

The Soviet authorities do have a preference for the more "progressive" and "antiimperialist" governments. Since the fall of Allende, sandinista Nicaragua and the Peruvian and Panamanian military governments have been their favorites, followed closely by Guyana and Jamaica when Michael Manley was prime minister. Democracies such as Venezuela and Colombia are preferred on ideological grounds over anti-Communist military dictatorships of the repressive sort, such as in Brazil. Because of Soviet economic interests and accommodation to the Argentine Communists, the Videla regime in Argentina received little criticism.

In the perspective of history, the USSR's greatest interests outside Cuba have been and are in Mexico and Argentina. Relations with Mexico have been based primarily on complementary political interests. Both governments have common revolutionary traditions, though these are different in kind, and Mexico was the first country in the Americas to recognize the new Soviet government, in 1924. Although it broke relations in 1930, Mexico was one of the first governments to establish diplomatic relations with the USSR during World War II, in November 1942. Unlike much of Latin America, Mexico did not break relations during the cold war and has had uninterrupted contact longer than any other country in the area. Cultural relations with Mexico have also been active. Although there have been many efforts to stimulate trade, the results so far have been disappointing.

Argentina has long been the major center of Soviet trading efforts in Latin America, beginning with the foreign trade agencies Amtorg and Iuzhamtorg in the late 1920s. Argentina established relations with the USSR in 1946, later than many other countries, because of its links to the Axis in World War II. But it maintained uninterrupted diplomatic contact thereafter. The main common interest has been trade, which has been greater than Soviet commerce with any other Latin American country, especially since the U.S. grain embargo on the USSR.

Brief treatments of the bilaterial relations of the USSR with a number of Latin American countries follow.

• *Mexico.* We have noted that the Soviet Union has had diplomatic relations with Mexico longer than with any other country in Latin America. Relations are also probably closer than with most other Latin American governments except Castro's. Yet the Mexican government has never been dominated or importantly influenced by the Mexican Communist party; nor can it ever have been properly characterized as pro-Soviet in the usual sense of that term. Curiously, the Cárdenas government, probably the most left-wing or socially "progressive" of all Mexican governments, refused to reestablish diplomatic relations with Moscow in the 1930s.

The reason for the relatively durable character of this bilateral relationship may be found in Mexican relations with the United States. Mexico is acutely conscious of its physical vulnerability to its powerful northern neighbor. That vulnerability is symbolized by the Mexican War (1845–1848) and Mexican dependence on U.S. markets, investments, and tourism. As a result Mexico has a traditional policy of maintaining access to great powers outside the hemisphere as a counterweight to U.S.

influence. In World War I and again on the eve of World War II, Mexico kept open its channels of communication with Germany and conducted an independent policy toward that country which had, from the Mexican point of view, a salutary effect on U.S. conduct.

Since 1945 the USSR has superseded Germany as the main rival of the United States. Mexico has therefore seen fit to maintain relations with the USSR throughout the entire postwar period, and is the only Latin American country other than Uruguay and Argentina to have done so. Mexican ties with the USSR have not been such as to pose any serious threat to the United States, nor have they been intended to. They have kept Mexican options demonstrably open. Mexico also strongly reiterated its independence by remaining the one nation in the hemisphere to retain diplomatic relations with Castro's Cuba.

Soviet and Mexican ideologies emerged from social revolutions even through their historical origins and content are different. Mexican experience with the United States has made antiimperialism an important thread of doctrine and policy. Mexico's record of opposition to Mussolini and Hitler reflects its antifascism. Like the USSR, Mexico was among the most ardent supporters of the Spanish Republic against Franco.

Mexico, too, has its own revolutionary traditions and a history of political action and rhetoric in favor of workers and peasants. Like the USSR, Mexico has been dominated by one party since the Revolution. This continuity of domestic and foreign policy, unmatched elsewhere in Latin America, accounts in part for the relative stability of the Soviet-Mexican relationship. During the cold war, when the USSR was anathema in much of the West, Mexico permitted the Soviet embassy to remain in Mexico City.

Moscow has long used Mexico City as a base for expanding its diplomatic, cultural, and political activities in the Caribbean and South America. Soviet cultural relations with Mexico have perhaps been more active than with any other Latin American government other than Cuba. Many Soviet writers and artists made their first visits to the hemisphere there and went on from Mexico City to other countries. And before Castro Mexico City served as an international headquarters for Parties in the region. Significantly, Soviet trade with Mexico is less than with other governments with whom the USSR has had far less cordial political relations. Mexico may also serve as a home for Soviet intelligence operations against the United States and Latin American countries.[4]

The Mexican authorities who deal with the USSR are rarely Communist; many have views which are decidedly not Marxist. However, the relationships appear to be fairly active and collaborative, if not intimate. For the most part, the Soviet side probably does the wooing and accepts any incidental benefits. The Mexicans are fully aware of what is happening, control the relationship closely, and are probably pleased with the results. The two governments deal on the basis of what appears to be a fairly durable sharing of limited common interests.

Among the most colorful periods in Soviet relations with Latin America is the 1920s, when the Bolsheviks were attempting to establish a foothold in Mexico. This period is richly treated in Soviet, Mexican, and American sources.[5] Dramatic personalities strode across this stage. For the USSR there were Mikhail Borodin, a founding father of the Communist International; Alexandra Kollontai, a revolutionary leader and ambassador; and Vladimir Mayakovsky, the flamboyant revolutionary poet. For the Mexicans there were such personalities as presidents Carranza and Cárdenas; Luis Morones, the labor leader; and Jesús Silva Hertzog, the academician and sometime Mexican ambassador to Moscow.

The Soviet Union had three ambassadors in Mexico City between 1924 and 1930. Kollontai was popular, but the other two ambassadors irritated the leading progovernment labor federation and were accused of interfering in domestic politics through the local Party. In the late 1920s, when the government swung to the right and began suppressing its leftist opposition, the International raised strong protests. The Mexicans held the USSR responsible for this and refused to accept the Soviet Foreign Office's formal disclaimers of responsibility. The Soviet ambassador was ridden out of town on a rail, so to speak; his treatment was so bad that Mexico's refusal to apologize was a barrier to the reestablishment of relations in the 1930s. Another source of friction was President Cárdenas's befriending of Stalin's enemy, Leon Trotsky. Mexico and the USSR took similar positions against the Axis, but when Cárdenas refused to sanction the Nazi-Soviet Pact of 1939 and sympathized with the

Finns in their war with USSR, it was clear the similarities of their earlier policies were purely coincidental.

The Nazi attack on the USSR of June 1941 set the stage for a resumption in diplomatic relations between the USSR and many Latin American countries. Mexico was the second such country to act, restoring relations in November 1942. K. A. Umanskii, the former Soviet ambassador to the United States, was assigned to the post in Mexico City. The Mexicans received him warmly, and he responded in kind, recreating for a short time the élan and excitement the Soviet embassy had inspired under Kollontai in the late 1920s. Perhaps the high point of Umanskii's short tenure was an address he delivered in Spanish to a joint session of the Mexican Congress. He was killed in a plane crash in Mexico in January 1945.

When the cold war began in the late 1940s, most Latin American governments broke diplomatic relations with the USSR. Mexico and Argentina were the two most important governments not to do so. Nonetheless, during most of these years relations between the USSR and Mexico were largely a formality. Soviet authors who have written about Soviet-Mexican relations have virtually nothing to say about this period.

When relations between East and West began to thaw in the late 1950s, symbolized by the Khrushchev-Eisenhower meeting at Camp David in 1959, the Soviet Union once again turned to Mexico to inaugurate its diplomatic offensive in Latin America. On the heels of the sputnik triumph, the USSR mounted an exhibition in Mexico City of Soviet achievements in science, technology, and culture. A. I. Mikoyan, as first deputy chairman of the Council of Ministers, led the Soviet delegation. On his return from Mexico, he stopped in Havana to establish the first high-level Soviet contact with Fidel Castro.

Since that time Mexico has been at the forefront of Latin American countries in establishing bilateral contacts with the USSR. The Mexican foreign minister visited Moscow in 1968, and presidents Luis Echeverría and Lopez Portillo did so in 1973 and 1978. The accords achieved on these visits were agreements on cultural and scientific exchange, on trade, and on scientific and technical cooperation. Parliamentary, trade union, and other delegations have been exchanged. During the Lopez Portillo visit, the USSR announced its decision to sign Protocol II of the Treaty on the Prohibition of Nuclear Weapons in Latin America, an act which attracted attention due to the absence of Cuban adherence to the treaty. Meanwhile, and unrelated to the Moscow visit, the Mexican authorities had taken steps to remove obstacles to the legalization of the Mexican Communist party. Mexico also has a formal agreement for cooperation with the Council of Mutual Economic Assistance, signed in 1975.

The most persistent and resistant problem in Soviet-Mexican relations has been the strengthening of economic ties. Since the Mikoyan visit in 1959, the two governments have sought to increase trade and contact at all levels. Considering the political importance of Mexico and the size of the Mexican economy, Soviet commentators have mentioned time and again the insufficiency of that trade. In 1976 the USSR exported 6.9 million rubles to and imported 11.1 million rubles from Mexico. Soviet turnover in 1980 did not exceed the 1976 level.[6] As early as 1964, the USSR and Mexico exchanged groups of oil specialists, and the USSR thereby had an early chance to assist Mexico in the current oil boom. Petróleos Mexicanos secured ten oil-drilling rigs and other equipment at that time. In spite of intermittent contact ever since, the USSR did not place any large sales of equipment for the oil industry in Mexico.

The USSR has also been attracted to Mexico because of the latter's independent foreign policy, particularly in relations with the United States. Soviet authors, for example, have noted Mexican criticism of U.S. policy in Guatemala in 1954 and in the Dominican Republic in 1965. In addition they have noted that Mexico has been the only country in Latin America to maintain normal relations with Cuba throughout the Castro period.[7] Altogether, Soviet-Mexican political ties have proved durable while economic ties have disappointed Soviet hopes.

• *Argentina.*   In many ways Soviet relations with Argentina are the obverse of relations with Mexico. The USSR has consistently placed emphasis on economic rather than political relations, regarding Argentina as a promising market. Soviet authorities have long looked to Buenos Aires as a base for expanding trade with other South American countries, especially Brazil, Chile, Bolivia, and Peru. The USSR has stubbornly pursued its goals of trading with Argentina in spite of disappointment with Argentine purchases and ideological differences.

The USSR has maintained demand over many years for Argentine exports: grain, hides, wool, quebracho extract, and other agricultural products. Although diplomatic relations between the two governments were not established until 1946, trade with Argentina, consisting mostly of Soviet imports, was usually far larger from the beginning than with any other Latin American country.[8] While some Argentine governments have been indifferent or hostile toward the USSR, others have encouraged this trade because the USSR has been a profitable customer for Argentine exports.

In 1925 the USSR began its trade relations with Argentina by establishing an office of the Soviet trading company Amtorg in Buenos Aires. The USSR bought skins, quebracho extract, and meat and sold the Argentines lumber, fur, and mineral oil. Since there was an unfavorable balance, Soviet negotiators offered the Argentines oil. The Argentine government and the head of the state petroleum company were much attracted to the Soviet offer because they were then engaged in an effort to lower the domestic price of oil, strengthen the state company, and break the dominance of foreign oil companies. The availability of Soviet oil provided an alternative source to give them some independence from the foreign companies.[9]

By 1930, however, a coup d'etat brought in a new government closely linked to the foreign oil interests. This government embarked on anti-Communist repression, and Argentina sharply cut its oil imports from the USSR. In 1931, the government closed down the offices of the Soviet trading company, then known as Iuzhamtorg, which moved across the estuary to Montevideo, Uruguay. Soviet-Argentine trade plummeted, and diplomatic relations between the two countries were not established during the interwar period.

Unlike most governments of Latin America which recognized the USSR during World War II, Argentina was an exception because of its wartime association with the Axis. In his campaign for the presidency in 1946, Juan Domingo Perón promised to create ties with the USSR and after his election did so in June 1946. Perón did little else to promote relations with the Soviet Union until 1953, when the Argentine economy was in serious trouble. In an effort to find new markets and better terms, Perón signed a trade and payments agreement with the USSR. In exchange for Argentine agricultural products, the Soviet Union was to supply oil, coal, machinery, equipment, steel, and iron.[10] Trade turnover rose nearly ten times to almost seventy million rubles in 1954.

Soviet interest has been based on the needs of the domestic Soviet economy for many Argentine exports, most particularly hides, wool, grain, and, more recently, wine. Soviet purchasing agents have continued to buy these Argentine exports even when the trade balance has showed a huge deficit. From the Soviet perspective, the key to a satisfactory relationship is greatly augmented Argentine purchases of Soviet machines and equipment, sales of which have been consistently disappointing. Were Argentina to sharply expand purchases of Soviet goods, further increases in Soviet purchases would be likely.

Soviet relations with Argentina have had their ups and downs, as reflected in annual trade turnover figures. Several governments (Frondizi, Illia, Lanusse, and Perón's second government) encouraged trade with the USSR, mainly, it seems, for economic advantage. While these governments may have viewed cooperation with the Soviet Union as strengthening their hand vis-à-vis the United States and Western Europe, they did not share Soviet political values.

Other governments, which Soviet writers termed oligarchic, militarist, repressive, and anti-Soviet, discouraged ties and trade with the USSR. These included the governments of Aramburu, Guido, Onganía, and at the end, Isabel Martinez de Perón.

Since Perón's first government fell from power in 1955, there have been intermittent trade and economic cooperation agreements, exchanges of governmental and parliamentary delegations, and visits by Soviet leaders to congresses of the Argentine Communist party. In 1958, Arturo Frondizi, who had criticized the government for not availing itself of Soviet oil in the early 1930s, became president and negotiated a very favorable 100-million ruble line of credit to finance the purchase of Soviet equipment for the oil industry.[11] The Argentines were to pay off any loans with agricultural exports.[12] The USSR was to supply equipment for geological exploration and drilling, transport vehicles, and so forth. In 1960 A. N. Kosygin, the deputy chairman of the Council of Ministers, visited Buenos Aires, and the two governments signed a protocol to the trade agreement providing for Soviet supplies of lift vehicles, road-building equipment, and metalworking machinery. When Frondizi was overthrown in a coup d'etat, and his successor terminated trade relations with the USSR, only 30 percent of the Soviet credit had been drawn down. Relations improved again under Illia but worsened again under the military dictatorships of generals Onganía and Levingston from 1966 to 1971. A new trade agreement, providing for economic cooperation, was signed in June 1971 when General Alejandro Lanusse was president. And in February 1974, after Perón's reelection, an agreement was signed for the delivery of Soviet machines and industrial equipment on a credit basis. In May 1974 two high-level trade delegations reached agreement with respect to Soviet equipment for Argentine power stations, one hydroelectric and one thermal. Agreement was also reached on Soviet participation in the construction and in training for Argentine industrial projects in the fields of energy, chemical industry, shipbuilding, and the construction of ports. On its side the USSR made commitments with respect to the purchase of meat, fruit, and fruit juice. Questions of marine and air connections were also discussed. In the fall of 1974, the two countries also signed an intergovernmental agreement on sports. But in July 1974, Perón died. In her short tenure, his widow did not carry out the Soviet-Argentine agreements, and once again Soviet objectives for cooperation with Argentina were defeated.

The overthrow of Isabel de Perón in March 1976 by General Jorge D. Videla resulted in a new period of Soviet-Argentine cooperation. Trade rose to new highs, and planning of joint projects, such as the large hydroelectric project in the Middle Paraná, went forward.

The greatest impulse to Soviet-Argentine ties was the American-imposed grain embargo on the Soviet Union following the military occupation of Afghanistan in late 1979. Unable to fill their needs for grain in the United States, Soviet buyers offered huge purchase contracts to Argentine exporters. In the past much of Argentine grain was exported through large firms, many of which were controlled by foreign capital. Now, under bilateral agreements with the USSR, a much larger share is sold directly. In spite of U.S. pressure and the visit of General Andrew Goodpaster, Argentine exporters refused to join the grain embargo. The Argentine government limited itself to mild criticism of the Soviet occupation of Afghanistan. Its concession to the United States was joining the boycott of the 1980 Olympics.

Soviet purchases of Argentine grain were historically unprecedented in volume and a huge bonanza for Argentine grain producers. By 1980 shipments to the Soviet Union constitute 60 percent of Argentine grain exports (wheat, corn, sorghum, and soybeans) and 22 percent of Argentine total exports. Soviet purchases of fresh meat equaled 50 percent of frozen meat exports and 25 percent of total meat exports in 1980.[13] The USSR became Argentina's greatest single foreign customer; Argentina supplied one-fifth of Soviet imports from developing countries in 1980. Argentina, however, bought very little in return. Significantly, Soviet exports to Argentina were less than 3 percent of Argentine imports in 1980.

Argentina is also attractive to the USSR as a market for its thermal, hydro, and nuclear power equipment. As chapter 3 indicates, the Soviet Union already participates in several power projects. Soviet engineers have an advantage over engineers from many other countries because the most important rivers of Argentina, like those of the Soviet Union, have gradual rather than steep descents. The Soviet Union has sold Argentina nuclear fuel in the form of heavy water and enriched uranium.[14]

The two countries enjoy a remarkable coincidence of economic interests. The USSR urgently needs grain, meat, wool, and other consumer materials and goods, and Argentina benefits greatly from such purchases. Argentina is also a good prospect for Soviet exports of machinery and equipment. Common economic interests are accompanied, however, by strong ideological and political divergencies. The Argentine military governments of recent years are firmly anti-Communist and antisocialist, authoritarian, and repressive. According to the UN Commission on Human Rights, there have been from seven to nine thousand *desaparecidos* in Argentina; that is, "disappeared persons," many of whom are believed to have been murdered by government authorities.[15] One of the main targets of President Carter's human rights program was Argentina, but the Soviet Union has abstained from votes on resolutions criticizing the Argentine government for human rights violations. For its part the Argentine government has softened its criticism of the Soviet role in Afghanistan and Poland. More important, although leftist parties were formally outlawed, the Argentine Communist party, like parties of the right and center, was allowed to retain its offices and equipment and function semilegally.

Argentina has been stregthening its military relations with the USSR by an exchange of military visits and of military attachés. No doubt the Argentine government is comforted to know that should it be denied access to Western arms manufacturers, the Soviet Union might well be an alternate source. Argentina has gone its own way before—during World War II and again right after the war under Perón. The close ties that now exist between Argentina and the USSR, firmly based on common economic interests, strengthen Argentina's negotiating position greatly. The Soviet Communists are dealing with the Argentine military, and the latter have the further assurance, already demonstrated in practice, that the Argentine Communist party, so long as it suits Soviet interest, is unlikely to be a severe critic of the military government and is unlikely to foment revolts against it.

During the Falklands/Malvinas Islands conflict of 1982, the Soviet delegates abstained from censuring Argentine seizure of the islands, because a negative vote would have condoned the use of force. But in other respects, the USSR tended to support Argentina against Britain and its allies in the West, giving the Argentines a powerful sympathizer to balance against their Western critics. Cuba, too, supported Argentina and led the nonaligned movement in backing the latter's cause.

• *Brazil.* The Soviet Union has long attributed great importance to Brazil because of its huge area, large population, and political influence in the world. In addition, the Brazilian economy produces many goods the USSR needs and also offers the largest market in Latin America for Soviet exports. For these reasons Soviet officials and scholars have long placed great value on diplomatic and economic relations with Brazil and have also followed with care political developments inside the country.

During most of Brazil's recent history, however, the Brazilian government has had a political complexion among the least propitious in Latin America for relations with the USSR. Before World War II there appears to be no evidence that Brazil ever seriously considered recognizing the USSR. The most prestigious Communist in Latin America, Luiz Carlos Prestes, resident in Moscow for most of the 1970s, led an unsuccessful armed uprising to overthrow the Brazilian government in 1935. At that time the Communist International and leading Soviet Communists strongly backed Prestes. As one would hardly find surprising, the Brazilian government was then a vocal critic of the Brazilian Communists, the International, and the Soviet Union.

Brazil recognized the Soviet Union in April 1945, partially in acknowledgment of the Soviet contribution to the defeat of the Axis, against whom the Brazilians fought in Italy. The period of formal relations proved short because after the war, on 20 October 1947, Brazil was the first Latin American government to break relations with Moscow. The diplomatic break was paralleled by government suppression of the Communist party. It was outlawed in May 1947, and its deputies and senators were ejected from Parliament in October 1947. Brazil continued to maintain diplomatic relations with Poland, Czechoslovakia, and Yugoslavia after the break.

In the ensuing ten years, the national discussion about ties with the socialist countries continued. On one side were opponents of such relations, who feared Soviet "penetration" of Brazil and the influence of the Brazilian Communist party. On the other side were nationalists who insisted that the question of relations with the Soviet Union was a strictly Brazilian decision and that trade with the socialist countries was in the national interest.

In the fall of 1959, the Brazilian government under President Kubitchek sent a trade delegation to the USSR. In December 1959 the two countries signed a trade and payments agreement for three years. The USSR was to supply Brazil with oil, petroleum products, wheat, machines and equipment, and chemical products in exchange for coffee, cocoa, and hides. The president of Petrobras told *Pravda* that Brazil acquired high-quality Soviet oil at lower prices than were available from other sources. A joint executive committee was formed to promote trade, and in May 1960 Gosbank, the Soviet state bank, and the Banco do Brasil signed a clearing agreement and made arrangements for the exchange of other products. In the spring of 1961, trade promotion offices were established in Moscow and Rio de Janeiro.

Meanwhile, Jânio Quadros, one of several presidential candidates, visited the USSR in 1959. In his campaign platform, the party proposed that Brazil establish relations with governments irrespective of their political structure. Quadros was elected, and relations between the two countries continued to grow as part of the new "independent foreign policy" with a more balanced and neutralist orientation. It was not until November 1961, after Quadros resigned and Vice President Goulart became president, that relations were formally reestablished. In May and June 1962, the USSR sponsored a trade and industrial exhibit in Rio de Janeiro which was the largest Soviet exhibit abroad in that year. Soviet authorities claimed that over one million Brazilians visited the exhibit. In April 1963 the two countries signed a new trade and payments agreement for 1963–65.

In 1963 two Soviet geologists, E. A. Bakirov and E. I. Tagiev, were invited to Brazil to help identify oil reserves. The Soviet specialists claimed that there were reserves in Brazil, especially in the north, and that these were sufficient to meet the nation's needs. Their report attracted much attention because earlier surveys made by American geologists had reached opposite conclusions. The Soviet press said that the American geologists had been associated with Standard Oil, which had an interest in exporting oil to Brazil. Brazil is still heavily dependent on foreign oil, and optimistic Soviet claims have not yet been proven.

Meanwhile, the Goulart government was in growing economic and political difficulties. Inflation was mounting rapidly, and there was labor and popular unrest in many cities. Goulart himself was moving leftward, and conservative groups in Brazil and the United States were concerned. Measures to nationalize certain public utilities caused alarm in the same quarters. In April 1964 Goulart was overthrown by the Brazilian military and fled the country.

In the period from Kubitschek to Goulart, Soviet trade with Brazil expanded substantially. Total trade rose from five million rubles in 1959 to sixty-five million rubles in 1963. This was a huge increase although the 1963 figure constituted less than 3 percent of Brazilian foreign trade. Soviet imports tended to run well ahead of exports, but not to the same extent as in many other Latin American countries.

The Castelo Branco government, which overthrew Goulart in 1964, closed the Congress and imprisoned or exiled many political leaders on the left, including the Communists. Brazil became a repressive anti-Communist military dictatorship. One of the first foreign policy acts of the new government was to break relations with Cuba. Brazilian policy toward the socialist countries in Europe, however, was quite different. In May 1964, in reply to a journalist's question, Castelo Branco maintained that Brazil would continue normal relations with other governments irrespective of their political system and that the Soviet embassy had normal relations with his government.[16] Defending this policy, Roberto Campos, minister of planning and economic coordination, explained that Brazil had heavy debts with the Western countries, which were saturated with Brazilian exports, while prospects for expanding trade with the USSR were good.[17]

In August 1966 the two governments signed a protocol about Soviet deliveries of machinery and equipment to Brazil on terms of commercial credit. The USSR agreed to take 25 percent of its imports from Brazil in finished or semifinished goods. The Soviet minister of foreign trade pointed out that this contract made possible both an increase in Soviet purchases of Brazil's traditional exports and purchase there of finished and semifinished goods at least equivalent to 25 percent of Brazil's purchases in the USSR. In 1967 the USSR brought soluble coffee from Brazil; some Brazilian purchases in the USSR were lathes, ball bearings, watches, and cameras. Oil was by far the largest Soviet export to Brazil in 1966, fluctuating greatly but sometimes about 90 percent of exports to Brazil.

In the years immediately following the military coup of 1964, Soviet-Brazilian trade dropped off but nonetheless continued to maintain a level far above the pre-1960 period. The military dictatorship continued to trade with the USSR, and in 1972 total trade exceeded the former record year of 1963 under Goulart. In 1971 the USSR had more trade with Brazil than with any other Latin American country except Cuba, thereby edging out Argentina as the Soviet Union's first trading partner in Latin America. In October 1972 the two countries signed an agreement on shipping to increase the quantity of their mutual trade carried on their own ships. In the meantime Brazil began to purchase new items of Soviet manufacture: power, excavating and cementmaking equipment, tractors, and cement. As noted in chapter 3, the Soviet Union has delivered generators to Brazilian power plants.

Brazil's economic difficulties, particularly its need to import most of its oil, have had a favorable impact on trade with the USSR. Brazil sought to expand exports and, as we have seen, became for a time the Soviet Union's largest trading partner in Latin America except for Cuba. Sales to the USSR have helped Brazil improve its balance-of-payments position. At the same time, the USSR has been dissatisfied with the volume of Soviet exports to Brazil and links future Soviet purchases to Brazilian purchases of Soviet products. Oil constituted most of Soviet exports to Brazil until 1978 when the USSR began reserving oil for its socialist and more politically favored customers.

Soviet authors have called attention to a constructive Soviet role in Brazil's economic crisis in 1974. In that year there was a steep drop in demand for shoes, partly caused by the imposition of a protective tariff in the United States. In 1975 the USSR agreed to purchase 120,000 pairs of shoes; this permitted some twenty-nine Brazilian factories to remain open and guaranteed employment for hundreds of workers.[18]

Soviet-Brazilian trade is planned and coordinated by a joint trade and economic commission which meets annually. The Brazilians sponsored an exhibit of light industrial products in Moscow in 1973, with over one hundred Brazilian firms exhibiting. Soviet initiatives to stimulate trade continued to rely on industrial exhibitions such as the one in São Paulo in August 1973.

Soviet commentators have called attention to the fact that Brazilian aims in the Soviet relationship are "quite limited," meaning that they prefer to keep ties strictly business. Soviet relations with Brazil are not close for a variety of reasons. In the first place, the authoritarian Brazilian military regime does not look kindly on socialism or the USSR. The Brazilians are happy to sell their products to the Soviet Union, but neither government or private corporations are making much effort to increase Brazilian imports from the USSR, which the Soviets hold to be essential to a large trade expansion. Nor does the Brazilian government wish to go much beyond economic relations; cultural relations, for example, are minimal. And the Brazilian government maintained its anti-Communist policies until 1982, including the repression of the Communist party and other parties on the left. Nonetheless, the USSR continues to have diplomatic and commercial relations with Brazil and appears to regard the results of those relations positively.[19] No doubt this is partly because Soviet leaders consider Brazil a large, powerful, and influential state where it is desirable to maintain a presence. This motivation helps explain why Soviet trade officials are prepared to buy far more from Brazil than they sell.

• *Chile*. Chile had no official contact with the USSR during the interwar period, but like most other Latin American governments, it established diplomatic relations toward the end of the war, in December 1944. In 1946 Gabriel González Videla was elected president of Chile with Communist support, and Communists joined his cabinet. Prospects for the expansion of relations between the two countries seemed promising. Plans were underway for direct steamship connections between Valparaiso and Vladivostok, and for the sale of Chilean nitrates and other products in exchange for Soviet equipment and raw materials.[20]

When the new president had difficulty in securing parliamentary majorities and as the cold war deepened abroad, his government swung abruptly to the right and outlawed the Communist party. On 21 October 1947, Chile broke diplomatic relations with the USSR.

In the years that followed, there was lingering concern in Chile that the absence of relations with the USSR was denying the nation a profitable market. In January 1960 the government of President Jorge Allessandri, the leader of a coalition of right-wing parties, sent a trade and industrial delegation to Moscow to look into economic opportunities. Meanwhile Chile suffered a severe earthquake in 1960, and the Soviet Union sent food and medicines. In 1961 Chile considered selling copper to the USSR, but opposition in political and industrial circles prevented sales from taking place. In 1963, however, Chile signed its first agreement for the sale to the USSR of several thousand tons of copper. Again in 1963 a Chilean economic delegation visited the USSR with no concrete results.

In the elections of 1964, the Christian Democratic candidate, Eduardo Frei, and the candidate of the Left, Salvador Allende, both favored reestablishing relations with the USSR. After Frei became president, the new Chilean foreign minister and the Soviet ambassador from Argentina signed an agreement on 24 November 1964, reestablishing diplomatic relations. In 1966 a Chilean delegation headed by the minister of labor and social welfare visited Moscow, and Politburo member A. P. Kirilenko attended the Thirteenth Congress of the Chilean Communist party in 1965. While in Chile, he was received by President Frei.

Progress in expanding relations was slow. On 13 January 1967, three agreements were signed in Moscow: a trade agreement, an agreement about deliveries of Soviet machinery and equipment, and an agreement for technical cooperation for the construction of industrial and other projects. The USSR agreed to use 30 percent of its receipts from these projects to buy finished and semifinished Chilean goods. In June 1968 these agreements were followed up by the visit of a Chilean trade delegation to Moscow. The two governments reached another agreement regarding expenditures under a Soviet credit of US $57 million for machines, equipment, and industrial construction.[21] Arrangements were made for Soviet specialists to travel to Chile to study industrial construction projects, modernization of the railroads, the equipping of a fishing port, and a factory for canning fish. On its side Chile agreed to sell the USSR wool, yarn, clothing, shoes, cellulose, fruit, and other products.

The Soviet authorities enthusiastically welcomed the election of Salvador Allende to the presidency and his assumption of power in October 1970. A member of the Socialist party himself, a Marxist, and enjoying the support of the Communist party, Allende was politically and ideologically closer to the Soviet Union than any Latin American president except Castro. Moscow moved to strengthen ties with his government. From the beginning it was clear to all, including Soviet leaders, that Allende faced an uphill struggle in an economic and political sense. His plans to move Chile rapidly toward socialism meant further shocks to an economy which was already in deep trouble. And his radical program and relatively narrow base of support raised serious questions whether the Chilean military would permit him to finish his term.

In spite of Allende's tenuous position, Soviet economic cooperation continued within roughly the same framework as in other friendly countries, such as the military government of Peru. This treatment included generous credits to promote Soviet exports, extensive purchases of the Latin American partner's traditional exports, technical assistance, and gifts for humanitarian purposes. During Allende's presidency the USSR authorized more credits, increased trade more rapidly, and helped the Chilean economy more than it had other Latin American countries except Cuba. But it did not move outside the traditional framework. The Soviet authorities, for example, did not follow the same policies as toward Cuba, that is, subsidizing Chilean exports and imports, providing free military equipment (Allende turned it down), absorbing huge trade deficits, or buying up much of Chilean exports.[22] Clearly neither Soviet nor Chilean leaders viewed their relationship as a repetition of Soviet-Cuban relations.

The tempo of the development of Soviet-Chilean relations was moderate. In the first place Allende and his leading associates had their hands full in Chile, nor did they consider inordinate haste in developing ties with the USSR seemly. On the Soviet side the bureaucracy operated ponderously and cautiously. The first step forward took place in May 1971 when the Chilean foreign minister paid a visit to Moscow. He was received by Chairman of the Council of Ministers Kosygin and by others of second rank. His visit led to the signing on 28 May of an agreement increasing Soviet credits to Chile within the framework of the 1967 agreement with the Frei government. The agreement also provided for a list of items for trade, the establishment of a Chilean trade mission in the USSR, and the creation of a Soviet-Chilean trade commission. The USSR also agreed to offer technical assistance in the construction of a factory to produce lubricating oil and an apartment construction facility, and for the study of the possibilities for cooperation in other fields, including fishing and the chemical industry.

In June 1971 a group of Soviet copper-mining specialists arrived to help restore the operation of mines which had been nationalized and from which American specialists had departed. In July the USSR gave the people of Chile, who had recently suffered a severe earthquake, a factory for the production of apartment buildings. The factory was designed to produce fifty-eight four-story apartment buildings a year or 1,680 units. It went into operation in July 1973, before Allende's fall. The factory, near Valparaiso, is perhaps the most important visible object of Soviet assistance to the Allende government which continues in operation under the military junta. Apparently there's not much else left.

Another important field of Soviet-Chilean economic cooperation was in fishing. A Soviet delegation of specialists headed by the minister of fishing visited Chile in August 1971. The two governments agreed on Soviet cooperation in planning and constructing or reconstructing fishing ports, studying Chilean fishing resources, training fishing personnel, and establishing schools for the preparation of subprofessional specialists.

On their side the Chilean authorities offered many of Chile's major ports to receive Soviet fishing vessels for rest, reequipping, and resupplying. Three large Soviet fishing trawlers were rented out on commercial terms to the Chilean company Arauco. With larger Soviet equipment, the catch was many times greater than Arauco previously made. Another important Soviet delivery to Chile was 3,180 tractors in 1972 and 1973.[23]

Political contacts between the two countries were frequent during the Allende period. Sh. R. Rashidov, a candidate member of the Soviet Politburo, attended the Twenty-third Congress of the Chilean Socialist party in Santiago in January 1971, and representatives of the Chilean Socialist and Communist parties took part in the Twenty-fourth Congress of the Soviet Communist party, also in 1971. Politburo member Kirilenko came once more to Chile, this time to help the Party celebrates its fiftieth anniversary on 2 January 1972. Several aspects of these visits were noteworthy. The Soviet Party welcomed the Chilean socialists into the bosom of international communism, an expedient move since Allende himself was a socialist and the socialists were the largest party in the government. Political ties increased under Allende: a soviet parliamentary delegation came to Chile in 1971, and a Chilean economic delegation visited the Soviet Union in 1972. The latter resulted in further agreements for economic and technical cooperation. While in Moscow the chief of the delegation commented on how helpful Soviet credits were, especially in the light of "the pressure of U.S. imperialism to smother our economy."[24]

The climactic moment of Soviet-Chilean relations came on 6 December 1972 when Salvador Allende visited Moscow and was received by Brezhnev, Podgornii, and Kosygin. It is of interest that his first visit as president came more than two years after his assumption of the post and nine months before his fall from power. He was accompanied by Foreign Minister Almeyda and the general secretary of the Chilean Party, Luis Corvalán. Army Commander Carlos Prats visited the USSR in May 1973.

Trade between the USSR and Chile grew rapidly during the Allende period (see table 2). By 1972, when momentum in the relationship began to build, most of Soviet exports to Chile were machinery, equipment, and transport vehicles. In 1973, however, economic conditions in Chile

Table 2
Soviet Trade with Chile, 1970–1973
(millions of rubles)

	1970	1971	1972	1973
Exports	0.5	7.0	11.6	16.0
Imports	0.3	0.8	7.3	12.6
Balance	0.2	7.0	4.3	3.4

Source: Vneshniaia torgovlia SSSR, statisticheskii sbornik for 1971 and 1973.

had worsened substantially, and the bulk of Soviet exports were consumer items, particularly wheat and frozen meat. In 1971 the USSR
imported iodine from Chile, but in 1972 and 1973 the major items were
copper and copper concentrate. Unlike Soviet trade with many Latin
American countries, the USSR had a trade surplus with Chile during the
Allende years. This is not surprising in view of the Soviet interest in
helping Allende through credits and economic cooperation. Yet the
Soviet trade surplus was relatively small, totaling less than 15 million
rubles in the three-year period. While that small figure may not reflect the
real value of Soviet aid to Allende, it does show its limited scope.

The Soviet trade surplus of about 15 million rubles is small compared
to the credits authorized for Allende. The latter came to about US $260
million.[25] Some of this may have been in hard currency, but the bulk
required Chilean purchase of Soviet products. As a result Soviet aid, or
more accurately, lines of credit, was of limited utility when Allende
needed hard currency to pay off the Chilean foreign debt and to pay for
products needed and contracted for in the West.

From a Soviet perspective, the USSR tried to aid Allende but only
within the framework of its traditional foreign economic policies, not as
it aided Cuba. Most of this assistance took the form of lines of credit and
technical cooperation in fishing, apartment construction, vehicles, and
mining. Allende welcomed Soviet moral and financial support, but it
contributed little to helping him solve his economic and political problems.

Shortly after Allende was overthrown in 1973, the USSR broke diplomatic and commercial relations with the military junta with no intention of reestablishing relations with that government.

• *Peru.* Unlike most of the larger Latin American nations, Peru did not recognize the USSR at the end of World War II. The Soviet Union had almost no contact with Peru until 1969, when diplomatic relations were established for the first time. During the interwar period and the first few years after World War II, Peru was an old-fashioned society dedicated mainly to agriculture and mining and displaying many symbols of its colonial past. In the 1970s, however, the Soviet Union achieved a broader and possibly closer relationship with Peru than with any other Latin American country except Cuba. The relationship is broader because Soviet-Peruvian relations cover not only trade but also cultural, economic, technical, financial, and most notably, military cooperation.

The usual Soviet preference for socialist or Communist governments was no obstacle to developing close ties with the Peruvian military regime. Since Marxist governments are few, the USSR is prepared to collaborate with governments that have an antiimperialist orientation, such as Peru from 1968 to 1980. The Peruvian military government which came to power in 1968 expropriated oil and other natural resources, imposed controls over foreign imports, introduced agrarian reform, and took other measures to improve the lot of the poor. General Velasco, who headed that government, took an antiimperialist line while rejecting explicitly both capitalism and communism for his country. He did favor relations with Moscow.

The USSR and Peru established diplomatic relations and signed a trade agreement in early 1969. Trade promotion offices were established in Moscow and Lima. The Peruvians expressed their hope that ties with an industrial state like the Soviet Union would create great opportunities for their national development in many fields. Beginning in 1971 ships began to travel twice a month between Baltic ports and the Pacific. In 1974 Aeroflot began the first Soviet commercial air service to South America. It flew to Lima by way of Frankfurt, Lisbon, and Havana.

In 1970 Peru experienced one of the worst earthquakes in its history. The Soviets gave helicopters, one hundred apartment buildings, road-building equipment, equipment for three kindergartens, medicine, and food. Moscow also sent a field hospital and medical personnel.

In December 1971 the two countries signed an agreement about economic and technical cooperation which was later implemented by protocols dealing with specific projects, such as those at Olmos, Paita, and Rentama, discussed in chapter 3. A Soviet export firm was to have supplied equipment and know-how for the construction of a steel plant at Nasca and for equipment at Arequipa, but fiscal problems forced postponement of these projects. The USSR has supplied Peru with helicopters, trucks, oil tanks, and ore-bearing freighters. The helicopters have proven especially useful in the construction of a pipeline in the north and for moving heavy tools into the jungle. Soviet vaccines have also been provided in large quantity. In the late 1970s, when Peru was suffering fiscal and balance-of-payments difficulties, many of the projects were stalled for lack of capital. For its part the USSR has imported light metals and their ores, coffee, sugarcane, wool, and fish meal from Peru.

The most distinguishing feature of Soviet-Peruvian relations is the fact that Peru is the only Latin American country other than Cuba to which the USSR has provided arms. Peruvian purchases come to several hundred million rubles for aircraft, tanks, surface-to-air missiles, and artillery. The government purchased two hundred fifty 54/55 tanks and thirty-six Su-22 fighter bombers and SA-3 and SA-7 surface-to-air missiles. In addition the Peruvian government has purchased twenty-three Mi-8 helicopters, two hundred T-62 medium tanks, and 122mm and 130mm artillery.[26] Peru maintains one of the few Latin American embassies in Moscow with a military attaché; he has the rank of brigadier general. U.S. government sources for the 1970s show almost one hundred Soviet military advisers in Peru and over six hundred Peruvian military in training assignments in the USSR.[27]

Unlike Cuba, which has received most if not all of its arms from the USSR free, Peru must pay, but on what are believed to be easy terms. In 1978, when Peru was having great difficulty servicing its foreign debt— payments of interest and principal were coming to 55 percent of exports—the Soviet Union was the first major creditor to reschedule its debt. The USSR put a moratorium on payments beginning with the equivalent of some US $60 million due in that year.[28] The moratorium lasted through 1980, payments resuming then until 1988, with the larger amounts to be paid later. Moscow placed no charges or conditions on this rescheduling and reportedly even expressed willingness to make further adjustments if conditions warranted. Peruvian officials have indicated that the generous Soviet attitude contributed to the softening of the position of Western creditors later in the year. To express appreciation for Soviet material and moral support in a time of national crisis, the Peruvian government awarded high decorations to Politburo members Brezhnev, Kosygin, Gromyko, and Andropov. Relations cooled, however, when Belaunde came to power in 1980, and Soviet-Peruvian cooperation generally ceased.

• *Grenada.*   Until the U.S. invasion in October 1983, Soviet relations with Grenada were probably more cordial than with any other nation in the hemisphere except Cuba and Nicaragua. In March 1979 the New Jewel Movement under the leadership of Maurice Bishop staged an armed coup overthrowing the corrupt, long-entrenched, and repressive dictatorship of Eric Gairy. Prime Minister Bishop and other leaders were pro-socialist and pro-Soviet from the beginning: they had grown up under the influence of radical thinkers like Frantz Fanon, Malcolm X, Fidel Castro, and Lenin and naturally took their place among the pro-Soviet governments of the Third World.[29] Holding out socialism as a rather distant but desirable ideal, the Bishop government sought to put Grenada back together after the ravages of Gairy's rule.[30]

Given its social and political orientation, forged from political action as well as reading, the New Jewel Movement appeared to have concluded that the Communist world would supply Grenada's needs better than the United States. Grenada's radicalism and location in the U.S. Caribbean sphere meant that it should not have been difficult to raise in the East sums that would have a great impact on the development of a country with only about one hundred thousand people. The pro-Soviet stance was expressed rhetorically and also more substantively in Grenada's negative vote on the UN resolution deploring the Soviet invasion of Afghanistan. The Reagan administration's indignation over that vote partially explained Washington's opposition to international bank financing of Grenada's new airport, nine thousand feet long and capable of accommodating wide-bodied jets, designed to boost the nation's tourist revenues.[31] The Cuban government provided equipment, material, and 270 workers to build the airport. Other countries that came to Grenada's aid included

Algeria, Libya, Iraq, and Syria. Venezuela, Czechoslovakia, Bulgaria, and East Germany also provided assistance.[32]

After the invasion, U.S. officials discovered secret Grenadian documents describing in detail relations with the Soviet Union. The documents suggest that the Grenadians aggressively wooed the USSR and other Communist nations. For example, they modeled their political system on the one-party Communist societies, creating a politburo and mass organizations and using Communist terminology. Soviet leaders had decided, probably correctly, that the best way for them to develop a long-term position in Grenada was through its political leadership. That helps account for the emphasis on party-to-party relationships—they joined with the Cubans in helping build a new party headquarters—and on people-to-people programs in the USSR: student scholarships, training of civilian and military officials, familiarization visits, rest and recreation visits, and the like.

Next to party relations and approval of ties with other socialist governments, the Soviet military aid program was probably most important. The two countries signed several comprehensive secret military agreements which provided the Grenadians with a wide range of small arms, transport vehicles, anti-aircraft weapons, communication and other technical equipment, and so forth.[33] Shipped through Cuba, these weapons were numerous enough to arm most of the local population. Their most important purpose may have been to quell a domestic uprising or to repel an invasion by the opposition. There is no suggestion in the documents that Grenada intended to foment guerrilla operations elsewhere in the region. Its lack of naval vessels and aircraft support this view.

The Soviet Union provided Grenada with relatively little economic assistance.[34] For example it granted some $1.4 million in steel, flour, and other goods in 1982, but was unwilling to help Bishop complete his most pressing project, the airport.

In the political struggle preceding Bishop's assassination in October 1983, the Soviet Union appears to have favored Bernard Coard, who had been a frequent visitor to the Soviet Union. Bishop, on the other hand, was a close friend of Fidel Castro, who was saddened and angered by his death. The outcome of the Bishop-Coard struggle, however, appears to have been decided mainly by Grenadians.

• *Other Countries.* Soviet relations with many other Latin American countries are also worthy of extended and separate treatment, but space in this volume does not permit it. Here are short summary statements.

The USSR had trade relations with Uruguay soon after the Bolshevik Revolution, and Uruguay recognized the USSR in 1926. The level of trade has been rather high relative to other Latin American countries over the long term. That is because Uruguay, like Argentina, has many products the USSR wants to buy. There has been some trade even in periods when political relations have been difficult, for example in the 1970s.

Economic ties with Bolivia have been expanding as rapidly as with almost any other Latin American country. This trend was established even before the authoritarian military regime of General Banzer was overthrown. Bolivia became the USSR's fourth trading partner in Latin America except Cuba in 1977, largely because of Soviet purchases of tin ore. Soviet provision and financing of a plant to process low-grade tin ores was successful, and construction of another plant followed. The USSR increased scholarships for poor Bolivians, who appreciated these opportunities to improve their lot in life.

Guyana under Forbes Burnham and Jamaica under Manley courted the USSR, most particularly to secure Soviet loans and technical assistance for the refining of bauxite. The Soviet Union purchased much bauxite from both countries from 1973 to 1975, and they have been negotiating for technical assistance of other kinds, such as in construction and fishing. Burnham and Manley have both visited the USSR. On his visit in April 1979, Manley got a commitment from the USSR to buy large qualities of alumina from Jamaica's new plant. The Jamaican and Guyanese brands of socialism were politically and ideologically closer to Soviet socialism than those of most other Latin American countries, and the three governments have similar views on a number of international questions, most particularly in Africa. Guyana has applied for membership in the socialist nations' Council for Mutual Economic Assistance, and Burnham's People's National Congress wanted association with the Soviet Communist party, perhaps as a counter to the existing association of the Guyanese Communists led by Dr. Cheddi Jagan. Soviet relations with the Seaga government, which succeeded Manley in Jamaica, have cooled.

Soviet purchases of Colombian coffee have given the latter country an opportunity to diversify its foreign markets. The USSR provided and financed equipment for a US $200-million hydroelectric plant at Alto Sinú. The two governments had an easy political relationship with active cultural relations and a large number of Colombian students in the USSR.

The USSR appears to be interested in Venezuela primarily for political reasons, that is, as a means of access to and influence on a leading Third World nation. Relations were not established until 1970. Venezuela finds a Soviet tie useful in strengthening its bargaining position with the United States and in the Caribbean, where there has been rivalry with Cuba. Trade between the two countries has been only slight, but with the Soviet Union having a tiny, but rare for Latin America, trade surplus. President Perez visited Moscow in late 1976. To save transportation costs on both sides, Venezuela agreed to provide Cuba with oil, and the USSR agreed to supply an equivalent amount to Spain.

Although without diplomatic representation, the Soviet Union has maintained an interest in Panama and was a supporter of the Panama Canal treaties. The USSR usually has a trade surplus with Panama, selling, for example, large quantities of watches and other consumer durables, probably for resale to transit visitors. Soviet officials would probably like to have diplomatic relations but appear to understand that such a tie might place Panamanian interests with the U.S. in jeopardy.

Soviet relations with Central America are discussed in chapter 6, and conclusions about Soviet relations with Latin America in general are given in chapter 7.

III   The Stubborn Trade Deficit: Economic Relations

The most significant aspect of Soviet economic relations with Latin America (except Cuba) is the large continuing trade deficit (table 3). In recent years Soviet trade deficits with Latin America have fluctuated between 200 and 1,400 million rubles a year, and the Soviet global balance has been between 4 billion rubles plus and 2 billion minus. Thus Latin America has contributed heavily to the negative side of the Soviet balance of payments.

Soviet import agencies have been buying hundreds of millions of rubles of consumer goods and nonferrous metals every year, paying for them in hard currency (table 4). Recently, more than three-quarters of these purchases have been from Argentina and Brazil. The Latin American countries are not buying back Soviet exports in comparable volume (table 5). Latin American purchases from the USSR at best are less than a third of Soviet purchases in the area, and in some years they are as little as one-tenth.

The most dramatic purchases in the history of Soviet trade with the area came in 1980, when the USSR sought alternative suppliers after the imposition of the U.S. grain embargo for the occupation of Afghanistan. Soviet purchases of Argentine grain, frozen meat, and other items produced a deficit with Argentina alone of over 1.1 billion rubles. That figure was more than twice the Soviet deficit for all Latin America in 1979.

Even in the absence of emergencies, why are Soviet agencies able and willing to continue purchasing at such relatively high levels? Probably the main reason (this has been confirmed independently from various Soviet sources) is that Moscow finds Latin American offerings attractive. In order to examine alternative markets, I selected the items imported by the USSR in the largest quantities and checked the geographic distribution of these items in the official Soviet foreign trade yearbook. Two groups of items were prominent in that search. The first, including

Table 3
Soviet Trade Deficit, 1960–1980
(millions of rubles)

	1960	1970	1971	1972	1973	1974	1975	1976	1977	1978	1979	1980	1970–1980
Argentina	-6.9	-26.5	-28.5	-22.1	-67.7	-125.5	-283.0	-216.9	-179.5	-286.4	-263.4	-1131.7	-2638.6
Bolivia		-3.1	-9.0	-1.7	-8.2	-7.3	-6.6	-8.1	-24.1	-29.0	-27.2	-14.5	-138.8
Brazil	5.8	-18.4	-39.7	-58.7	-107.2	-22.0	-209.05	-293.5	-105.2	-95.3	-140.1	-230.8	-1320.2
Chile		1.9	6.2	4.3	3.4								15.8
Colombia		-7.9	-3.2	1.5	-8.5	-3.3	-5.2	-1.6	-5.5	5.4	5.2	-2.9	-26.1
Costa Rica		-6.2	-2.2	-2.8	-4.9	-1.0	0.5	-1.6	-3.4	5.5			-12.7
Dominican Rep.				-2.8	-15.6								-18.4
Ecuador		-0.6	-3.3	-2.2	-0.5	-3.9	-12.3	-7.0	-9.4	-27			-41.9
El Salvador				-2.8	-3.7		0.1		1.1				-5.3
Guatemala					-4.3								-4.3
Guyana				0.3	-6.9	-4.3	-24.5		-1.6	-3.5			-40.5
Jamaica		-0.7	-2.3	-1.0	-3.9	-9.5	-11.2						-28.6
Mexico	-2.4	0.4	-8.9	-7.2	0.4	-0.2	2.7	-4.2	-0.5	-8.6	-3.4	1.0	
Panama							2.6	3.8	5.7	5.2	0.4	4.9	22.6
Peru		-0.1	-0.2	-1.6	-11.1	-0.1	-61.9	-4.2	6.0	1.1	-7.1	-7.1	-84.7
Suriname									-2.4	-1.1			-3.5
Trinidad-Tobago				-8.4					-1.8				-10.2
Uruguay		-0.2	-0.4	-1.0	-4.5	-23.9	-13.0	-1.6	-7.4	-11.5	-10.1	-19.0	-92.6
Venezuela				-4.0		0.2	0.2	0.3	2.7	0.7			0.1
Total	-3.5	-61.4	-91.5	-110.2	-243.2	-200.8	-621.1	-534.6	-325.4	-420.2	-446.2	-1401.0	-4483.0

Note: Prepared by Aldo Isuani and Silvia Borzutzky from annual volumes of *Vneshniaia torgovlia SSSR, statisticheskii sbornik.*

Table 4
Soviet Imports from Latin America, 1960–1980
(millions of rubles)

	1960	1970	1971	1972	1973	1974	1975	1976	1977	1978	1979	1980	1970–1980
Argentina	19.5	28.2	30.4	22.9	72.2	131.5	293.7	225.4	192.9	308.8	288.7	1162.1	2776.3
Bolivia	—	3.1	9.0	2.5	12.2	11.4	9.6	12.3	27.7	34.3	32.4	20.0	174.5
Brazil	8.4	20.8	41.7	65.8	116.5	112.0	302.8	369.4	209.6	130.2	160.0	252.9	1790.1
Chile	—	0.3	0.8	7.3	12.6	—	—	—	—	—	—	—	21.0
Colombia	—	9.4	4.3	1.2	9.3	4.3	7.1	3.3	7.4	0.1	3.0	12.0	61.4
Costa Rica	—	6.2	2.2	2.8	5.1	1.6	—	2.2	3.6	5.6	—	—	29.3
Dominican Rep.	—	—	—	2.8	15.6	—	—	—	—	—	—	—	18.4
Ecuador	—	0.7	3.3	2.3	0.7	4.4	12.9	7.4	9.8	3.3	—	—	44.8
El Salvador	—	—	—	2.8	3.7	—	—	—	—	—	—	—	6.5
Guatemala	—	—	—	—	4.3	—	—	—	—	—	—	—	4.3
Guyana	—	—	—	—	6.9	4.5	24.5	—	1.6	3.5	—	—	41.0
Jamaica	—	0.7	2.3	1.0	3.9	9.5	11.2	—	—	—	4.1	1.9	28.6
Mexico	3.0	0.3	9.2	7.8	0.1	1.3	1.7	11.1	1.7	11.0	9.9	10.2	53.2
Peru	—	0.2	0.2	1.8	15.4	4.7	90.2	18.1	20.4	15.7	—	—	186.8
Suriname	—	—	—	—	—	—	—	—	2.4	15.7	—	—	18.1
Trinidad-Tobago	1.2	1.0	—	8.4	—	—	—	—	1.8	—	—	—	10.2
Uruguay	—	—	1.3	2.2	5.3	24.7	14.0	4.1	8.6	12.4	11.7	21.4	107.9
Venezuela	—	—	—	4.1	0.6	—	—	—	—	—	—	—	4.7
Total	32.1	70.9	104.7	135.7	284.4	309.9	767.7	653.3	487.5	540.6	509.8	1480.5	5377.1

Note: Prepared by Aldo Isuani and Silvia Borzutzky from annual volumes of Vneshniaia torgovlia SSSR, statisticheskii sbornik.

Table 5
Soviet Exports to Latin America, 1960–1980
(millions of rubles)

	1960	1970	1971	1972	1973	1974	1975	1976	1977	1978	1979	1980	1970–1980
Argentina	12.6	1.7	1.9	1.8	4.5	6.0	10.7	8.5	13.4	22.4	24.8	30.4	138.7
Bolivia	—	—	—	0.8	4.0	4.1	3.0	4.2	3.6	5.3	5.2	5.5	35.7
Brazil	14.2	2.4	2.0	7.1	9.3	9.0	93.3	76.1	104.4	34.9	19.9	22.1	394.7
Chile	—	0.5	7.0	11.6	16.0	—	—	—	—	—	—	—	35.1
Colombia	—	1.5	1.1	2.7	0.8	1.0	1.9	1.7	1.8	5.5	8.2	9.1	35.4
Costa Rica	—	—	—	—	0.2	0.6	0.5	0.6	0.2	0.1	—	—	2.2
Ecuador	—	0.1	—	0.1	0.2	0.5	0.6	0.4	0.5	0.6	—	—	3.0
El Salvador	—	—	—	—	—	—	0.1	—	1.1	—	—	—	1.2
Guyana	—	—	—	—	—	—	—	—	—	—	—	—	0.5
Mexico	0.6	0.7	0.3	0.6	0.5	1.1	4.4	6.0	1.2	2.4	0.7	11.9	30.3
Panama	—	—	—	—	—	—	2.6	3.8	5.7	5.2	10.3	15.1	42.7
Peru	—	0.1	—	0.2	4.3	4.6	28.3	13.9	26.4	16.8	2.8	3.1	100.5
Uruguay	1.2	0.8	0.9	1.2	0.8	0.8	1.0	1.3	1.2	0.9	1.6	2.4	14.1
Venezuela	—	—	—	0.1	0.6	0.2	0.2	0.3	2.7	0.7	—	—	4.8
Total	28.6	7.8	13.2	26.5	41.2	28.1	146.2	116.8	162.1	94.8	73.5	99.6	838.4

Note: Prepared by Aldo Isuani and Silvia Borzutzky from annual volumes of *Vneshniaia torgovlia SSSR, statisticheskii sbornik.*

wool and corn, was purchased heavily in hard currency markets. It was a question of buying from Latin America or, as in the case of wool, from hard currency sources like Australia or New Zealand. The second group, composed mainly of nonferrous metals, was not shown in the geographic distribution statistics. Its absence suggests that these products may be considered strategically sensitive. Some may be in short supply or involve delicate issues of access.

Soviet officials also consider Latin America a potentially large market for their machinery and equipment. Incidently, their major interest appears to be selling manufactures, not raw materials. Latin America is regarded as more highly developed than most Asian and African countries and thus better able to absorb Soviet finished products. Soviet specialists also consider the prospects for growth in Latin America relatively good. Partly for these reasons, Soviet officials have been willing to incur large trade deficits in order to establish themselves in a potentially good market.

In the past Soviet trade has sometimes been regarded in the West largely as a political instrument of the Soviet state, as a means of penetrating other areas. It may be that one of the reasons for carrying high trade deficits has been to expand economic and political influence in the region. My own opinion is that Soviet resources are still so limited as to discourage purely political use. Domestic needs for resources are so great that the USSR cannot afford to take many losses in Latin America for purely political purposes. Moreover, other geographic areas closer to home take priority. In any case Soviet trade and influence in the area (except Argentina) to date are low both in absolute and relative terms.[1]

• Trade Structure

Soviet trade with Latin America, which fluctuated between 600 and 900 million rubles recently, ran to 1.6 million rubles in 1980 as compared to 60 million in 1960. Preliminary figures for 1981 show turnover with Latin America doubling to over 3 billion rubles, with most of the gain due to a doubling of Soviet imports from Argentina and, at a much lower level, from Brazil. Soviet trade with Latin America was about 2 percent of Soviet global turnover in 1980 and 3 percent in 1981.[2]

The trade deficit with Latin America represents the reverse of Soviet experience with developing countries as a whole, with which the USSR has been running large surpluses. That surplus was 1.8 billion rubles in 1980. Soviet imports from Latin America constituted nearly 30 percent of imports from the developing countries in 1980, and Soviet exports to Latin America were only 1 to 2 percent of exports to developing countries. Soviet trade with Latin America experiences wide variations, but these generalizations hold in a gross sense from year to year.

Argentina was among Moscow's earliest trading partners in the hemisphere, and with one exception it has traded more with the USSR than any other Latin American country. The exception is Brazil, which moved out front during the Goulart years (1961–1964) and from 1971 through 1977. In 1978 Brazil's trade dropped to half its earlier levels, possibly due to curtailment of Soviet exports of oil, and Argentina forged ahead. One of these two countries has often been among the USSR's leading trading partners from the developing countries, but ordinarily behind Egypt, India, Iran, and Iraq.

The Soviet Union has bought a wide variety of consumer goods from Argentina: wool, yarn, and clothing as well as grain, frozen meat, and wine (table 6). In the late 1970s, Soviet purchases hovered between 200

Table 6
Principal Soviet Imports from Argentina, 1979–1980
(thousands of rubles)

	1979	*1980*
Fine sheep wool	38,944	43,882
Upper leather for footwear	1,525	1,296
Semifinished leather	16,810	12,496
Wheat	13,452	314,181
Corn	129,817	295,844
Sorghum	—	145,013
Soybeans	—	112,480
Fresh frozen meat	43,221	123,940
Linseed oil	27,691	31,859
Total (all imports, in millions of rubles)	288.7	1.162.1

Source: Vneshniaia torgovlia SSSR, statisticheskii sbornik for 1980.

and 300 million rubles. It is striking that before 1978, Argentine purchases from the USSR did not reach 14 million rubles, a small fraction of Soviet purchases. Argentine purchases jumped to between 20 and 30 million rubles in 1978–1980. Most were power equipment, machinery, storage tanks, and various types of industrial vehicles (table 7). In spite of these purchases, the Soviet trade deficit with Argentina has been huge.

The most dramatic jump in Soviet purchases came in 1980 after the United States embargoed grain sales to the USSR in protest of military occupation of Afghanistan. Soviet need provided Argentina with a great commercial opportunity. The USSR purchased ten times as much wheat and nearly twice as much corn as in 1979. Argentina also sold Soviet purchasers sorghum, soybeans, and other grains not traded in 1979. Sales of frozen meat more than doubled. Nineteen eighty-one was an even better year, with annual turnover at 2.4 billion rubles. The Soviet Union became Argentina's best customer and took about 33 percent of Argentine exports in 1980.[3] Meanwhile, Argentina purchased only about 30 million rubles of Soviet goods, much of it power equipment, as contrasted with Soviet purchases of nearly 1.2 billion rubles.

Brazil is Moscow's other major trading partner in Latin America (tables 8 and 9). Soviet purchases have been heavy in consumer items such as coffee, cocoa, rice, and wool as well as some clothing. Soviet

Table 7
Principal Soviet Exports to Argentina, 1979–1980
(thousands of rubles)

	1979	1980
Machinery, equipment, and vehicles	21,187	25,853
Power equipment	7,798	16,867
Hoisting equipment	2,708	1,230
Antifriction bearings	80	212
Trucks	3,486	—
Spare parts for trucks (except motors)	1,839	681
Sodium dichromate	2,325	2,843
Total (all exports in millions of rubles)	24.8	30.4

Source: Vneshniaia torgovlia SSSR, statisticheskii sbornik for 1980.

Table 8
Principal Soviet Imports from Brazil, 1979–1980
(thousands of rubles)

	1979	1980
Sisal hemp	745	3,405
Wool yarn	5,081	1,043
Castor oil	17,979	10,607
Oitidica oil	2,678	2,574
Soybeans	13,461	24,026
Soybean oil	8,485	14,968
Coffee (natural)	995	6,796
Cocoa beans	81,290	38,598
Cocoa oil	8,650	11,775
Sugarcane	10,056	99,958
Leather footwear	—	907
Medicines	640	2,484
Motion pictures	5	6
Total (all exports, in millions of rubles)	160.0	252.9

Source: Vneshniaia torgovlia SSSR, statisticheskii sbornik for 1980.

exports to Brazil used to be far larger than to Argentina—sometimes as much as 90 percent were oil or oil products. Exports of Soviet machines and equipment to Brazil have usually been below exports in these categories to Argentina. Because the USSR has heavy demands of its own for oil at home and its allies abroad, it has found it impossible to continue supplying oil regularly to Brazil. Unless Brazil can be persuaded to buy other Soviet exports, trade between the two countries will suffer. In fact it already has: the total turnover in 1980 did not reach the level of the mid-1970s.

In the mid-1970s, Peru was the third best customer of the USSR in Latin America. The Soviet relationship with Peru under the military government was broad and involved extensive economic cooperation in many sectors. Large Soviet military sales tended to offset Peru's substantial export surplus (military sales are not shown in Soviet trade statistics). Soviet imports from Peru in 1976 and 1977 included nonferrous metals, wool, fish meal, and coffee beans. It is of interest that almost all Soviet exports to Peru were machinery and equipment. In the late 1970s, Peru

Table 9

Principal Soviet Exports to Brazil, 1979–1980

(thousand of rubles)

	1979	*1980*
Machinery, equipment and vehicles	18,576	14,932
Metal-cutting machine tools	1,290	1,210
Power equipment	8,541	7,661
Antifriction bearings	669	444
Potassium salts	960	5,987
Total (all exports, in millions of rubles)	19.9	22.1

Source: Vneshniaia torgovlia SSSR, statisticheskii sbornik for 1980.

was by far the largest purchaser of such items in Latin America. Among the exports were storage tanks, ships, and aircraft, including helicopters.

Soviet trade with Bolivia was distinguished by the fact that Soviet imports were almost exclusively tin. The direct bilateral relationship was to both parties' advantage since they do not need to pay a commission to a middleman as had been the case before commercial relations were established. Bolivian purchases from the USSR were almost exclusively machinery and equipment, especially for mining and transport. Bolivia moved ahead of Peru in 1978 as the third ranking trading partner of the USSR in Latin America.

Uruguay has been one of the more active partners from time to time as was Chile during the Allende (tables 4 and 5). Much effort has been expended in Mexico, but despite its size, Mexico has never been an important trading partner.

Trade with Venezuela is distinguished from that of most other countries in that the USSR almost always has a surplus, though small. It buys little or nothing in Venezuela and sells the Venezuelans ammonia sulphate and granular urea as well as luxury items like canned crabmeat, caviar, vodka, and motion pictures. Trade has been too small for yearbook entry.

In spite of an absence of formal diplomatic or trade relations, the USSR has been selling Panama several millions of rubles a year in consumer items, no doubt for sale to travelers. These include vodka, watches, cameras, and television sets. Soviet autos and other products are also transhipped to the United States.

• Trade Composition

The Soviet Union has mainly bought the traditional agricultural products of Latin America: hides and wool from Argentina and Uruguay, coffee from Brazil and Colombia, cocoa from Brazil and Ecuador. More recently the USSR has begun to buy nonferrous metals from Peru, alumina from Jamaica and Guyana, and tin from Bolivia. The purchasing pattern is irregular with wide variations in quantity from year to year, and sometimes trade in a popular item is cut out entirely. The list of items traded is relatively short.

At peak years Latin America has sometimes provided the USSR with 50 percent of its coffee, 25 percent of its cocoa beans, 100 percent of its linseed oil, 60 percent of its tung oil, 30 percent of its coarse hides, and 15 percent of its wool.[4] The USSR has bought wheat and corn in Argentina and corn and rice in Brazil. As an expression of its policy favoring the purchase of finished or semifinished goods from developing countries, Moscow has bought semifinished hides, wine, cloth, and shoes in Latin America. Soviet purchases of manufactures and semimanufactures, however, are insignificant in the total volume of the Latin American sales of these products.

The USSR has tried to promote the sale of its machinery and equipment in Latin America. As table 10 shows, Soviet sales of such equip-

Table 10
Soviet Exports to Latin America of Machinery, Equipment, and Transport, 1970–1980[a]
(millions of rubles)

	1970	1975	1976	1977	1978	1979	1980
Machinery, equipment, and transport	3.6	44.2	28.6	44.4	59.1	56.2	62.9
All exports to Latin America	7.8	146.6	116.8	162.2	94.8	73.5	99.6

Source: Strany SEV i Latinskaia Amerika, problemy ekonomicheskogo sotrudnichestva (Moscow 1976), table 3, p. 28. Figures for 1975 and later were calculated and rounded from the Soviet foreign trade yearbooks *Vneshniaia torgovlia, SSSR statisticheskii sbornik*.
[a]Except Cuba.

ment constitute a growing share of total exports. Such exports include hydroelectric and thermal power equipment, mining equipment, metalworking machines, construction equipment, and vehicles. A substantial part of Soviet exports are still in raw or semifinished materials. Other popular Soviet exports include watches, which have sold in huge quantities to Panama and Venezuela, caviar, vodka, and motion pictures.[5]

• Trade Promotion

In order to reduce the huge trade deficit with Latin America, Soviet officials have been attempting to increase exports to the area. This urgent interest is reflected in virtually all the government and scholarly literature and in interviews with Soviet officials and scholars. Soviet trade promotion efforts are highly formalized, and the same or similar patterns are followed with almost all countries, including the Latin American. Among the standard devices for export penetration is the Soviet industrial exhibition. The first in Latin America was in Buenos Aires in 1955. Another important exhibition was held in Mexico in late 1959. Anastas Mikoyan, deputy chairman of the Council of Ministers, visited that exhibition before his first trip to Cuba under Castro. Also under the sponsorship of the USSR Chamber of Commerce and Industry is Soviet participation in the world trade fairs, such as in Buenos Aires (1976), Bogotá (1978 and 1980), and Lima (1979). In recent years the USSR has usually been represented at only one major trade fair in Latin America.

Fundamental to establishing trade ties is an intergovernmental trade agreement, sometimes referred to as a framework agreement. Such accords are extremely important to the Soviet Union because they constitute evidence of willingness by the Latin American partner to trade. If such willingness is absent or fitful, Soviet trade organizations know through long experience that obstacles to trade are likely to become so great as to nullify their efforts. Equally important, individual units of the Soviet bureaucracy do not ordinarily operate on their own. They need a juridical basis and policy decisions for such action. The bilateral trade agreements provide the official authority and mechanism for engaging the huge Soviet bureaucracy concerned with foreign trade. The USSR has trade agreements with most Latin American countries.[6]

The next step is to expand Soviet trade specialists in the countries concerned, either under commercial counselors at the embassies or by appointing trade representatives in the two capitals. The trade representatives may have a larger staff and separate office space. The USSR maintains representatives with responsibility for encouraging trade in the majority of the countries. The trading partners usually also establish mixed commissions which meet annually to plan trade expansion. These arrangements are vital to the Soviet side since trade is conducted through the state monopoly.

Agreements for the purchase of Soviet machinery and equipment often come on the heels of the trade accords. These usually are open-ended lines of credit on prearranged terms. Some of the recent agreements provide for installment payments over a ten-year period on the basis of interest now up to 6 percent for government organizations and 6.5 percent for private businesses. A down payment due at specified times after signature of contracts under the agreement has often totaled 15 percent. In some cases the 15-percent down payment may be borrowed from Western banks and the remaining 85 percent financed by the Soviet side. Payments are usually made in convertible currency.

Such agreements exist with all of Moscow's major trading partners in Latin America, and the USSR appears to stand ready to sell its machinery and equipment to buyers in most Latin American countries on these very favorable terms. Originally many of these agreements provided for credit up to a certain amount, such as US $100 million, but were wide open as to date. Now the tendency is to leave the amounts open but to specify the date of availability. According to one source, Latin American countries have drawn down only US $525 million of the US $2.4 billion of credit from Communist countries extended between 1958 and 1978. About 40 percent of those credits were extended by the USSR.[7]

The USSR has been counting on big projects to bolster trade with the area. Clearly such projects involve purchases of Soviet machinery and equipment, more than can ordinarily be sold piecemeal through private Latin American importers. But perhaps more important, projects of such dramatic size and economic impact attract attention to the sales capacity of the Soviet economy. And of course these huge projects demonstrate Soviet scientific, technological, and managerial talents. If successful, the projects can attract business not only from the host country but from countries throughout the hemisphere who send observers to the site. The first Soviet-built steel mill in India is given credit, for example, for much of the subsequent expansion of Soviet economic relations with India. Soviet officials responsible for such projects look favorably on Latin America as more advanced than Asia or Africa. One Soviet economic cooperation official commented that in Soviet–Latin American cooperation, unlike that in Africa, "one doesn't have to bring positively everything with you." In Latin America some partial Soviet participation in huge ventures has taken place, and the USSR has begun to design and bid on others, but no big project has been completed.

The big projects are coordinated by the State Committee for Foreign Economic Ties. Some are complete plants, that is, turnkey ventures in which the USSR provides all manpower, equipment, and supplies. The most promising field in Latin America for such Soviet projects is hydroelectric stations designed for irrigation and power generation. Designs for the largest of those, the Urrá hydroelectric project on the Alto Sinú in Colombia, were completed in 1978.[8] The Soviet Union has also explored similar construction in Brazil, Uruguay, Argentina, Peru, and Costa Rica. There are smaller projects which while not sufficiently complex to require the participation of the State Committee do involve large sales and a useful demonstration effect.

One pathbreaking Soviet project has been the supply of generators of 165,000 kilowatts each for the hydroelectric plant Capivari, the first station in Latin America using Soviet equipment. On the basis of an agreement signed in 1971, the Soviet trading firm Elektromashexport began deliveries of equipment in 1973 and within a year supplied the fourth and last hydrogenerator, produced in Leningrad. The plant, which has a capacity of 640,000 went into operation in March 1977. In 1975 Elektromashexport agreed to supply the Brazilian power company, San Francisco, with five Soviet power hydrounits of 178,000 for the hydroelectric station Sobradinho in the state of Pernambuco. This complex has a huge water reservoir, second only to Lake Titicaca in South America, and will serve irrigation and other purposes.[9]

Soviet trading organizations have also been working with Argentine officials and power companies. In 1973 the Argentines gave the Soviet bidders an order for fourteen turbines and generators for a hydroelectric station at Salto Grande on the Uruguay River being built jointly with Uruguay. The USSR is also supplying thermal electric stations at San Nicolas, Luján de Cuyo, and Constanera.

The largest Soviet opportunity in Argentina is a hydroelectric project on the Middle Paraná River, involving a complex series of dams from Corrientes to Santa Fe. A Soviet firm prepared a design for the project; this gave the USSR the inside track on a contract to supply turbines and generators for the dams worth about US $2.5 billion.[10]

Most other Soviet projects have been located in Peru. One of these was an effort to realize an old Peruvian dream of bringing water from the Amazon Basin across the Andes to irrigate the dry Peruvian north coast. The project was expected to irrigate fifty-six thousand hectares of land and have a generating capacity up to 520,000 kilowatts.[11] The most difficult part of the project is the completion of a tunnel twenty kilometers long. In 1979 the USSR had completed the preliminary work for the tunnel, but in spite of larger Soviet offers, arrangements for financing the huge work were not made.

The USSR also collaborated with Peru in the construction of a fishing complex at Paita on the Peruvian north coast. The USSR supplied fishing and refrigeration equipment, icemaking facilities, generators, and repair shops. The fishing complex never went fully into operation because ecological disturbances along the Peruvian coast caused the fish to disappear.

Soviet specialists have also been helping Peru design hydroelectric stations on the Marañon and other rivers. One such station, at Rentama, has a projected capacity of 1.5 million kilowatts. Soviet specialists also helped Peruvian specialists explore for oil. A Soviet firm assisted in the expansion of a steel mill at Chimbote and in planning a new mill at Nasca. Soviet-Peruvian projects came to a halt in the late 1970s due to financing problems and a change in government.

• Export Prospects

Soviet authorities maintain that any significant expansion in trade with the region depends now on Latin American willingness to expand purchases from the USSR, an understandable argument in view of the current imbalance in trade. What is the likelihood of such expanded economic ties?

Discrimination against the USSR on political and business grounds continues to plague bilateral trading relationships. Visas are sometimes delayed, and political criticism of the USSR rubs off on Soviet trading representatives. Nevertheless, political discrimination is gradually subsiding in many countries and has now become more of a nuisance than an absolute barrier to trade.

The Soviets have found it hard to expand exports for several reasons. Among them are business prejudices, assumptions that Soviet goods are inferior, and the difficulty of integrating Soviet machines and equipment into industrial plants of Western origin. Mistakes in judgment also hurt Soviet sales. Their tractors proved too light for Mexican needs, for example, and the contract had to be terminated. This put a damper on future business. Since most Latin Americans are used to imports from Western Europe or North America, the USSR is breaking into these markets slowly.

Yet Soviet machinery and equipment does have advantages for certain areas, such as the Andean countries. Since it tends to be less complicated, maintenance requires less highly trained personnel. Soviet prices are often lower and credit terms better. Nor are hard currencies necessary, especially when purchases in the USSR can be offset by sales there.

Latin Americans sympathetic to trade with the USSR are beginning to insist that the latter provide better guarantees and local servicing. Although Soviet sales do not seem likely to increase dramatically, it should not prove too difficult to increase exports gradually over the existing low levels. From the Soviet perspective, gradual increases may be most prudent because the overheated Soviet economy would probably have difficulty filling a wave of new orders to several items, such as turbines and generators.

The Soviet Union has many years of experience that improve its prospects for competing with the West in certain lines. Hydroelectric power and irrigation projects, of which there are many huge examples in the USSR, are strong offerings and needed by Brazil, Argentina, and the Andean countries. Soviet mining and oil equipment might also serve the Andean countries well; Bolivia's preliminary experience with the Soviet smelter appears to be good. As a major producer of oil, the USSR has many skills and heavy equipment available. It has produced durable and useful vehicles such as trolley buses, trucks, taxis, and helicopters. The USSR has much experience in fishing, most recently augmented by its dramatically successful collaboration with Cuba.

In the immediate future, progress hinges on the outcomes of negotiations with certain countries. Brazil has a system and political outlook that have proved discouraging to Soviet suppliers. Some Brazilian officials may have opposed Soviet business, thereby reinforcing existing anti-Soviet prejudices. With the USSR less and less able to sell oil to Brazil, short-term prospects there are not encouraging.

Argentina, and particularly the Middle Paraná project, offer the USSR its best immediate prospects. Many Argentines have an anti-Communist cast of mind but have no trouble separating business and politics, especially when business with the USSR is profitable. Part of the problem in Argentina is that changes in political and governmental personalities, legal delays, and the like have been holding up progress.

The Peruvian military governments used to have close relations with the USSR, but the second Belaúnde administration was not favorably disposed to economic relations with the Soviets. At present Peru is on hold or worse. The USSR went ahead and built more smelting plants for the Bolivians, but it seems cautious about grandiose involvements due to the limited fiscal capacity and stability of the Bolivian government. Jamaica and Guyana need help, but the defeat of Michael Manley dimmed prospects in Jamaica. The small populations and limited resources of these countries have made the USSR cautious. The same applies to Costa Rica, which wanted but did not get Soviet financing in developing large dams and hydroelectric projects in the south.

Mexico and Venezuela are both partners prized by the USSR, probably because both have oil, sophisticated economies, and close ties to Europe and the United States. Especially considering the size of their economies, their trade with the USSR has been disappointing. Mexico is collaborating with the USSR in many fields, but until more concrete results are achieved, skepticism seems warranted with respect to trade. The Soviet economy is less complementary to these oil-producing states than to other countries in the area.

Two countries where there has been little trade in the past, Colombia and Ecuador, may offer good prospects for the future. The hydroelectric project in the Alto Sinú is an example. Both countries can use help in hydroelectric power, oil, mining, and transport.

Soviet traders concerned with Latin America are not buoyantly optimistic about the future. They have worked so hard and long with modest results that they are discouraged. Nonetheless, they continue doggedly ahead, and progress is made little by little.

My own view is that Soviet hydroelectric, mining, transport, and other equipment should meet the needs of some Latin American countries, especially in the Andes, and that the USSR wants trade with these countries enough so that capital goods and related services can be priced attractively. Over the long term and in the absence of global disturbances, the Soviet share of Latin American trade should rise considerably. After all, the base now is 1 or 2 percent. It is difficult, however, to conceive of circumstances when the Soviet share would exceed Latin American trade with the United States or leading Western European nations in the region as a whole.

Some readers may have noticed that I have made scarcely any reference at all to Soviet "aid" to Latin America. There are two reasons for this. First, outright grants are very few and often limited to national disasters when the USSR sends medical equipment, personnel, and various forms of reconstruction facilities. Second, what most analysts refer to as Soviet aid is in fact Soviet lines of credit for the purchase of machinery and equipment. The down payment and the interest terms are low and the repayment period fairly long. Compared to commercial terms in the West, Soviet terms are concessionary. Yet I am not convinced that these lines of credit should be counted as aid, and if they are, their nature should be understood. Often governments have used little of this credit because they have not wanted to buy Soviet machinery and equipment. My own tendency is to regard these credits primarily as an inducement to Latin American governments to buy Soviet goods; they are thus similar to Export-Import Bank credits. I believe that Soviet officials have a similar view of these credits and regard them as a form of "economic cooperation."

The relatively low volume of Soviet exports to Latin America—the cause of the extreme asymmetry in balance of payments and of the slow growth of balanced trade—is not due only to insufficient Soviet entrepreneurial spirit. As Gerard Fichet of the Economic Commission for Latin America has pointed out to me, Soviet traders do not meet their competition on even ground. They may not be permitted to participate in bidding, or if they do, have time to mobilize the huge Soviet trade bureaucracy within required deadlines. Nor may they compete for infrastructure projects of the World Bank or the Inter-American Development Bank that require bidders to be members of these two institutions. The Soviet Union also does not participate like Western companies in economic and industrial cooperation, technology transfer, mixed enterprises, or tripartite cooperation, nor does it provide the same maintenance agreements for projects sold. No wonder then that Latin American buyers tend to prefer their traditional markets and make use of such a small share of Soviet credits offered. Soviet trade with Latin America will grow as long as the USSR has urgent need of exports, such as Argentine grain; parallel growth of imports and exports will require much time and work.

It is not surprising, therefore, that the Soviet trade turnover with Latin America, except for Cuba and Nicaragua, was about the same, or less, in 1986 as it was in 1980.

Alexandra Kollontai, an old Bolshevik, famous feminist, and Soviet ambassador to Mexico, 1927–1930, the high water mark in Soviet–Latin American relations before World War II. Library of Congress

Arturo Alessandri Palma (r), president of Chile (1920–1925, 1932–1938), meets uneasily with his longtime political rivals, a delegation of Chilean Communists headed by Party President Elias Lafertte (2nd from l) and poet and senator Pablo Neruda (l).

Gabriel González Videla (l), president of Chile (1946–1952) embraces Carlos Contreras Labarca, secretary general of the Chilean Communist Party, a member of the winning coalition in the 1946 presidential elections.

Carlos Rafael Rodríguez, now Cuba's leading "old" Communist and economic coordinator, meets in 1962 with Nikita Khrushchev (r) and Anastas Mikoyan (l). TASS from Sovfoto

Salvador Allende, president of Chile (1970–1973), pays his respects at the Tomb of the Unknown Soldier near the Kremlin wall in December 1972, his only visit to Moscow as president. Fotokhronika TASS

Carlos Andrés Perez, president of Venezuela, visits Red Square in Moscow in November 1976. Fotokhronika TASS

Foreign Minister Gromyko, Chairman of the Council of Ministers Kosygin, and General Secretary Brezhnev bid farewell to President and Mrs. López Portillo of Mexico in May 1978. Fotokhronika TASS

Daniel Ortega Saavedra, leader of the Junta of the Nicaraguan Government of National Reconstruction, during his visit to Moscow in May 1982. Fotokhronika TASS

Luiz Carlos Prestes, leader of the Brazilian armed insurrection of 1935 and longtime general secretary of the Brazilian Communist Party has spent many years in exile in Moscow.

Raúl Castro (r), minister of the Revolutionary Armed Forces of Cuba, accompanied by Soviet Defense Minister Dmitry Ustinov, reviews an honor guard in Moscow, February 1979. TASS from Sovfoto

Vasily Kuznetsov (1), alternate member of the Soviet Politburo, presents the People's Friendship Order to Rodolfo Ghioldi, leader of the Argentine Communist Party in Moscow, June 1978. TASS from Sovfoto

Argentina's Minister of Economics José B. Gelbard (l) shakes hands with a Soviet official in Moscow in May 1974, formalizing the signing of a series of commercial agreements that served as the springboard for a rapid expansion of Soviet-Argentine trade relations. TASS from Sovfoto

During the Brezhnev era Boris N. Ponomarev (l) served as CPSU secretary for the non-ruling Communist and Workers' parties and Konstantin V. Rusakov (r) as CPSU secretary for liaison with the Communist and Workers' parties of socialist countries. Eastfoto; Fotokhronika TASS

Yuri Andropov, general secretary of the CPSU (r), meets with Fidel Castro in Moscow, November 1982. TASS from Sovfoto

Jorge Schafik Handal, secretary general of the Communist Party of El Salvador. Prensa Latina

Salvador Cayetano Carpio, Comandante "Marcial" of the Farabundo-Marti National Liberation Front in El Salvador, 1983, before his suicide following internal strife in the FMLN. Prensa Latina

IV Many Roads to Power: Party Relations

The USSR is the only great power, and also the only government, which has sponsored, supported, and guided political parties in almost every Latin American country. Many of those Parties were founded by emissaries of the USSR. Marxism-Leninism is their bible, and the Soviet Union is their model state. Studying Soviet relations with Latin America without studying the relations between the Communist party of the Soviet Union (CPSU) and the Latin American Parties would be as unrealistic as ignoring multinational corporations in examining U.S. policies toward the area.

• Soviet Doctrine

The Soviet leadership is irrevocably committed to national liberation movements and the ultimate achievement of socialism in Latin America. The Soviet commitment in all official institutions to these goals is probably more firmly held, carefully articulated, and consistently pursued than is the U.S. commitment to encourage democracy and free enterprise abroad. In the past the Parties in Latin America have been perceived as instruments of Soviet policies, and they still are today, with an occasional exception. Obviously it is necessary to exclude *non-Soviet* Marxist groups such as the Trotskyites, Maoists, certain Castroites, and in part the Cuban Party itself from the list. While disputes arise within the international Communist movement, the policies of the remaining Parties, the so-called pro-Soviet Parties, are rarely distinguishable from the policies of the CPSU. For these reasons it is necessary to go to the authentic source of Soviet policies, the congresses of the CPSU, to learn how the Soviet Communists plan to achieve socialist revolutions.

The post-Stalin Soviet position on this subject has been expressed at the Party congresses, beginning in 1956. A key issue has always been whether armed struggle or political participation is the appropriate road to power in a particular country. The most authoritative statements were by Party leader Nikita Khrushchev and his successor, Leonid Brezhnev. The Party line is clear; what changes over the years is emphasis and tone. Here is my oversimplification of the Soviet position: (1) The local Communist parties may take either the armed or nonarmed road, or some combination thereof. Local conditions determine which road is followed. (2) Communists should take the nonarmed road where feasible. If armed opposition appears, the Communists will probably have to resort to arms to defend the Revolution. This formulation puts the onus for the resort to force on the opposition.

Here is how Khrushchev treated this issue in 1956 at the Twentieth Party Congress:

> In present-day conditions the working class in many capitalist countries . . . uniting around itself the working peasantry, the intellectuals and all the patriotic forces . . . has an opportunity to defeat the reactionary anti-popular forces, to win a firm majority in parliament and to turn the parliament from an agency of bourgeois democracy into an instrument of the genuinely popular will. [This] would create conditions for the working class of many capitalist and formerly colonial countries to make fundamental social changes. Of course, in those countries where capitalism is still strong, where it possesses a tremendous military and police machine, a serious resistance by reactionary forces is inevitable. The transition to socialism in these countries will take place amid sharp revolutionary class struggle.[1]

Brezhnev had a most interesting application of this line to the failure of the Allende government in Chile, which was overthrown in September 1973. It will be recalled that the Allende government was the first socialist government in history to come to power with the Communists as junior partners in free elections. Many observers interpreted Allende's failure to serve out his term as proof that the peaceful, or more accurately, nonarmed road to socialism will not work. Brezhnev and other leading Communists interpreted Allende's experience quite differently, and in so doing defended the established Soviet position on roads to socialism:

The tragedy of Chile does not fail to reinforce the conclusions of the Communists about the possibilities of various roads of revolution, including the peaceful road, if for this, the necessary conditions exist. But it was a forceful reminder that revolutions ought to know how to defend themselves.[2]

Soviet doctrine on these points is reiterated at the conferences of Communist and worker's parties and the regional conferences of the Parties of Latin America and the Caribbean. At the Moscow conference in 1957, for example, the attending parties agreed that

> The forms of transition of various countries from capitalism to socialism may be different . . . the working class has the possibility on the basis of worker and national fronts . . . to gain state power without civil war and guarantee the transfer of the means of production to the people. . . . In conditions in which the exploiting classes resort to force against the people, it is essential to keep in view another possibility, the nonpeaceful transition to socialism. In each country the actual possibility of one or another form of transition is determined by concrete historical conditions.[3]

At the Havana meeting in 1975, the Latin American Parties took a similar position:

> The utilization of all legal possibilities is an indispensable obligation of the anti-imperialist forces. . . . Revolutionaries are not the first to resort to violence. But it is the right and duty of all people's and revolutionary forces to be ready to answer counter-revolutionary violence with revolutionary violence.[4]

Official Party statements on this subject are difficult to interpret, but the change of emphasis and tone in the last twenty years is evident. When Khrushchev first enunciated this line, one had the impression that the nonarmed road was perceived as desirable but less likely because of opposition to the Communist movement. In the late 1970s, Party statements suggested that the nonarmed road was more feasible than before because local conditions had improved and world communism was stronger. The addition of further detail about the nonarmed or, as is sometimes said, parliamentary road supports this interpretation. The classic organizational device for the nonarmed approach since the 1930s has been the national or popular front, that is, a coalition of left and center parties that share certain common views, most particularly antiimperialism or antifascism. At the Twenty-Fourth Congress in 1971, for example, Brezhnev specifically mentioned left-socialists as qualifying for inclusion in these fronts.[5] At the Twenty-Fifth Congress in 1975, the Party spectrum was explicitly broadened to include revolutionary-democratic parties.[6] Khrushchev earlier had been cautious about recommending ties with such parties.

At the Twenty-Sixth Congress in early 1981, Brezhnev stressed the permissive side of Soviet policy, noting that "all the socialist countries carried out a revolution in their own way, using forms dictated by the alignment of class force within each of these countries, by national life styles and the external situation."[7] He indicated that some national liberation movements came to power in armed struggles and others without them; that some succeeded quickly and others slowly; that some came with struggles against an external power and others without them. The congress essentially extended the policy on revolution of earlier years. With respect to Latin America, the new element was the success of armed force in Nicaraguan Revolution and the rapidly developing opportunity in El Salvador. These events gave new hope and confidence to the international Communist movement. They suggested that by using force, national revolutionary movements outside Communist control may have better prospects of seizing power than the Parties themselves, but that the latter might benefit from joining them.

• Regional Apparat

Most of the authoritative statements of the Latin American Parties are consistent with the elements of Soviet doctrine already described as well as with Soviet doctrine in general. How is this confirmity achieved?

The responsible Soviet body is the Latin American staff of the Central Committee of the Soviet Party. The Central Committee has about thirty professionals concerned with Latin America under the leadership of Mikhail Fedorovich Kudachkin. That group is responsible not only for bilateral relations with the Parties but also for keeping abreast of all aspects of Soviet–Latin American relations since the Party is ultimately responsible for coordinating and approving government policies toward the area. Kudachkin's group works within the Party's international department headed by Politburo candidate member Boris Ponomarev.

Under the Communist International in the 1920s and early 1930s, there were cadres of Eastern European, Western European, and American radicals who brought the Communist movement to Latin America and ran it for Moscow. Those who left their mark on the Latin American movement included M. N. Roy, Mikhail Borodin, Sen Katayama, Bertram Wolfe, Jules Humbert-Droz, Vittorio Codovilla, and Fabio Grobart. In the 1930s Stalin purged many of the Comintern agents. Others have since died, and only a few, like Fabio Grobart in Cuba, have gone on to honorable retirement.

Many of the Cominterns' leading agents were articulate intellectuals who had many years' residence in Western Europe or the United States. They were well read and knew many languages. Most important, they had the evangelical and entrepreneurial spirit vital for attracting political support. It was a time for freewheeling and risk taking. Such cadres have never been replaced. Few of the early agents were actually Russians, and most of those were émigrés. People raised in the Soviet Union, no matter how talented, cannot easily make up for the life experience the early Comintern agents had.

Most Soviet Latin Americanists are homegrown. They have spent years studying the area and its languages, they have much book knowledge, and many speak Spanish remarkably well. Yet of the dozens I have met, only a handful had actually lived in the region. Some had made an occasional visit. Many had hardly any knowledge of day-to-day living in particular countries: what customs are, the nature of prejudices, political habits, manners—all the things that are essential for operations in the field. Soviet diplomats and journalists with experience in Latin America probably know the area, but there are only a few since diplomatic and press relations are rather new in most countries. And Soviet diplomats live more isolated lives than the diplomats of Western nations.

More important, however, is the absence of independent operational experience in the region on the part of most Soviet Party members. They are all members of some huge, hierarchical organization in which authority flows from the top down. The Latin Americanists I met in the Academy of Sciences and in the ministries were employees or officials. The result is that it is hard to conceive of these agents leading revolutions, nor is it likely that this has occurred to them. I suspect most support the abstract, almost rhetorical goal of socialist revolution, and they will welcome it when it comes to individual countries. I doubt that many feel committed personally to any particular Latin American revolutionary movement.

The Latin Americanists on the Central Committee staff have more authority, political scope, and, presumably, self-starting qualities. This group, however, appears small and has continuing management responsibilities. As a result the real leadership of the Parties in most countries rests with the recognized local leadership, as it should anyway. While Soviet Party officials visit the Parties occasionally and there may be local Soviet liaison representatives, much of the influence and coordination appears to be exercised through visits to Moscow.

The leaders of the Latin American Parties come to Moscow, some frequently. A few, such as Luiz Carlos Prestes, lived there many years. In addition to their contacts with the Central Committee staff, such leaders have informal ties with the Foreign Office, and many visit institutes of the Soviet Academy of Sciences, such as the Institute of the Workers' Movement and the Institute of Latin America. Here they lecture and lead discussion groups with specialists.

The leaders of almost all Communist parties make speeches at congresses of the CPSU. These speeches serve a disciplinary function since the contents almost invariably support the approved Soviet line. Another means of coordinating Soviet and Latin American Communist policies is through the official journals of the international movement published in Prague. These are the *World Marxist Review* and its separately published *Information Bulletin*. Prague is a site where Soviet influence is strong, and there is an international staff which is responsive to Soviet guidance. Conferences on various themes are called from time to time with participation of Party members from around the world.

Coordination is achieved in Latin America through congresses of the local Parties. When a particular Party has its national congress, leaders from around Latin America and from the Soviet Union usually attend. Such gatherings provide further opportunities for ensuring common adherence to the international line. There are also the international conferences of the Communist and workers' parties, such as the meetings of 1957, 1960, and 1969, and there were regional conferences in Havana in 1964 and 1975.

The patterns I have described do not have as tight an organizational form nor the formal obligations of the old Communist International. The Soviet leaders probably compromise occasionally, and may learn from their comrades abroad. The foreign Parties are so numerous, however, that the Soviet leaders are almost forced to set the line to maintain cohesion in the movement. Most Parties fall in line. The Mexican Party sharply criticized Moscow over the Soviet invasion of Czechoslovakia, and there are no doubt other deviations, most of which are not permitted to surface.[8] With few exceptions the facades remain remarkably uniform.

The Parties in Latin America (except Cuba, of course) are small and weak compared to Parties in Italy, France, and Spain. Most Communists have spent their lives struggling in what are essentially hostile environments. Members are both poor and few. How could they have continued to function all these years without Soviet help? How could they have published a daily newspaper or a monthly journal when few or no other political parties of comparable size have been able to do so? And that support can be moral as well, for example, from fellow Communists in neighboring countries, and from the ultimate source of strength, the USSR.

The Communist parties have had remarkable continuity in leadership compared to other Latin American political parties. Members make a career of communism, serving in most cases their entire lives. Old-timers such as Luiz Carlos Prestes, Manuel Mora Valverde, Blas Roca, Rodolfo Ghioldi, Gilberto Veira, Pedro Saad, Jorge del Prado, and Rodney Arismendi served or have been serving for decades, some since before World War II. Provided they don't misbehave, these cadres can count on the Soviet Union to make an international issue of their arrest; to provide them rest and refreshment; to supply medical care; to help them in old age; and to commemorate them in death. The relationships are reciprocal. Is it so surprising that small Communist parties are faithful to the international Communist movement's central leadership?

As the Parties grow stronger, however, central controls become more difficult to maintain. For one thing, the local memberships become larger, more complex, and less responsive. Second, the party leadership has a stronger political and financial base and therefore is less dependent on outside assistance. That explains in part why the Cuban Party is probably the most independent in Latin America.

The international Communist movement under Soviet sponsorship has been working in Latin America since 1919. When one compares its progress with that of other ideological movements (socialist, fascist, Christian Democratic), international communism has not done badly. What other nation state has political parties espousing its cause in almost all the countries of Latin America and elsewhere in the world? Yet if one compares Communist membership with that of other parties in individual countries that membership is very small in almost all cases except Cuba (table 11). The table does not show another important trend, namely that since the 1950s, a number of radical Marxist parties on the left (Castroite, Maoist, and others) have grown up to challenge the orthodox Communists for control of the revolutionary movement.

The figures on Party membership in table 11 are only estimates and should be read with caution. But they are probably the best available. Membership appears to have increased sharply in Mexico and, as one would expect, in Cuba. Otherwise, membership trends generally appear to be level or declining.

Table 12 shows Communist participation in elections and parliaments. Even in Chile under Allende, the Latin American government that has come closest to Castro, the Communists only had about 17 percent of the vote. Significantly, they received 23 percent of the seats in Guyana. Or, take countries where Soviet economic ties are most important. In Argentina the Communists got 2 out of 312 seats and in Peru 6 out of 100. In Brazil and Bolivia, the Communists made no independent showing at all, a result due more to the political system than to a complete absence of Communist sentiment in those two countries.

Table 11
Pro-Soviet Communist Party Membership in Latin America, 1962, 1973, 1982

	1962	*1973*	*1982*
Argentina (PCA)	50,000	70,000	70,000–125,000
Bolivia (PCB)	4,000–5,000	—	500 (1980)
Brazil (PCB)	25,000–40,000	6,000	10,000
Chile (PCCh)	18,000–20,000	120,000	—
Colombia (PCC)	8,000–10,000	10,000	12,000
Costa Rica (PVP)	300	1,000	3,200
Cuba	27,000	120,000	434,143
Dominican Republic (PCD)	—	470	—
Ecuador (PCE)	2,000–3,000	500	1,000 (1979)
El Salvador (PCES)	500	100–150	200
Guadaloupe (CPG)	—	3,000	—
Guatemala (PTG)	1,000–1,100	750	750
Guyana (WPVP) (PPP)	—	100	500 (PPP)
Honduras (PCH)	1,500–2,000	300	1,500
Martinique (CPM)	—	1,000	—
Mexico (PCM)	5,000–6,000	5,000	100,000
Nicaragua (PSN)	200–300	60 (PSN)	1,200
Panama (PCP)	150	500	500–600
Paraguay (PCP)	5,000	3,000–4,000	3,500
Peru (PCP)	5,000–7,000	2,000	3,200
Uruguay (PCU)	3,000	22,000	7,500
Venezuela (PCV)	20,000	3,000–4,000	—

Sources: For 1962, U.S. Department of State, Bureau of Intelligence and Research, *World Strength of the Communist Party Organizations* (Washington, D.C.: U.S. Government Printing Office, 1962); for 1973, ibid. (1973); for 1982, *Yearbook of International Communist Affairs 1982* (Stanford, Calif., 1982).

Note: Prepared by Aldo Isuani and Aldo Vacs.

— = not available, unknown.

Tables 11 and 12 show that outside of Cuba, membership in the local Communist parties and Communist participation in legislative bodies is low. Both characteristics suggest that Communist political influence on the electorate is not great.

• Communist Armed Struggles

Communist revolutionaries have been active in Latin America now for about sixty years. All have maintained as a long-term goal overthrowing the existing order, by force if necessary. Yet the pro-Soviet Communists in Latin America resorted to organized insurrections (as distinct from sporadic use of force) on only three occasions: (1) in a revolt in El Salvador in 1932, which was quickly suppressed, (2) in an insurrection in

Table 12
Electoral Strength of Pro-Soviet Communist Parties in Latin America, 1971–1981

	Percentage of Votes	Seats in the Legislature
Argentina		2 of 312 (1973)
Bolivia[a]		
Brazil		5 (1981)
Chile	16.90 (1971)	29 of 200 (1970)
Colombia	1.9 (1978)	3 of 311 (1978)
Costa Rica	7.0 (1978)	3 of 57 (1978)
Dominican Republic	—	—
Ecuador	3.2 (1979)	11 of 69 (1979)
El Salvador	—	—
Guadaloupe		7 of 36 (1976)
Guatemala	—	—
Guyana		10 of 43 (1980)
Haiti	—	—
Honduras	—	—
Jamaica	—	—
Martinique	—	3 of 36 (1979)
Mexico	5.4 (1979)	18 of 300 (1979)
Nicaragua	—	—
Panama		1 (1980)
Paraguay	—	—
Peru	5.9 (1978)	6 of 100 (1978)
Uruguay[b]	6.0 (1966)	
Venezuela	9.0 (1978)	22 of 195 (1978)

Sources: Yearbook of International Communist Affairs, 1982 (Stanford, Calif., 1982), except for Argentina, ibid., *1974*, p. 227, and *La Prensa* (Buenos Aires) 12 March 1973: Chile, *Yearbook, 1973*, p. 305; Uruguay, ibid., *1972, p. 429*.

Note: Table prepared by Aldo Isuani and Aldo Vacs.

[a]In the 1980 elections, Communist candidates were absorbed into the Unión Democrática Popular.

[b]In the 1971 elections, Communist candidates were absorbed into the Frente Amplio.

—means either that the party did not participate in the election or that it received no recorded votes. A blank space has been left in column 2 when the party participated as part of another group and its own total is unknown.

Brazil in 1935, also quickly suppressed, and (3) in unnsuccessful guerrilla movements in Venezuela, Guatemala, and Colombia in the 1960s. So far the Communists' use of force has always failed. The case of Castro in Cuba does not count because the Communists opposed Castro during much of his armed revolt and were not important participants. The Nicaraguan and Salvadoran revolutions do not really qualify either because in both cases the pro-Soviet Communists joined the rebel forces late, formed a small minority, and were not among the top leaders.

The first Latin American Communist insurrection took place in El Salvador in January 1932. In that month the Communists took part in municipal and congressional elections and claimed to have won, challenging the official results. When the government refused to review the ballot count, the Communists attempted to seize power. They had developed a following within the armed forces and organized the uprising in military units. President Martínez received a warning of the impending revolt and quickly arrested many of the participants, including the leader, and silenced the Communist press. Party leaders sought to prevent the insurrection from taking place but word did not reach all the units in time. Many of the Party's leaders were captured and shot. The Party was largely destroyed and was unable to reorganize for several years.[9]

The insurrection in Brazil in 1935 was similar in many ways. Under the leadership of the famous Communist Brazilian military hero Luiz Carlos Prestes, the Party sponsored a popular front organization called the National Liberation Alliance. The alliance appeared to be gaining political influence rapidly, particularly among organized labor. President Vargas was strongly opposed to the alliance and declared it legally dissolved. In the face of this government action, the alliance decided to revolt and declared Prestes president of Brazil. The Brazilian army quickly suppressed uprisings in Rio de Janeiro and other cities and arrested most of the leaders of the Brazilian Party. The Party was then forced underground.[10]

After the crushing of the Brazilian insurrection of 1935, Soviet Communist leaders were not faced with acute problems of armed revolutionary strategy until the Cuban Revolution. Castro and his closest lieutenants, not the Communists, overthrew Batista and seized power. Castro found the Communists (the Popular Socialist party) useful, in-

cluded them in his government in a subordinate capacity, and in 1965
absorbed them into his own larger and more powerful revolutionary
movement as a newly formed Communist party.

Castro thus made his revolution independently of the local Communists, winning immense authority among revolutionary movements
around the world, especially in Latin America. He viewed himself as a
great liberator whose achievements had global significance and applica-
bility in many Third World countries. Yet the orthodox Communists had
long criticized his strategy, emphasizing the need for years of political
recruitment and mobilization and extensive propaganda to meet the political prerequisites for an armed takeover.

The orthodox Communist leaders felt threatened by Castro. Many
were old or otherwise unfit for partisan warfare; they were political
organizers and propagandists, not *guerrilleros*. If the insurgents won, the
old guard would be swept from its position of leadership. Besides, they
doubted that Castro's strategies would work in their countries, and they
knew local conditions better than the Cubans. Moreover, partisan warfare in their countries put their lives and political networks in grave
jeopardy. The central theme of the developing dispute between Havana
and Moscow was over the relative emphasis to be given the armed and
unarmed strategies.

Fresh from the victory of his struggles in the Sierra Maestra, Fidel
Castro provided the theory, the model, and the impetus for guerrilla
movements in other Latin American countries. Shortly after overthrowing Batista, Castro launched armed assaults on a whole series of Caribbean dictatorships, all of which failed. It was then he turned his attention
to reformist governments against which the guerrilla movements of the
1960s were directed. In the mid-1960s, bloody partisan warfare broke out
or was continued in Peru, Colombia, Venezuela, Guatemala, and
Bolivia. These armed challenges to the status quo were perceived as
serious in the United States, and President Kennedy organized counterin-
surgency units to train Latin American soldiers to suppress the *guerrilleros*.

The bitter dispute over revolutionary strategy between Castro and
Castroite movements which sought to emulate him in many Latin American countries presented the Soviet Communists with a dangerous and

delicate challenge. On the one hand, they could hardly oppose Castro and the one revolutionary strategy that had worked since the Communists seized China. Nor could they risk being outflanked on the left. Castro's experience and strategies were sufficiently close to the Chinese experience that they also feared losing ground to the Chinese within the international Communist movement. On the other hand, they seriously doubted that Castro's strategies would work, genuinely believing that unless political conditions were ripe for revolution, the seizure of power would be short-lived. Nor could they repudiate the pro-Moscow network which opposed Castro, and which had been created as their own instrument.

Venezuela became the main arena for competing strategies since Cuba found it conveniently nearby for pursuing the objectives of national liberation. In the early 1960s, the Communist party of Venezuela (PCV) joined up with a radical faction (the MIR) of the governing Acción Democrática in a guerrilla organization called the FLN. The Communists' formal commitment to armed struggle lasted from 1962 until 1965, when they began a retreat from armed warfare.[11] During those years violence in Venezuela escalated, and the government decisively put it down in 1964 and early 1965. Partly for this reason, the Venezuelan Communists, that is, the main group of the pro-Soviet Party, decided to suspend armed action. Meanwhile, Douglas Bravo, one-time member of the Politburo of the pro-Soviet Party, led a group favoring continued armed action out of the PCV.

A compromise formula was reached at a conference of Latin American Communist parties in Havana in December 1964. The Chinese and their Parties in the hemisphere were excluded, and "splinter tactics" within the Communist movement were denounced. The conference communiqué called for active support of freedom fighters of six countries: Venezuela, Colombia, Guatemala, Honduras, Paraguay, and Haiti.[12] In the other countries, the orthodox Parties with which Castro was expected to deal would follow traditional strategies.

The compromise reached in 1964 fell apart at the Tricontinental Conference in Havana in January 1966. The Soviet main concern at the conference was to outmaneuver the Chinese in this three-continent Third World forum, and the USSR had hoped that Castro would orchestrate a Chinese setback. That he did by a sharp attack on China's trade policies with Cuba and by excluding the Chinese from a leadership role in the Tricontinental organization. But to Soviet surprise, Castro also excluded pro-Soviet groups. As the Soviets had hoped, he denied pro-China movements in Latin America invitations to Havana, but he excluded most of the orthodox Communist parties as well. Castro increased his militant calls for support to armed national liberation movements.[13] That was followed in January 1967 with Regis Debray's statement of Castroite revolutionary doctrine, *Revolution in the Revolution*. A close adviser to Castro, Debray identified as the central revolutionary organization a politico-military leadership in a rural guerrilla vanguard organization, a strategic mobile force.[14] Thus he emphasized the guerrilla force, not the Party, as having priority. Such a formulation was unacceptable to the Soviet leadership, who consistently reiterated the importance of the Party, the establishment of broad antiimperialist fronts, and the flexible use of various forms of struggle.

A retrospective Soviet appraisal of the Venezuelan Communists' involvement in the partisan movement is most revealing. It is contained in an authoritative textbook used in Party schools dealing with the history of the international workers' and national liberation movements:

The government of Leoni tried to carry out a more flexible foreign and domestic policy but opposition in the country to the anti-democratic regime continued to grow. However, the Communists at that time made a serious mistake. They concentrated all their strength in the development of the partisan struggle and significantly weakened their work in the masses, which led to growth in the party of sectarian tendencies.

Anarchist and putschist attitudes grew in the partisan detachments. The opinion was spread that the partisan detachments were the embryo of "the real Communist party" and the partisan movement, the decisive strength of the national revolutionary struggle.

A difficult situation in the Communist Party developed. At the end of 1966 the Party was forced to begin the gradual rolling up of the partisan movement.

In the Eighth Plenum of the Central Committee in April 1967, the Communist Party of Venezuela was subject to criticism for its mistakes and worked out a new political line. That line was directed at the development of the mass movement for satisfying the economic demands of the workers, against the terror and repression, for the liberation of political prisoners, and the legalization of the Communist Party of Venezuela and the left revolutionary movement.[15]

In a sense the Soviet critique of the Venezuelan movement serves as a symbol, to a greater or lesser degree, of Soviet attitudes toward other failed Latin American partisan movements.

Guatemala was another country where members of the pro-Soviet Communist party, called there the Guatemalan Labor party, were one of several left-wing radical groups to form the partisan movement called the Rebel Armed Forces. The relationship between the Party and the leaders of the partisan detachments, in which several organizations split and reformed, was difficult from the start. The military commanders insisted on controlling the partisan groups and placed far greater emphasis on paramilitary activities than the Party leadership, which stressed political organizational activities. By 1968 there was a split between the Guatemalan Labor party and the partisan forces with the former emphasizing the necessity of mobilizing mass support by appealing to the needs and interests of the masses. The partisan forces, on the other hand, said that "armed struggle is . . . the only path to complete liberation and independence."[16]

The Colombian Communist party is a special case in that it has long combined both electoral and violent political strategies. In the 1950s and earlier, the Party backed partisan warfare against the then dictator Rojas Pinilla.[17] Subsequently, under the National Front, Communists have expressed sympathy or solidarity with the guerrilla movements but have not participated directly as an organization. Since 1966 they have maintained close ties, and possibly formal control, over the Fuerzas Armadas Revolucionarias de Colombia (FARC), whose leader Mario Marulando Velez was once on the Party's Politburo.[18] In fact, the Party and its long-time leader Gilberto Veira give priority to legal political activities and the electoral struggle while maintaining that the Party's strategies may also include armed struggle. Communist leaders saw little hope for the few armed bands operating in the interior but were reluctant to pay the political price that dissociation would involve.[19]

The Communists were even less closely associated with the partisan movement in Peru than in Colombia. In 1965 the Peruvian Communists did not view the local situation as revolutionary, nor did they consider themselves strong enough to influence it decisively.[20] They did not accept Debray's thesis that the *foco* could create the conditions for revolution.[21] The partisan movement had a brief life from about 1963 to 1965, in which year it was crushed.

The most dramatic conflict between the pro-Soviet Party and the partisans took place in Bolivia. Here Mario Monje, the secretary-general of the Bolivian Party, refused to subordinate it to Ché Guevara's leadership and Guevara's partisan movement went forward without Party support.[22] As a result he lacked the men, arms, and supplies or much other support from the countryside. His historic conversation with Monje took place at the end of December 1966, and Guevara was executed in October 1967.

The guerrilla detachments in the Andean countries and Guatemala had been largely if not totally wiped out by 1967, the date of Ché Guevara's death. Their failure to attract more fighters to their detachments or to expand the political struggle largely bore out the criticism directed against them by local Parties. Now, however, the focus shifted to the east coast of South America, and especially to the cities.

The most famous of the urban partisans were the Tupamaros operating in Montevideo. The original leaders of the group came from left-wing socialists and anarchists with a strong Marxist-Leninist cast to their programs. Yet the Tupamaros operated independently of the Uruguayan Party and have now been largely wiped out by police action. The Tupamaros' counterpart in Brazil was the National Liberation Action, formed by dissidents of the Brazilian Communist Party, most particularly Carlos Marighela. He broke with the Brazilian Communists over the use of armed force and has expressed his agreement with Castro on this subject.[23] Similarly, guerrilla groups in Argentina, like the Montoneros, began from political organizations opposing the pro-Soviet Communists, such as the left-wing Perónists, Castroites, and particularly Trotskyites. Through these years the Argentine Communists have concentrated their efforts on the "mass struggle," that is attracting popular support through legal means.

The orthodox Communists also criticized the proponents of guerrilla warfare on other fundamental grounds. The Communist purpose is not simply to wrest power; the real objective is to make a socialist revolution. That means seizing the means of production and placing them in the hands of the state to serve the working class and the peasantry. Such a revolution requires more than a weak grip on the state organs; it requires broadly based political support. To seize power prematurely, before the social transformation can successfully begin, also sets back progress toward the ultimate goal.

Castro's prestige and capacity to sponsor partisan detachments in various Latin American countries presented the Soviets with a complicated challenge. The Left was badly split. Not only were there Castroites, but there were also Maoists and Trotskyites who shared Castro's attachment to armed struggle. The latter groups, although small, were part of a challenge to Soviet preeminence in the global, not just the hemispheric Communist movement. The Soviet leadership could not afford to be outflanked on the left. Had Moscow openly attacked the partisan movements prematurely, it would have isolated itself from what was then one of the most dynamic sectors of the revolutionary movement. As a result the orthodox Communist Parties supported the guerrillas briefly in Guatemala and Venezuela, turning against them later. By the end of the 1960s, the pro-Soviet Parties were aligned against the guerrilla movements and were themselves following the contrasting line of legal political and electoral activities and the building of widely based popular fronts.

In their respective accounts, Soviet authorities explicitly condemn the leaders of the guerrilla forces as having been guilty of "left opportunism." These views are elaborated at length in a book entitled *The Great October [Revolution] and the Communist Parties of Latin America*, edited in 1978 by M. F. Kudachkin, chief of the Latin American section of the Secretariat of the CPSU. According to this source, the ultraleftist mood came to prevail among new participants in the revolutionary struggle and took the form of an attack on elements of the Parties. "The partisan movements in many countries of Latin America failed not so much because of imperialism and reaction, but because of isolation from the working class, the laboring masses as a whole, through mistaken tactics and forms of struggle."[24] Soviet Communist leaders believed that the guerrillas underestimated national factors, lacked faith in the revolutionary potential of the working class, and refused to make a realistic appraisal of the existing balance of forces and needs of the moment. In this view all these errors, and making armed struggle an absolute value, led to failure and dealt the national liberation movement a serious blow.[25]

In the end events proved Moscow and the orthodox Communists right. The guerrilla movements in Guatemala, Venezuela, Colombia, and Peru were decisively crushed. Other parties on the left, including the Communists, were badly hurt in the process. The coup de grâce against the Cuban-supported guerrilla strategy came in Bolivia with the failure and execution of Ché Guevara in 1967. Castro was convinced for the time being that armed struggle in most Latin American countries would not work. Until Nicaragua, Soviet leaders concerned with Latin America and Castro concentrated most of their efforts on the united front and other forms of political recruitment within existing legal frameworks.

• The Lessons of Chile

Many of the controversial strategic issues concerning the seizure of power reappeared in new form under the Allende government in Chile (1970–1973). Castro had learned many lessons during the 1960s and, in contrast to his more flamboyant and romantic earlier views, urged caution on Allende. But the new president was forced to deal with radical elements on the left who sought to push the revolution ahead far and fast.

The actions of the Chilean Communist party during its participation in the government and the pro-Soviet Communists' retrospective analysis of the Chilean Revolution are among the most authoritative indications of the international Communist movement's policies about the path toward Communism. The Communist party was the sponsor and motive force behind the coalition of left-wing Chilean political parties that backed Allende for president unsuccessfully in 1964 and unsuccessfully in 1970. The Communists worked hard to maintain unity inside the leftist coalition, directed their main efforts at mobilizing popular support for their program, and competed actively in the country's various elections. In general they defended the Constitution and civil liberties, partly because the democratic framework provided them with protection and the best opportunity to expand their political base.

In the policy and political struggles of Allende's government, the Communists opposed ultra-Leftists who sought to force the pace of social change more rapidly than the Communists believed realistic. The Communists feared correctly that violent methods would alienate the middle class and other groups whose support Allende needed.[26] They felt that moving too precipitously would deprive the Allende government of critical support, a view that was confirmed by events.

In an authoritative assessment of the lessons of the Communist achievement in Allende's Chile, the leading Chilean Communists did not repudiate the peaceful road to socialism. They reaffirmed the validity of that road in the Chilean case by pointing out that Allende was elected to the presidency and important strides forward made during his tenure.[27] They also reaffirmed their policy of moderation and support for Allende against the ultra-Leftists. Soviet retrospective appreciations of the ultraleftist Chilean political party, the MIR, are harsh. The MIR, it will be recalled, while not a member of the Allende government, attempted to push it leftward and served as a kind of rival movement. It was responsible, for example, for illegal land seizures. A Soviet source explained how "the Chilean Communist party repeatedly unmasked the traitorous and provocative role of the MIR, which by its irresponsible seizures of small private enterprises and lands pushed a significant part of the middle sectors into the camp of reaction, facilitating the implementation of the fascist coup in the country."[28]

In fact, the orthodox Communists identify the main problem of the Allende government as political, that is, the failure of his government to maintain sufficiently broad support. As one member put it, "The key problem . . . was to achieve monolithic working class unity and gather round it, under its leadership, a strong alliance of the intermediate sections of the populations, above all the peasants, and also the middle strata of the urban population."[29] Interestingly enough, in the light of Communist criticism of U.S. interference, this member also held that "the key to success" lay with internal factors.[30] For these purposes the Communists frequently emphasized their own efforts to work with the Christian Democrats as well as Marxists parties on the left.

The Chilean Communists are equally emphatic that the Chilean experience does not and should not indicate that the peaceful and violent roads to revolution are mutually exclusive. Instead they emphasize that the Chilean experience shows the need at times to *combine* methods and be prepared to switch flexibly from one to another as circumstances dictate.[31]

• The Late 1970s

The most authoritative recent treatment of the strategies of the Latin American Communist parties is contained in Kudachkin's book. This work states that the activities of Latin American Communists should be determined by "the strategic line designed to complete the tasks of the anti-imperialist and democratic revolution."[32] This means that the Communist parties should orient their activities against imperialism, most particularly U.S. imperialism, and carry out the "democratic" revolution. The latter involves the achievement of broad economic and political rights for the masses but falls short of the socialist revolution. Presumably the democratic revolution provides the Communist parties with the best opportunity of expanding their political influence and protects them against repression from the Right. It is a stage which supposedly precedes the socialist revolution.

In the present stage of political development of Latin America, Soviet leaders view the situation as extremely dangerous for the working class. They recall the tragedy in Chile, and they point out existing threats to efforts at revolutionary transformation in Peru and Panama and fascist tendencies in Argentina and other countries. As a result they seek "the widest unity of Democratic forces." The Latin American Communist parties are to create "wide anti-imperialist and democratic coalitions, popular fronts."[33]

In describing the strategies of the various Latin American Communist parties, the Soviet specialists divided countries as of 1978 into three categories: (1) where patriotic circles of the armed forces are in power and are carrying out an antiimperialist and democratic transformation (e.g., Peru, Panama); (2) where liberal reformist bourgeois circles are in power (e.g., Venezuela, Colombia, Costa Rica, Mexico, and Argentina); and (3) military dictatorships (e.g., Chile, Brazil, Bolivia, Paraguay, Guatemala, Uruguay, Prerevolutionary Nicaragua, and Haiti).

In Peru the Communist party sought the widest possible alliance of "progressive" military, worker, and peasant forces and supported the "progressive" measures of the government, thereby seeking to promote the further transformation of society. The Parties' cooperation with the government continued after the more conservative Morales Bermúdez succeeded Velasco Alvarado as president. Relations cooled when Fernando Belaúnde became president. The Communists usually supported the late General Omar Torrijos in Panama. In Peru and Panama, the Communist parties with other democratic parties and organizations collaborated with the military government forming "temporary political blocs and coalitions."[34]

In the countries with liberal reformist governments, the Communist strategy was "to unite the democratic and patriotic forces, isolate the right and liquidate the threat of coups d'etat, [and] preserve and expand democratic freedoms and the social achievements of the people."[35] Such parties sought to build broad alliances in order to establish a united front of popular forces, capitalizing in part on the lessons learned in Venezuela in the 1960s. Such a front included the left wing of the traditional bourgeois parties, socialists, Christian Democrats, independent left radicals, democratic social movements, labor unions, and organizations of the middle sectors.[36] In Argentina the Communist party was threatened immediately following General Jorge Videla's coup against Isabel Perón. When the new military government "refused to pursue Communists and Peronists," the Party continued its "struggle for the union of democratic and patriotic forces on the basis of a program of democratization of political life, the freeing of political prisoners, and the ending of the terroristic activities of the ultra-right and ultra-left."[37] Settling for progress towards democratization as a preliminary goal, the Party favored a military civilian government with broad backing and a capability for making structural changes. Such was the Party's formula for avoiding open conflict with the military regime. The Argentine Communists have sought to avoid direct confrontations with the government or personal attacks on the President, General Videla. Instead they identified two competing trends within the government, one fascist and one democratic, and tried to assist Videla in following the latter trend. Their objectives involve conventional democratic freedoms, including the release of political prisoners of whom some one hundred out of several thousand are Communists. The Party also supported Videla's foreign policy, particularly relations with the socialist countries.[38]

The Colombian Party went into opposition against the "promonopoly" course of Liberal President López Michelsen and joined in the National Opposition Union (UNO), which was supposed to be a first step toward the formation of a patriotic front of national liberation. The UNO put up a candidate in the 1978 elections but won only 1.9 percent of the popular vote. The Popular Vanguard party, the Communists of Costa Rica, are a small group with relatively little influence. In Mexico, the Communist party carried the tactics of the broad front to an extreme, merging in 1981 with other leftist parties into the Unified Socialist party. The latter's candidate in the 1982 presidential elections won only about 6 percent of the votes.[39]

Military dictatorships constitute the third category of Latin American regimes used by Soviet analysts. Perhaps the first thing one notes about this category is the absence of Argentina although military men have been ruling there since the overthrow of Perón's widow in 1976. Argentina was listed among the liberal reformist regimes even though the government took police action against some Marxist-Leninist groups. No doubt the Soviet analysts omitted Argentina from the military dictatorship category partly because the pro-Soviet Argentine Party has announced support for the government on selected issues and Argentina appears to have been chosen as the central focus of the Soviet economic offensive in South America.

According to the Soviet analysts, the main task of the Communists in the military dictatorships is "to promote the formation of wide antidictatorial and anti-fascist fronts designed to overthrow reactionary regimes, establish citizens' rights, and achieve a matured socio-economic transformation."[40]

The list of the dictatorships falls naturally into two categories: those with which the USSR has diplomatic relations (Bolivia, Brazil, and Uruguay) and those with which it does not (Chile, Paraguay, Guatemala, and Haiti). In Bolivia, where the USSR has a large tin-refining project and fairly extensive cultural relations, the Communist party has been collaborating with many other left-wing parties in an effort to restore a civilian democratic government. In the confusing electoral and political events of 1979, the Party supported ex-President Hernán Siles Suazo.

In Brazil the Communists have been subject to much suppression, and the Party leadership was forced to go abroad.[41] Luiz Carlos Prestes, now a very old man, lived in Moscow until late 1979, when the government relaxed relations with the Communists. The Party characterizes the present regime in Brazil as military-fascist. The Communists support the Brazilian Democratic movement, the only opposition group allowed by the government. It has participated successfully in elections defeating government candidates. A small and persecuted group, the Brazilian Communists have few options. This may partially explain why "we Communists consider participation in elections important for the working class and the working people. . . . We see them as one of the ways of inflicting defeat on the dictatorship . . . obviously, in a crisis situation everything will depend on the development of subsequent events."[42] Calling elections "one" of the ways to defeat the dictatorship left the way open eventually to the use of force. The Party's demands include restoration of constitutional standards, repeal of all repressive legislation, release of all political prisoners, freedom to form parties, including the Communist party, direct elections including presidential elections, and the calling of a constituent assembly. The Communists seek a free political climate in which they can reorganize and broaden their political following. In 1980 a revolt in the Party led to the ouster of Luiz Carlos Prestes as secretary-general, a remarkable development whose full consequences are difficult to predict. In the early 1980s, the Communists broke up into competing factions, supporting different candidates.

In the past some have seen contradictions between the high level of Soviet purchases in Brazil, for a while the largest in Latin America, and the vigorously anti-Communist policies of the Brazilian military government. Others have complained about Soviet "aid" to Brazil in reference to the large credits offered to finance Soviet sales. In fact, economic relations between Brazil and the USSR have been limited mainly to trade. Some knowledgeable Brazilians believe that neither side has come close to realizing the potential benefits of that trade primarily because of the anti-Communist prejudices of Brazilian businessmen and the anti-Communist policies of the government. As an indication of the naiveté of Brazilian businessmen, one Brazilian industrialist visiting Moscow was overheard protesting to a countryman that "I am not a Communist."[43] As to the credits offered, these are designed primarily to promote Soviet exports—not to help Brazil.

The Uruguayan Communist party, and most particularly its leader, Rodney Arismendi, has been among Moscow's most reliable collaborators in Latin America. The Party has only a few thousand members and attempts to make its influence felt through the Frente Amplio, its long prohibited but active opposition on the left. The Communists want to expand participation in the Frente by attracting collaboration from the National party, which is also against the military government.

The other military dictatorships, which do not have diplomatic relations with Moscow, are even more authoritarian and repressive and have forced the Parties underground. Under such conditions political organization is barely possible. In Chile the Communists look to their alliance with the Socialists as the cornerstone of an antifascist front. Other Parties which were in the Popular Unity government of Allende are also included, but the Communists want to make the organized opposition even broader, including the Christian Democrats.[44] Soviet treatment of Communist opposition in Chile uses rather vague political terms; nonetheless, the use of the term *resistance* and other indications suggest that eventually the Communists view an armed uprising as possible, or likely, when opposition to the junta is strong enough. In Paraguay and Guatemala, the small Communist parties also seek to organize opposition to the entrenched military dictatorships. Their leadership meets secretly, and their underground activities are likely to lead eventually to armed resistance as long as conventional political campaigning is outlawed.

• Communist Strategy

The lessons of the Nicaraguan Revolution have had an impact on the tactics and strategy of the Soviet-led Communist movement in Latin America. The impact has been mainly of emphasis rather than kind. The victory in Cuba of a broad national movement with roots in guerrilla warfare, and without significant Communist participation, used to be considered an "exceptional case." Now, with the triumph over Somoza, another such movement sought power in El Salvador too. Sergo Mikoyan put it this way:

> Military political fronts of the type of the 26th of July movement in Cuba and the Sandinista National Liberation Front in Nicaragua showed (and now one can say proved) that they are capable in certain cases of replacing political parties of the proletariat as a revolutionary vanguard. . . . The political activity of these fronts, operating with close links to the masses, on the basis of military and military-organizational power, turned out to be so effective that they, being at first purely military organizations, gradually acquired in fact the functions of political parties. And on the contrary, in both cases, not a single political party, including the Communists, was able even to come close to them in their potential as a vanguard.[45]

The Communist parties in Latin America are being forced to come to terms with the reality that such broad, loose, national fronts are leading and winning revolutions almost without them. Whereas they used to refer to such groups as "ultra-Leftists," "putschists," "petty bourgeois extremists," and the like, they must now accept them as effective revolutionary organizations. Put another way, if the Communists can't beat these radical nationalists, it is better to join them. Not only has this meant that their competitors have seized their revolutionary banners, but also that the Communists have found it desirable to subordinate themselves to their one-time rivals. Once this becomes the policy of the pro-Soviet Communists, and when such movements are identified, the local Communists can be counted on to fall briskly in line. Such a policy can be justified in terms of the interests of the national revolution and of the international Communist movement. It is the policy, for example, in El Salvador, where the general secretary of the Communist party, Shafik Jorge Handal, has swung into line behind the Popular Forces of Liberation Farabundo Martí.[46]

In the latter half of the 1970s, the Communist movement in Latin America lacked direction and dynamism. Allende's victory in Chile showed that Communists could come to power through elections, and the coup against him did not disprove that. The lesson of the coup was that once in power, Communists needed to know better how to defend themselves. After Allende, Soviet leaders concerned with Latin America surveyed the continent and found no attractive opportunities to come to power either peacefully or by force. The Party apparatchiks and their associated officials and scholars dug in their heels for the long pull, writing, organizing, and waiting patiently for better days. In the late 1970s, the mood in these circles was depressed and cynical with no developments in Latin America to brighten an otherwise drab existence. Then came the Nicaraguan Revolution and hard upon that the civil war in El Salvador. The pages of *Latinskaia Amerika* brightened noticeably as an aroused bureaucracy once again could see opportunities in the Americas.

The Sandinista victory in Nicaragua and the civil war in El Salvador once again raised the issue of Soviet military aid to rebel movements. Ordinarily, Moscow has been cautious about providing such aid. One reason is that successful revolutionaries usually need to be strong enough to win on their own. Another is that such aid can have damaging effects on Soviet relations with third powers. These reasons are largely pragmatic: clearly, the Soviets favor revolutionary causes as a matter of principle.

Initially, the Communist parties in Nicaragua and El Salvador were rivals of the leaders of the revolutions. Since the Soviets were supporting their own Communists, competitors in the revolutionary movements, Soviet access was not easy. Castro, on the other hand, knew the Central American nationalist leaders well and provided arms to them in the late 1970s and early 1980s. So, for that matter, did Costa Rica, Mexico, and Venezuela. For a variety of reasons the Soviet Union usually prefers to supply arms and otherwise support revolutionary movements in such countries as El Salvador through third parties, like the Cubans and East Germans.

Although the Nicaraguan Communists were outmaneuvered in the late 1970s, the victory over Somoza gave new hope for revolutionaries in the Americas and new authority to the armed road to power. The Sandinistas' success emboldened the Communists in El Salvador to break with their commitment to legal tactics. General Secretary Handal said, ''Our decision is a bit late, but we're in time.''[47] He explained how difficult it had been for the Party to switch from legal to illegal methods. The timing of the Party's action assured Handal a place on the coordinating committee leading the revolt. Interestingly, Handal also pointed out that the leader of the revolutionary army, Salvador Cayetano Carpio, had broken with the Communist party earlier in order to set up the Popular Forces of Liberation Farabundo Martí.

The Soviet Party has become more sensitive than ever to the opportunities that radical, revolutionary fronts offer the Left. Accepting as fundamental to victory the organization of as broad a national front as possible in certain revolutionary situations, the local Communists will play the role of mediators and peacemakers among leftist factions. Popular fronts, national fronts, and the like are not new to the Communists—they go back to the mid-1930s and before—but their organization for *paramilitary* purposes will receive greater emphasis. Parties and leaders other than Communists may organize and control many such fronts, but the Communists will be more willing than in the past to make the compromises necessary for joining them.

At the same time, Soviet policy has by no means given up the "peaceful" road. On the contrary, it is still the preferred strategy. Party strategies will be determined by "objective conditions" in the country concerned. It is now possible to envisage at lease three models of Communist strategy in Latin America vis-á-vis old regimes:

1. Military dictatorships, type 1. There will be explicit or tacit collaboration with military dictatorships having important economic ties to the USSR and support for a civil-military solution. The Communist party will have limited opportunities to recruit, circulate publications, and compete in certain elections. Example: Argentina before 1983.
2. Democratic reformist regimes. Communists will follow the peaceful road. They will accept the constitutional order, compete for votes and popular support, and collaborate closely with other legal leftist parties. Example: Venezuela.
3. Military dictatorships, type 2. There will be armed revolutionary opposition. Communists will collaborate with, and where possible participate in, revolutionary leadership. They will accept non-Communist leadership. Example: El Salvador before 1982.

The fact that the USSR has swung behind violent revolution in Central America does not mean that it will change its policy in Mexico, Venezuela, or Colombia, nor necessarily toward Argentina and Brazil, where it has strong Soviet economic interests. It will give moral and sometimes material support to revolutions where victory seems possible and desirable. Such countries, in addition to El Salvador, include Chile, and perhaps Paraguay. The strong rhetorical support the Soviet Union has given the Nicaraguan and Salvadoran revolutions has paid dividends. The local leaders know perfectly well where power lies within their own movements, but uninformed observers abroad have identified the USSR with these movements, attributing to it a role and influence not consistent with the facts. The effect of that interpretation and U.S. policies hostile to these revolutions have tended to draw revolutionary forces closer together in the face of the common "imperialist" danger, exaggerate Soviet influence, and enhance the prestige of the USSR in many parts of the world.

V Cuba: Political Asset, Economic Liability

In over sixty years, the Soviet Union has had few successes in Latin America. The Allende government in Chile seemed promising for a few years until its life was ended by a military coup. So Communist successes in Cuba, an enduring bright spot in an otherwise dark hemisphere, have seemed sweet to the USSR.

Cuba may be the Soviet Union's most important political windfall since World War II. As already noted, it was Castro and his 26th of July movement which did the fighting that caused Batista to collapse. The Cuban Communists and the USSR contributed little or nothing. As will be pointed out later, the Soviet Union's economic and military assistance to Castro began about eighteen months *after* he seized power.

Cuba has played a unique role in bolstering the authority and appeal of Soviet doctrine, the universal claims of which require intermittent validation. Communist Cuba has helped make the Soviet contention that communism is the wave of the future more believable. Thus the Marxist-Leninist regime in Cuba has strengthened Soviet influence, most particularly in the Third World. But Cuba has had more than a demonstration effect; Castro sought to mobilize revolutionary forces around the world and supported, where it suited him, Soviet political objectives. Soviet leaders have been particularly pleased that Cuba introduced the first Communist state into the Western Hemisphere, and it has been a useful ally in political competition with the United States.

The political benefits flowing from a Communist Cuba did not come cheaply. Soviet economic and military aid permitted Castro to survive, and his regime has required several billion dollars of Soviet aid each year (table 13). As will be discussed later in this chapter, the cumulative cost of Soviet economic aid to Cuba came to at least US $16 billion by 1979. Although Soviet aid continues to escalate, the Cuban economy manages to keep its nose barely above water. Cuba also is a military strategic liability for the USSR although rarely viewed as such in the West. Similarly, South Korea and West Berlin are strategic liabilities for the United States. These themes will be discussed further.

• The Coming of Soviet Influence

The Soviet Union maintained a presence in Cuba long before Castro came to power through the Cuban Communist party, called for many years the Partido Socialista Popular (PSP). The Cuban Communists, together with the Chilean, were the most politically powerful Parties in Latin America during the 1930s, dominating their respective national labor movements and with an impressive though small electoral following until the late 1940s.[1] Leading Cuban Communists served in President Batista's cabinet during World War II. Throughout its life the Cuban Party loyally followed Moscow's political line.

It is not surprising, therefore, that when Castro first burst upon the scene, some observers declared that he was part of a secret Communist

Table 13
Cuban Economic Reliance on the USSR, 1961–1980

Indicators	Amount or Percentage	Period
Soviet economic aid to Cuba	$16.7 billion	1961–1979[a]
Soviet military aid to Cuba	$ 3.8 billion	1961–1979[b]
Cuban debt to the USSR	$ 5.7 billion	1961–1979[a]
Cuba's percentage of total trade with USSR	66%	1977–1980[c]
Soviet share of Cuba's trade deficit	51%	1961–1980[c]
Percentage of Cuba's sugar exports to the USSR	55%	1975–1979[c]
Percentage of Cuba's oil needs supplied by USSR	98%	1967–1975[c]
Percentage of Cuba's foreign trade carried by Soviet ships	45%	1975

Source: Carmelo Mesa-Lago and June S. Belkin, eds., *Cuba in Africa* (Pittsburgh, 1982), p. 4. Reprinted by permission of the editors.

[a]Cumulative.

[b]Estimate of cumulative military aid calculated on basis of the amount granted in 1961–1968 ($1.5 billion); the total probably is much higher.

[c]Annual average.

conspiracy to take over Cuba. Put another way, this view holds that the USSR, using the Cuban Communists, and the latter using Castro, engineered a successful plot to take over Cuba as a Soviet instrument in the hemisphere. That version of events is not supported by the facts nor by the leading scholars of this period. On the contrary, Fidel Castro and his 26th of July movement took over the Cuban Communists, using them to strengthen their hold over Cuba and to facilitate beneficial relations with the USSR. Such an interpretation is borne out by events both before and after 1 January 1959, when Castro came to power.

In the struggle against Batista, the main disagreement over political strategy between Castro and the 26th of July movement, on the one hand, and the pro-Moscow Communists, on the other, concerned timing and the priority given to the use of armed force. Castro recruited, armed, organized, and put his partisan forces into the field with relatively little attention to conventional propaganda and organization. Castro, for example, had no established political party as such. The Communists, on the other hand, who kept their small political organization together, contributed little and late to the armed struggle against Batista. In a retrospective account of this period, Blas Roca, the PSP leader, explained that the Party correctly believed that mass actions can be transformed into an armed struggle or national armed uprising but that "we took no practical measures to realize this possibility for a long time. We thought [this could happen] spontaneously. We didn't train or arm our cadres . . . that was our mistake."[2]

At crucial points in the Revolution, the Communists did not act decisively to support Castro. They viewed his attack on the Moncada barracks in 1953 as "putschist" and "bourgeois" since the political organization to follow up such an attack, if successful, had not been achieved.[3] Similarly, the 26th of July movement quarreled with the Communists over the general strike Castro called on 9 April 1958. The Communists criticized some of the violent acts ("arson" and "repression") of the Castro forces while the latter attacked the Communists for being slow in organizing strike actions.[4] The strike was led by Castro, and the Communists have since wanted to be associated with it, especially since their contribution was probably of marginal value. The strike failed.

A precise understanding of this period is difficult to achieve because commentators probably have been highly selective in the use of the little material available. One of the most useful sources is a letter from a Comrade P. Lopez (probably a pseudonym) to the Soviet periodical *Partinaia zhizn*. It represents a position that must have been approved by the Moscow leaders and was published before Castro came to power.

The letter stressed that the PSP's strategy was "mass mobilization" and not the "terrorist acts and adventuristic activity" of some members of the 26th of July movement.[5] The PSP did not back Castro's armed expedition to Cuba on the grounds that political conditions were not ripe, but it did give aid once the survivors of the landing began to attract popular support. The letter also criticized Castro's forces for "completely unexpectedly organizing a putsch in Havana with an unsuccessful attack on an arsenal."[6] In spite of the failure to organize this action with broad support and its ill-timing, the letter said the PSP supported the strike and Fidel Castro.

The sharp criticism of Castro's tactics and clear resentment that the Communists had been left out of the planning showed that the PSP was separate from the 26th of July movement and offered its support late and grudgingly. As Blas Roca explained, the Cuban revolution is "the first socialist revolution that was not made by the Communist Party."[7]

The position of the old-guard Communists was uneasy when Castro took over Cuba in early 1959. None of them led a major partisan detachment, the Party had always been critical of the 26th of July movement, and their contribution to the Cuban Revolution was minimal. None of the old-guard leaders held top administrative or political positions in the Castro regime in the early years. When various Castro-approved political parties merged into a newly formed Communist party in 1965, the old PSP leaders had no place on the eight-man Politburo and only two of the five places on the new Party's Secretariat. As late as 1980, only two old PSP leaders, Blas Roca and Carlos Rafael Rodríguez, served on the sixteen-man Politburo. Castro took over the Communists, not the reverse.

After Batista's fall, the Soviet Union did not rush to establish close relations with the Castro regime. It extended formal recognition on 11 January 1959 but did not make a substantial contact until A. I. Mikoyan visited the island on 13 February 1960, at which time a trade and credit agreement was signed. Provisions for an exchange of ambassadors were not announced until 8 May 1960, sixteen months after Castro came to power.

The Eisenhower administration set the stage in 1959–1960 for the close Soviet-Cuban relations that followed. In March 1960 the president authorized a series of measures designed to lead to Castro's overthrow: (1) the termination of U.S. sugar purchases, (2) the end of U.S. oil deliveries, (3) the continuation of the arms embargo, and (4) the organization of a paramilitary force of Cuban émigrés to assault the island and overthrow Castro. Such measures soon became known, and the Cuban government used this information to persuade the USSR to extend aid.[8]

Antonio Nuñez Jiminez, head of a Cuban economic mission, arranged for Soviet supplies of oil and petroleum products and for cultural and technical cooperation on a visit to the USSR in June 1960. Shortly thereafter Raúl Castro, minister of the Revolutionary Armed Forces of Cuba, secured a Soviet commitment "to satisfy completely Cuban needs in exchange for Cuban products." On 12 July Khrushchev agreed to buy the unused portions of the U.S. sugar quota. Later the Soviet government committed itself to providing the "necessary aid" in case of armed intervention.[9] These Soviet commitments made it possible for the Castro government to survive U.S. sanctions, with the two governments achieving far closer relations than ever before. Bolstered by Soviet arms, the Cuban government repulsed the American-backed émigré landing at the Bay of Pigs.[10] United States sanctions against Castro provided the rationale and the catalytic action which accelerated close economic, military, and political relations between Cuba and the USSR.

• The Antagonistic 1960s

Soviet relations with Cuba can only be understood if the conflicts between the two governments are taken into account, conflicts which both governments usually try to keep confidential. Since the West has devoted little attention to them and has little knowledge of them, they will be discussed at length. At the same time, it is essential to bear in mind that the Soviet government and the Castro regime have had fundamental interests in common. The first is that Castro survives any potential domestic or foreign efforts to overthrow him. His overthrow, hardly likely in the early 1980s, would surely lead to Cuba's estrangement from the Soviet model at home and from international communism abroad. The second is that Cuban socialism prospers. Only then can the heavy Soviet aid burden be lightened and can Cuba begin repaying its huge debts.

Serious Soviet-Cuban differences first surfaced at the time of the missile crisis in 1962. Angry because Khrushchev settled the crisis without Cuban participation, Castro refused to allow an inspection team to verify the removal of the rockets. In addition, he said Cuba would shoot down airplanes violating Cuban air space. Nor were the Cubans ever fully satisfied by pledges of Soviet military assistance in the event of a U.S. attack. From 1962 until 1968, there were sporadic conflicts between the Soviet Union and Cuba over the latter's domestic and foreign policies.

• *Domestic Policies.* In the early 1960s, Castro went overboard in an industrialization campaign requiring heavy investment, large inputs of raw materials and fuel, and high levels of imports beyond Cuba's capacity to pay. The USSR was unwilling to subsidize such ambitious and unrealistic programs. Faced with their own errors and Soviet criticism, the Cubans later veered to the other extreme, pressing sugar output toward the unrealistic goal of ten million tons by 1970. In spite of herculean efforts and the sacrifice of other economic sectors, only 8.5 million tons were produced in 1970. The Soviet advisers were also dismayed by the erratic and disorderly management of the Cuban economy, not to mention Castro's own impulsive and inexpert personal intervention. Ineffective policies and mismanagement were reflected in annual average economic growth rates of minus 0.4 percent in 1962–1969.[11]

Symbolic of Castro's domestic political supremacy during the 1960s was his summary treatment of old-guard Communists. When Aníbal Escalante, a leader of the PSP, became too powerful in 1962, Castro dismissed him and sent him abroad. Only one old-guard Communist remained at the top of this organization, and many of the rank and file were purged.[12] Castro turned against the old PSP leadership once more in 1964 (the Marcos Rodríguez affair) and again early in 1968. In the latter case, a "microfaction" was charged with conspiring against the

Revolution by taking a critical line, a line actually similar to Moscow's.[13] Escalante and others were sentenced to prison for from ten to fifteen years. In this way Castro eliminated some of Moscow's strongest supporters within the old Cuban Party. Conveniently, Soviet agencies were explicitly absolved in the controversy.

• *Foreign Policies.* Castro has long sought and has failed to receive an iron-clad Soviet guarantee to defend Cuba from the United States. That issue first arose in July 1960 when he sought Soviet aid against U.S. sanctions. Khrushchev said then "in a figurative sense, if it became necessary, the Soviet military can support the Cuban people with rockets and weapons."[14] His offer was figurative, hypothetical, and referred literally to Soviet capacity, not intention. For the next weeks Khrushchev pointedly watered down the statement, offering to send "necessary aid." Soviet spokesmen did not refute such interpretations since they welcomed the deterrent effect they might have on the United States. The effect, clearly, was insufficient to prevent the Bay of Pigs landing in April 1961. Krushchev sent a message to President Kennedy saying that he would give "to the Cuban government all the necessary assistance to repel aggression."[15] The landing collapsed so quickly that the Soviet hand was not called.

The next time a Soviet military guarantee became a major issue was in the Cuban missile crisis. The Soviet Union maintained at the time and frequently since that the missiles were sent to Cuba at Cuban request.[16] Castro, on the other hand, prefers to explain the deployment as a matter of mutual agreement.[17] The question is intriguing since an answer would throw light on the question about the extent of Soviet "expansionism," "adventurism," "agressiveness," and the like in Latin America.

Suárez offers his personal belief that Castro eagerly sought missiles beginning in 1960 in order to realize his own plans to secure his home base and bolster his antiimperialist campaign elsewhere in the hemisphere.[18] This plausible explanation, if true, would show what an important impact client states may have on their sponsors, the North Korean attack on South Korea being another case in point. Anyway, Khrushchev clearly had many reasons of his own for undertaking this gamble. As a result of disagreements over the missile crisis, Soviet-Cuban relations were strained until February 1963, when a new economic agreement with the USSR sweetened the atmosphere.

• *China.* The USSR began competing with China for influence in Cuba virtually from the beginning of the Revolution. Not surprisingly, the Chinese were attracted by Castro's guerrilla strategies, his rural-based revolutionary movement, and his radical brand of communism. They therefore sought to win him to their side in the international Communist movement. This posed a sharp challenge to Moscow not only with respect to Cuba itself, but also in regard to Soviet influence over other Communist parties, especially in Latin America. For his part Castro used his relations with the Chinese early on to gain leverage over Moscow.

On different occasions, when in deep trouble, Castro tried to manipulate the two Communist superpowers. The Chinese never were able to offer economic inducements approaching those of the Soviet Union, and Castro usually ended up supporting the USSR in international Communist controversies. When the heavy U.S. sanctions were imposed on Cuba in the 1960s, the Soviet Union bought almost three times as much sugar as China and supported Cuba in many other ways. Cuba began to tilt toward Moscow. In 1963 the USSR, seeking to smooth Castro's feathers ruffled during the missile crisis, made so much more favorable trade agreements that Castro was willing to risk offending the Chinese by his visit to the USSR.[19] In November 1964 Castro played host to a conference of Latin American Parties in Havana to which the Chinese were not invited, and which passed a resolution inferentially critical of Peking. Perhaps the bitterest Cuban-Chinese polemic occurred in early 1966 on the eve of the Tricontinental Conference in Havana. Castro berated the Chinese for cutting off supplies of rice urgently needed in Cuba and for interfering in Cuban domestic affairs. His tirade helped him shape the outcome of the conference so as to protect his Soviet relationship while maintaining his area of maneuver. Castro's fundamental policy dispute with the Chinese was over Cuba's position in the Sino-Soviet conflict and the strategy of the world revolutionary movement. In the early 1970s, China's rice sales to Cuba grew substantially, but Cuban participation on the other side in the Angolan War angered the Chinese.

In the meantime, too, Cuba's economic, political, and military interests had become so intermeshed with those of the USSR that Ché Guevara's one-time wish that Cuba mediate the Sino-Soviet controversy seemed whimsical. Except for the middle 1960s, Cuban trade with China rarely exceeded, and was often less than, 10 percent of its total trade.[20]

Soviet and Cuban leaders also disagreed over revolutionary strategy in Latin America. In the mid-1960s, Castro favored armed action by guerrilla *focos* against established governments in the manner of his own rebellion. Such strategy, if successful, probably would have meant the end of the leadership of the pro-Moscow Parties, an outcome Soviet leaders could not accept. This subject is treated briefly later in this chapter.

• *Czechoslovakia.*   Soviet-Cuban tensions reached a climax at the time of the Soviet invasion of Czechoslovakia in 1968. The Cuban economy was floundering, not having been able to sustain prerevolutionary output in several important sectors. None of the guerrilla forces Castro had backed in various Latin American countries had succeeded, and several were wiped out, most notably the group of Ché Guevara in Bolivia. Meanwhile, Soviet leaders, dismayed by Cuba's erratic economic performance, which they were subsidizing, and by Castro's divisive role in the international Communist movement, were dragging their feet in bilateral economic negotiations. Most hurtful was a Soviet slowdown in oil deliveries at a time when Soviet oil supplies were known to be adequate.

The Soviet invasion provided Castro an opportunity to vent his ire and open the door to reconciliation with his Soviet patrons. Although expressing his reservations about armed intervention, he approved the use of Soviet force to defend Czech socialism and oppose imperialism.[21] He appeared to fear U.S. armed action against Cuba in retaliation for Soviet action in Czechoslovakia. Castro made it clear that if the United States intervened, he would welcome Soviet military assistance. After 1968 Cuba and the USSR steadily moved closer on virtually all fronts, most particularly the planning and management of the Cuban economy and relations with Third World countries.

• The Collaborative 1970s

Castro's mismanagement of the Cuban economy and its dismaying performance in the 1960s, the failure of Cuban-sponsored armed struggle in many Latin American countries, continuing dependence on high levels of Soviet economic and military assistance, and Cuba's failure to regain access to U.S. markets led to collaboration between the USSR and Cuba on a broad front in the 1970s. Collaboration was based on a genuine convergence of interests between the leaders of the two countries. Their cooperation is best known on international issues, but Cuban society was reorganized in the 1970s on the Soviet model.

Following Soviet experience and practice, central planning and control of the Cuban economy was strengthened, more rational use of manpower and capital encouraged, material incentives given priority over moral incentives, and planning goals made more realistic. In 1972 Castro introduced a layer of deputy prime ministers, constituting the Executive Council of the Council of Ministers, to coordinate the work of clusters of ministries. And in 1976 Cuba's new socialist constitution was established, modeling state and governmental structure on that of the USSR. The effect of these changes was to depersonalize day-to-day governance and institutionalize Cuban socialism. Since the Communist party of Cuba held its first congress in 1975, membership has been expanded and leadership changed following Soviet models.[22]

Similarly, Soviet support and influence over Cuba was increased in 1970 with the formation of the Soviet-Cuban Commission for Economic, Scientific, and Technical Collaboration. This instrument was designed to maximize for Cuba and the USSR the benefits of Soviet aid, more favorable long-term arrangements for which were made in 1972. Cuba joined the socialist countries' Council for Mutual Economic Assistance (Comecon) in 1972, thereby providing for stronger Cuban links with Eastern European economies. Cuba would have preferred the security guarantees that membership in the Warsaw Pact would have conferred, but Comecon membership was the next best thing. It also regularized and legitimized Cuba's dependence on Comecon markets. For the USSR, Cuba's membership in Comecon guaranteed greater Soviet influence on Cuban economic planning and policies than ever before.

Cuba and the USSR have been collaborating for more than a decade, not only on Cuban domestic policies but also on a broad range of regional and global issues. To explain that collaboration as simply a function of the island's extreme economic and military dependence on the USSR is to underestimate Castro's political capabilities and to misunderstand that collaboration. It might be tempting to attribute Castro's qualified approval for the Soviet invasions of Czechoslovakia in 1968 and of Afghanistan in late 1979, as well as Soviet sponsorship of military suppression in Poland in 1981, to Cuban servility and Soviet dominance. In fact, Castro's support has usually been qualified and sometimes delayed. Castro has his own reasons for approving Soviet military support for faltering socialist governments. He would hope to have such support if the Cuban government were similarly threatened.

The main justification for Soviet military suppression is that socialist regimes are being threatened with "foreign intervention" by "imperialist" nations. Massive domestic opposition to socialist regimes can hardly be publicly admitted. In the European cases, there has been little evidence to support charges of such foreign intervention, but Castro's fears, at least for several years after the Bay of Pigs invasion, were not groundless. Thus, if Castro is counting on the USSR to protect him from "imperialism" (or local forces linked to "imperialism"), he must necessarily approve the Soviet defense of "socialism" elsewhere.

Cuba has been a valuable partner for the USSR within the international Communist movement. Since the mid-1960s, Cuba has tended to take the Soviet side in the Sino-Soviet conflict. That is no small matter because the USSR has so much more to offer Cuba in trade and aid than China. Also, the pro-Soviet Communist parties tend to be more numerous, larger, and more powerful than the pro-Chinese. As a result, Cuba has pressed the Soviet cause against the Chinese in Third World forums. Many of Cuba's ideological and political positions, which were originally closer to the Chinese, have shifted toward the Soviet model. As a result Cuba has taken a resolute anti-Chinese stance on most issues, recently, for example, against Chinese incursions into Vietnam.

• *Africa*. Soviet-Cuban collaboration took a historically unprecedented turn and reached new levels of intimacy in Africa beginning in

1975. Never before had the two countries engaged in combined military operations. The Cubans supplied most of the troops and the USSR the field commanders, combat advisers, weapons, and financial support (table 14). Cuba has had about forty thousand troops in Africa.

In the 1960s Cuba had closer ties with many African revolutionary leaders, such as Ben Bella and Nkrumah, than did the Soviet Union. Castro provided hospitality to these leaders and trained their followers in Cuba. Cuba sent military missions and combat contingents to several African countries, such as Algeria and Congo (Brazzaville). Castro tried unsuccessfully to launch a tricontinental organization of revolutionary movements in Asia, Africa, and Latin America.[23]

Ché Guevara, who tried to organize revolutionary movements in the Portuguese colonies, first made contact with Agostinho Neto, leader of

Table 14
Soviet, Eastern European, and Cuban Technicians in Selected African Countries, 1979
(number of persons)

	Military		Economic	
	Soviet and Eastern European	Cuban	Soviet and Eastern European	Cuban
North Africa				
Algeria	1,015	15	11,500	100
Libya	1,820	—	23,500	1,000
Sub-Saharan Africa				
Angola	1,400	19,000	2,760	6,500
Equatorial Guinea	40	200	—	—
Ethiopia	1,250	13,000	1,500	450
Guinea	85	50	645	200
Guinea-Bissau	60	50	50	40
Madagascar	—	—	110	25
Mozambique	525	215	800	600
Nigeria	—	—	1,725	10
São Tomé and Príncipe	—	—	15	200
Tanzania	—	—	140	80
Total	6,195	32,530	42,745	9,205

Source: U.S. Central Intelligence Agency, National Foreign Assessment Center, *Communist Aid Activities in Non-Communist Less Developed Countries, 1979* (October 1980), pp. 15, 21.

the Popular movement for the National Liberation of Angola (MPLA) in Congo (Brazzaville) in 1965. Cuba provided the MPLA with arms and training thereafter.[24] When the Angolan civil war began to escalate and South African troops entered Angola in August 1975, the USSR was reluctant to provide the MPLA arms whereas the Cubans promptly sent troops. The latter arrived under their own steam in converted freighters and obsolete aircraft in the concluding months of 1975.[25] The Cuban military involvement shown in table 15 was an independent decision based on long and close relations with the MPLA.

Soviet relations with the MPLA had blown hot and cold over the years. More important, Soviet caution was due, on the one hand, to Angola's limited strategic value, and on the other, to the negative impact Soviet participation could, and in fact did, have on détente, arms control negotiations, and relations with the West generally.

If the Cubans took the lead in Angola, it was the Soviet Union that took the initiative in the intervention to buck up the military dictatorship of the dergue in Ethiopia in 1978. The dergue was under attack in the West by the self-proclaimed Marxist-Leninist government of Somalia which sought irredenta in Ethiopia's Ogaden province. In the north of Ethiopia, the Eritrean secessionists, divided into Marxist and other factions, have been intermittently capable of separating their territories along the Red Sea coast from Ethiopia proper. The Ethiopian government has troops stationed throughout the country but pacification in any complete sense had not yet been achieved in late 1982.

Cuba lacked the language and cultural ties with the Ethiopians that it had with Angola. Its relations with the government leaders were slight, and the Cubans did not relish taking sides against their long-time revolutionary comrades in Somalia and Eritrea. The USSR gave Ethiopia, commanding as it does the Horn of Africa, a higher priority than Angola. Ethiopia has the Red Sea ports in Eritrea and lies near oil states of the Middle East. The USSR took command, in a manner of speaking, of the defense of the Ethiopian government and persuaded the Cubans to bring in seventeen thousand troops, many from Angola. The Cubans, with a thousand Soviet military advisers, including generals, turned back the Somali attack. Soviet military leaders closely coordinated the defense with Cuban and Ethiopian troops and provided transport for the Cubans.

Table 15
Cuban Military Presence in Africa and the Middle East, 1966–1978

	Number of Troops and Military Advisers				
	1966[a]	1974	1976	1977	1978
Angola			13,000	19,000	19,000
Benin				10–20	20
Congo (Brazzaville)	700–1,000	50–100	1,000[b]	300	500–600
Equatorial Guinea		80	200–500[b]	150–200[d]	100[d]
Ethiopia				400	16,000–17,000
Guinea-Bissau			25–300[b]	60–120	100–150
Guinea-Conakry	50–100	200	100–300	300–500	400–500
Iraq				150	20
Libya			150	100–125	200
Madagascar				30	
Mozambique			1,200	650–750	1,000
Sierra Leone		10–25	20–25	120–125	10–15
Somalia			15–1500[c]	200	
South Yemen		600–700	200		300–400
Tanzania		150	500		50
Uganda				25[d]	60[d]
Zambia					15–60[e]
Estimated total	750–1,100	1,100–1,250	16,450–18,700	21,500–21,950	37,800–39,200
Total excluding Angola & Ethiopia	750–1,100	1,100–1,250	3,450–5,700	2,100–2,550	2,800–3,200

Source: William M. LeoGrande, "Cuban-Soviet Relations and Cuban Policy in Africa," in Cuba in Africa, ed. Carmelo Mesa-Lago and June S. Belkin (Pittsburgh, 1982), p. 43. Reprinted by permission of the editors.

[a] 1966 represents the high point of the Cuban presence during the 1960s.

[b] Staging and transshipment points for Angola.

[c] Represents an expansion of the Cuban presence in Somalia during 1976 rather than the margin of error in estimation.

[d] In December 1977, Fidel Castro denied that Cuba had any military advisers in Uganda and put the number in Equatorial Guinea at 8–10 rather than the 150–200 estimated in the November 1977 NSC report (see New York Times, 7 December 1977).

[e] Covertly, training guerrillas of the Zimbabwe Patriotic Front and/or Southwest African People's Organization (SWAPO).

Raúl Castro, Cuban minister of defense, and other Cuban military leaders coordinated operations with the Red Army leaders in Moscow. Soviet-Cuban military collaboration was decisive against the Somalis. The Cuban and Soviet forces refused to take to the field against the Eritreans, favoring a negotiated rather than an imposed solution in this conflict. The Ethiopian government, however, pressed forward the armed suppression of the Eritreans, subduing but not defeating them.

Soviet military intervention and Soviet-sponsored Cuban combat operations in Angola and Ethiopia prevented the defeat of the MPLA and the dergue. The political and military situations in these countries were still fragile in early 1982, when both governments were threatened at home and abroad. South Africa still makes military incursions into Angola territory, and Somalis are a continuing threat to Ethiopia. Jonas Savimbi, supported by Western governments, maneuvers with armed support against the MPLA inside Angola, and the Eritreans have prevented the dergue from pacifying the Ethiopian north. The USSR and Cuba believe that a strong socialist Angola is important in promoting social change in nearby Namibia and Zimbabwe, and both countries are determined to defend their gains in the Horn of Africa. Many observers believe that the Angolan and Ethiopian governments would fall without foreign support. As a result Soviet military advisers and the main force of Cuban troops remained in both countries in early 1983.

Soviet and Cuban military intervention bolstered the cause of blacks and social revolution in southern Africa. The verdict is less clear in the Horn since most of the participants in Ethiopia were either revolutionaries or self-proclaimed Marxists. Soviet-Cuban support for the dergue protected Ethiopia territorial integrity. Soviet-Cuban military victories gave both countries greater stature in Africa. Both African countries, however, made no progress or suffered setbacks in their relations with the United States and Western Europe. Cuba's Africa interventions, especially in Ethiopia, were a major factor blocking the full normalization of trade and diplomatic relations with the United States, its natural economic partner.

The Soviet Union and Cuba had a genuine partnership in Angola and Ethiopia. The USSR clearly was stronger and could have acted alone; Cuba could not have done so. Yet in a sense, Cuba may have made the larger contribution, in providing most of the manpower. Cuba was more interested in Angola, the USSR in Ethiopia. Cuba could hardly have been correctly characterized as a proxy in Angola although one could make a stronger case about that with respect to Ethiopia. But even there, the Cubans could not have been forced to fight against their will.

• *Nonalignment.* Nowhere, perhaps, have Soviet and Cuban values and interests come closer to coinciding than in relations with developing countries. The Soviet Union continues to press patiently and relentlessly for the establishment of Marxist-Leninist regimes on the Soviet model, or the next best thing, in developing countries. On the Soviet side, the goal has a long-term, doctrinal, and institutional character. For the Cubans it is more personal; Castro seeks to fulfill his self-image of liberator on a unique historic and global stage.

The USSR and Cuba have used the nonaligned movement as a principal public forum to influence the Third World. Castro's Western critics often scoff at his posing as "nonaligned" while hoping the USSR will defend Cuba, and while Soviet leaders try leaving the impression that they would do so. But the USSR has not made an unequivocal commitment to defend Cuba, and Cuba is not a member of the Warsaw Pact, and these facts are good technical grounds for claiming that Cuba is nonaligned. In practice Cuba has been working hand-in-glove with Soviet leaders within the nonaligned movement for years.

Cuba is an ideal sponsor for Soviet policies within the movement, reliable partly because of its dependence on Soviet economic and military assistance. Castro's antiimperialist credentials are impeccable, and the Latin-African character of Cuban society gives it credible ties beyond the Americas. The Cubans can now quite happily accept most Soviet policies, not because of Soviet pressure, but because there are many common interests. Castro, for example, would find it difficult to play his large, flamboyant role if he did not have solid Soviet support behind the scenes as well as the cooperation of other pro-Soviet states within the movement. One might refer to the Soviet-Cuban relationship as a marriage not only of convenience but also of convergence.

Cuba played host to the sixth summit of the nonaligned movement in 1979 and, as host, had administrative control of the organization. With the aid of several Marxist states like Vietnam, South Yemen, Ethiopia, and Angola, Castro managed to produce a draft conference declaration that sided with Soviet views on many subjects such as "imperialism," "racism," "human rights," and "Zionism." The opposition, led by President Tito of Yugoslavia, succeeded in changing this draft, and most particularly eliminating a statement that the Soviet countries and the nonaligned movement are "natural allies." A number of important questions dividing the movement down the middle were deferred until a later meeting. Nonetheless, the Havana summit shifted the movement left toward Castro's concept of nonalignment as antiimperialism.[26]

• Central America

The Soviet Union and Cuba have similar policies and goals in Central America just as in Africa. They favor opposition to old capitalist regimes linked to metropolitan powers and the defense of young socialist regimes. And they are, of course, sympathetic to revolutionary groups, most particularly those with a Marxist cast.

Castro and other Cubans know Central America far better than their Soviet comrades because the Cubans share a common culture, language, and geographical home with nations in the area. And unlike the Soviet Communists, the Cuban leaders have themselves fought a revolution recently. They had far better reasons, personal and political, to spring to the assistance of the Nicaraguan and Salvadoran rebels than Soviet Communists living in Moscow.

According to U.S. intelligence sources, the Cubans provided training, arms, and advice to the Sandinistas before Somoza's fall.[27] And Castro was reportedly active in bringing about the unification of the conflicting opposition groups against Somoza.[28] The unification of leftist forces has long been a standard strategy of the international Communist movement and is explicitly advocated by Soviet and Cuban leaders. Nor is there much doubt that such a strategy was vital to the Sandinistas' victory over Somoza.

It is difficult to find evidence that Castro was decisive in implementing such a strategy in Nicaragua. In any case the Nicaraguans themselves claim credit for the unification of anti-Somoza forces. Nor does the fact that the Nicaraguans organized a broad front against Somoza, a political and military strategy found effective by forces of many political complexions, means that Castro controlled the Sandinistas or that they are his puppets.

Since Somoza's fall the Cubans have been among the most active supporters of the new Sandinista government. By early 1980 Cuba had sent to Nicaragua twelve hundred teachers, about three hundred military and security advisers, and several hundred medical, construction, agricultural, media, and other specialists.[29] Castro has repudiated Vice President Bush's charge that there were five thousand advisers in Nicaragua. He maintained there were less than three thousand, mostly teachers and technicians.[30] The Sandinistas have been building up their security and military forces as hostility has grown in certain neighboring countries, as hostile paramilitary forces have been organized by the United States, and as the tone of the new U.S. administration turned belligerent.

The Soviet government and Party applaud Cuban help for the Sandinistas, and that help promotes Soviet objectives in the area. No doubt there is an exchange of information between Cuba and the USSR on these subjects. Also, since the Cuban economy is weak, the USSR probably takes into account the Cuban effort in Nicaragua in determining its own aid to Cuba. Convincing evidence that the Soviet Union controls the Cuban or Sandinista efforts in Nicaragua is not available. Besides, the issue of control is secondary; the Cuban effort suits Soviet needs and interests without control.

Soviet and Cuban policies run parallel in El Salvador as in Nicaragua. Both nations favor the overthrow of the military junta and the coming to power of the revolutionary front. The rebels have captured many arms from the Salvadoran armed forces and have accumulated large funds from kidnappings and ransoms which they use to bribe local officials or to buy arms from abroad. Most of the arms in the possession of the Salvadoran rebels are of U.S. or Western European manufacture; the former are often captured weapons supplied under U.S. aid programs to countries such as South Vietnam and Ethiopia. In a report dramatically presented to the public by the Department of State in February 1981, it was charged that two hundred tons of arms were covertly delivered to the Salvadoran rebels through Cuba and Nicaragua.[31] The main thrust of the argument was that the socialist countries were fomenting the Salvadoran insurrection through Cuba. Castro flatly denied that Cuba was sending its own or Soviet weapons to El Salvador or that it was sending advisers.[32]

The State Department report focused attention primarily on Cuba as serving as point man for the Communist effort. The Soviet Union was given a prominent but not dominant place. The report suggests that Cuba has been taking the lead in this attempt and has widespread socialist support. As this book went to press, U. S. pressure from Honduras against Nicaragua mounted, there was growing political polarization in Nicaragua and El Salvador, and Cuban and Soviet ties with the Sandinistas and Salvadoran rebels strengthened.

• Soviet Aid

The Soviet share of Cuban trade has hovered around 50 percent but has risen much above that figure in some years. In 1978, for example, it was 69 percent. Cuba often takes about 5 percent of Soviet trade. The share of all the socialist countries together has sometimes been over 80 percent of Cuban trade. Cuba has exported a narrow range of commodities to the Soviet Union, mainly sugar, nickel, rum, fruit, and cigarettes. The shape of Soviet exports to Cuba is immense, with machinery, equipment, vehicles, and oil being among the largest categories. In most years Cuba has had a large trade deficit with the USSR, which has usually also absorbed much of Cuba's global deficit (table 16).

We have seen that because of these massive trade deficits, Soviet economic assistance was essential in preventing the collapse of the Castro government in the early 1960s. It has been required ever since to keep the Cuban economy functioning. Cuba lacks natural resources; it has no oil and few minerals. It has little of value to export except sugar, nickel, tobacco, fish, and fruit, the proceeds from which are insufficient to pay for everything the country needs. The Soviet Union has been making up the difference, now running at the equivalent of several billion dollars a year.

The Soviet Politburo ultimately can decide how much help to give Castro, and barring some exceptional economic crisis, that decision will

Table 16
Cuban Balance of Trade with the USSR, 1959–1980
(millions of pesos)

	USSR	
	Global Balance	Soviet Balance
1959	− 39	13
1960	28	23
1961	− 12	38
1962	−238	−190
1963	−322	−297
1964	−305	−135
1965	−175	−105
1966	−327	−247
1967	−294	−216
1968	−451	−382
1969	−555	−436
1970	−262	−161
1971	−527	−427
1972	−419	−490
1973	−310	−334
1974	11	−214
1975	−166	411
1976	−488	148
1977	−521	205
1978	−141	178
1979	−187ᵖ	−154
1980	−542ᵖ	−558

Sources: Carmelo Mesa-Lago, *The Economy of Socialist Cuba: a Two Decade Appraisal* (Albuquerque, 1981); *Guía Estadística* (Havana, 1980); Banco Nacional de Cuba (Havana, 1981).
p = preliminary.

not be challenged at home. Certain Party and government specialists know about these huge capital transfers, deplore their size, seek their reduction, but don't know how to avoid them. Most citizens will be aware of them vaguely at best, and the most they are likely to do is grumble about Soviet largesse to national liberation movements made at their own expense.

The USSR has granted Cuba far more comprehensive, sustained, and massive economic assistance than any other developing country outside Moscow's Eurasian orbit. Third World countries, and particularly the two most favored recipients, India and Egypt, appear to have received far less Soviet assistance.[33] Soviet aid to Cuba is particularly generous in its subsidies for Cuban exports of sugar and nickel. In recent years Soviet prices have varied from about ten to thirty-five cents a pound above world market prices. Because many buyers from market economies pay preferential prices below the so-called world market price, that price is not a fair basis for comparison. Even if table 17 exaggerates, the Soviet subsidy is still considerable. Similarly, the USSR has been paying Cuba for nickel at prices pegged sometimes as much as 50 percent above the world market price. The USSR also subsidizes the prices charged Cuba for oil, virtually all of which must be imported. Following the Comecon pattern, prices are set by averaging world prices (for oil) over a specified period so that prices charged in rising markets necessarily lag behind world

Table 17
Soviet Subsidies of Cuban Sugar, 1970–1980
(U.S. dollars per lb.)

	Price Paid by the USSR	*World Market Price*[a]
1970	6.11	3.68
1971	6.11	4.50
1972	6.11	7.27
1973	12.02	9.45
1974	19.64	29.66
1975	30.40	20.37
1976	30.95	11.51
1977	35.73	8.10
1978	40.78	7.82
1979	44.00	9.65
1980	—	28.66

Source: Commisión Económica para América Latina, "Cuba: Notas para el estudio económico de América Latina" (Mexico, 1980), p. 24.
[a]Price of the International Sugar Agreement.

prices. Lately these various price subsidies appear to have been fixed to help even up the Soviet-Cuban balance of payments.

Cuban deficits were so high and persistent up to 1972 that the USSR deferred the repayment of principal and interest on the Cuban debt from then until 1986. Thus Cuban use of these monies during a thirteen-year period constitutes a substantial gift in itself. Soviet economists judged correctly that the Cubans would not be able to keep current annually, much less repay the already accumulated debt.

Soviet-Cuban economic cooperation is coordinated by the Soviet-Cuban Commission for Economic, Scientific, and Technological Cooperation. The commission met for the first time in Havana in 1971 and alternately in the two countries ever since. Carlos Rafael Rodríguez, a pre-Castro Communist, has headed the Cuban delegation for many years. The commission, together with Cuban representatives at Comecon and with other Comecon countries, also links the Cuban five year plans with those of the USSR and other Comecon countries.

• *Sectoral Development.* The assistance of the USSR and other socialist countries has probably been most massive in the sugar industry. This is not surprising since sugar constitutes Cuba's main export and nearly one-quarter of its national income. Sugar is, moreover, Cuba's principal means of payment to the socialist countries. The USSR has provided Cuba with technical assistance in virtually all stages of the sugar industry: planting, cultivating, harvesting, milling, and transport. Soviet scientists have collaborated with the Cubans in protecting sugarcane from disease and developing the best-yielding strains suitable for Cuban soil and climate. The two other main concerns of Soviet assistance have been to mechanize the harvest and to boost sugar-milling capacities.

Harvesting has been mechanized in order to increase the efficiency of the industry and save manpower. By 1980, 45 percent of the sugarcane harvest was cut mechanically. Soviet specialists were deeply involved with the Cubans in the invention of automatic loaders for collecting cut cane. By the early 1970s, there were ten thousand Soviet automatic loaders in service. In addition, the USSR took the lead in the design of tractors and harvesting combines to cut as well as load cane. Soviet advisers helped Cubans build a plant in Holguín which produced five hundred KTP-1 combines in 1980. Before the Revolution almost all the cutting and loading of cane was done by hand. By 1980 almost all the cane was loaded mechanically and about half cleaned mechanically.[34]

Another major thrust of Soviet assistance in the Cuban sugar industry has involved the renovation and expansion of existing mills. When Castro took over Cuba, all mills dated from before the Great Depression. Renovation was urgent, and the Cubans sought Soviet help. The costs of the initial renovation, together with improvements to associated rail and truck transport and to storage and port facilities, were estimated at eight hundred million pesos. In helping the Cubans shoulder this huge task, the USSR assumed responsibility for supplies, transport and assigning specialists to design, build, and operate these enterprises. Soviet help continues on sugar projects, with four new mills completed or nearing completion in 1981.[35]

Soviet-Cuban collaboration in the fishing industry has been especially successful, no doubt in part because Soviet fishing enterprises could advance their own interests measurably while helping the Cubans. The Cuban catch rose rapidly from 22,000 tons in 1958 to about 212,000 tons in 1978.[36] Collaboration began in 1962 when five Soviet trawlers and two smaller Polish trawlers served as the nucleus of a modern fleet to which was shortly added five Japanese ships. Initially almost all the commanders of these ships were Soviet fishermen. Other fishing fleets were formed, and the number of Cuban ships grew rapidly. Many but not all were of Soviet manufacture.

Meanwhile, specialists from the USSR in collaboration with Cubans began to explore not only local waters but also the Gulf of Mexico, the western Atlantic north of the Bahamas, and farther points in the Caribbean basin. The two countries published scientific reports on their joint endeavors. The major purpose of these efforts was to locate the best fishing grounds, establish the best season for catches, and identify the most effective fishing methods. The Soviets, for example, claim to have introduced the Cubans to fishing with electric lights.

As a result of a 1963 agreement, the USSR helped Cuba build a large fishing base in Havana harbor with mooring, refrigeration, storage, dry dock, repair, and radio facilities. The USSR itself provided large dry docks for ship repair. In exchange for Soviet assistance, the Cubans agreed to service Soviet fishing vessels for a period of ten years.

Next to sugar, nickel is Cuba's most valuable export product. Since

Cuba has some of the largest reserves in the world, nickel also holds much promise as a future source of foreign exchange. After the Castro government seized the nickel mines at Nicaro and Moa Bay from U.S. owners in 1960, the American engineers and other administrative staff left the island. American sources of supply dried up, and processing plants closed down for six months. In order to get the mines working again, the Cubans signed an agreement in 1961 with the USSR. The Soviet government sent specialists to run the plants and supplied raw materials, equipment, and spare parts to operate the mines.

Another agreement for an expansion of technical cooperation was signed 1972. It involved the modernization of the plants at Nicaro and Moa Bay with a proposed new combined annual capacity of forty-seven thousand tons of nickel-cobalt concentrate. The USSR took responsibility for the design and exploratory work to build a new nickel-mining facility at Punta Gorda with a capacity of thirty thousand tons a year in its first unit. In addition, the members of Comecon, except Mongolia, planned a second facility of Soviet design to produce thirty thousand tons of nickel-cobalt concentrate annually.

Nickel output languished at the end of the decade. Cubans hope that once long-delayed production from Punta Gorda begins, Cuban nickel exports will mount rapidly. An important issue in Cuba's future is whether Soviet technology and the technology of other socialist countries will permit Cuba to capitalize fully on its huge nickel and related mineral resources without being dependent on its high-cost petroleum fuels.

By 1980 the USSR had provided technical assistance in more than 180 manufacturing enterprises, including steel, machine-building, chemical products (particularly fertilizer), and construction (the USSR gave the Cubans a factory for producing prefabricated dwellings).[37]

Soviet specialists have been intimately involved in the development of transport, communications, and power in Cuba since the beginning of the Revolution. One of the first steps, based on an agreement in late 1962, was to establish direct telephonic and telegraphic contact between Havana and Moscow using Soviet radio equipment. Assistance was also given to strengthen Cuba's communications elsewhere in the world, apparently with a marked increase in shortwave transmissions. Poland helped Cuba build a factory to produce radios, and Soviet specialists constructed repair facilities to service these and other communications equipment. In the early 1970s, plans went forward for Soviet cooperation in the mass production of television sets and transistorized radios. At about the same time, arrangements were made for Cuba to establish its own transmission and receiving facilities for telephonic, telegraphic, and television transmission via satellite, including exchanges of television programming between Moscow and Havana. Soviet specialists have also been active in the reconstruction of railroads and power stations and the construction of a nuclear power station.

• *Cumulative Economic Aid.* Table 18, prepared at the U.S. Central Intelligence Agency, shows the composition and volume of Soviet economic assistance to Cuba. An important part of that aid is Soviet absorption of Cuba's trade deficit. Cuba has had a deficit with the USSR, except for 1975–1978. Even in those years, the USSR continued to lend Cuba money for development projects. The sums may have ranged from the equivalent of US $115 million to US $295 million. In addition the USSR absorbed interest and other charges on a repayable basis.

Actually, Cuba's so-called trade surplus in these years was misleading. That is because sugar and nickel exports and oil imports were subsidized by the USSR and are shown as grants in the table. It appears that in 1979 the subsidized prices for exports were fixed at a level that would assure a positive Cuban trade balance, possibly on the grounds that Cuba would not be able to pay any increase in its Soviet debt in the foreseeable future anyway. The ratio of Soviet aid to the repayable Cuban debt was much higher in the late 1970s than in the early 1970s. But there may have been a reversal in the early 1980s, when more of the Cuban deficit may have been chalked up to Cuban debt and less to Soviet aid.[38]

We can note that the volume of Soviet aid increased steadily in the 1970s: in U.S. dollars it was several hundred million a year in the early 1970s; about $1 billion annually in 1975 and 1976; about $2 billion in 1977; and $3 billion in 1979. In 1979 Soviet aid was equivalent to 25 percent of the Cuban GNP.[39]

These figures probably do not include all Soviet expenditures for education, scientific research, cultural exchange, and the like. And most

Table 18
Soviet Economic Assistance to Cuba, 1961–1979[a]
(millions of dollars)

	Annual Average 1961–70	1971	1972	1973	1974	1975	1976	1977	1978	1979
Balance-of-payments aid	255	509	632	437	289	150	150	210	330	440
Trade and development aid	216	427	535	404	255	115	115	175	295	405
Interest changes	17	57	69	0	0	0	0	0	0	0
Other invisibles	22	25	28	33	34	35	35	35	35	35
Total repayable aid (cumulative)	2,550[b]	3,059	3,691	4,128	4,417	4,567	4,717	4,927	5,257	5,697
Subsidies	102	56	0	150	407	901	1,357	1,772	2,638	2,667
Sugar[c]	102	56	0	97	Negl.	580	977	1,428	2,435	2,287
Petroleum[d]	0	0	0	0	369	290	362	328	165	365
Nickel[e]	0	0	0	53	38	31	18	16	38	15
Total grants (cumulative)	1,018[b]	1,074	1,074	1,224	1,631	2,532	3,889	5,661	8,299	10,966
Total economic assistance (cumulative)	3,568[b]	4,133	4,765	5,352	6,048	7,099	8,606	10,588	13,556	16,663

Source: U.S. Central Intelligence Agency, National Foreign Assessment Center, The Cuban Economy: A Statistical Review (Washington D.C., 1981), p. 39.

[a] Estimates based on official Cuban and Soviet trade data.

[b] Cumulative aid and grant totals are for the entire period 1961–1970.

[c] The sugar and nickel subsidies are estimated as the difference between the values of sugar and nickel exports to the USSR and the value of these exports if sold at average world market prices. They are considered a grant and not subject to repayment.

[d] The petroleum subsidy reflects the difference between the value of petroleum purchased from the USSR and the value of these imports at world market proces. It is considered a grant and not subject to repayment.

important, they do not include military grants. Nevertheless the figures are impressive. The $16.6 billion cumulative total in 1979 compares to the magnitude of aid given to some of Washington's most favored client states (table 19).

• *Military aid.*   Soviet military aid was essential to the survival of the Castro regime. This assistance first helped it to defend itself from internal enemies and later to protect itself from external enemies. Following a Leninist precept, Castro destroyed the prerevolutionary Cuban army when he assumed power and built the new Cuban Revolutionary Armed Forces under his own leadership and that of his brother, Raúl Castro, as minister of defense. In early 1958 the United States placed an arms embargo on Batista because of his use of U.S. arms against domestic opponents. When Castro came to power, U.S. authorities kept the embargo in force and prevented him from buying arms from American allies in Europe. Knowing of the landings being prepared against him, Castro then turned to the socialist countries for arms and munitions. The USSR gave Cuba sufficient arms to crush domestic opponents and the American-sponsored forces that landed at the Bay of Pigs.

In 1970 Castro said that the Soviet Union had already given Cuba military aid in the amount of 1.5 billion pesos.[40] By now it seems likely that many times that much has been given. While we do not know the total of such aid, we do know that Cuba now has one of the largest and best

Table 19
U.S. Loans and Grants to Selected Countries, 1946–1978
(millions of dollars)

	Economic	Military
Iran	760.0	1,404.08
Israel	4,009.4	7,904.2
Taiwan (ROC)	2,206.9	4,360.4
Vietnam	6,941.3	16,418.7

Source: U.S. Agency for International Development, *U.S. Overseas Loans and Grants and Assistance from International Organizations: Obligations and Loans, 1 July 1945–30 Sept. 1978* (n.d.).

equipped armed forces in Latin America. In fact, the armed forces have about 227,000 men (1981), up from 117,000 before the Angola war. In 1981 the army had some 650 tanks, 400 personnel carriers, and extensive artillery weapons including surface-to-surface and surface-to-air missiles. The navy, 11,000 strong, had dozens of patrol, gun, torpedo, and missile craft as well as 2 Soviet submarines. The navy also had 50 Samlet missile-equipped coastal defense units. The air force had 175 combat aircraft, including 3 fighter bomber squadrons and 8 fighter-interceptor squadrons. It is also liberally equipped with transports, helicopters, and trainers.[41]

A Soviet-equipped, modern Cuban military establishment has meant that no domestic forces have been able to unseat Castro or are likely to do so in the near future. While Cuba could not withstand a full-scale U.S. assault, its military strength is sufficient to extract a cruel price from any aggressor. This threat, combined with the prospective costs of military occupation, is a persuasive deterrent.

Soviet leaders have often implied that they would come to Cuba's aid if attacked, and Castro has sometimes interpreted their statements as a military guarantee. In fact, Soviet leaders have taken great care that their remarks do not constitute an iron-clad commitment. And, of course, Cuba's absence from the Warsaw Pact means it is not entitled to the guarantees of Soviet military assistance which that pact contains. Castro also sometimes makes it clear that Cuba is on its own. On 24 October 1981, discussing a possible U.S. attack on Cuba, he said, "What kind of revolutionaries would we be if we upheld our principles because we were expecting others to defend us? We defend our principles first of all with our own shield."[42]

• Soviet Balance Sheet

Cuba is a politically vigorous new member of the international Communist movement and has broadened its geographic scope. Castro has finally adopted the Soviet model at home and accepted the Soviet Union as a senior partner abroad. He has championed the Soviet cause in the Third World, and with most effect globally, in the nonaligned movement. Cuba's most concrete support for objectives both nations share has been in Angola, Ethiopia, and Central America. Reluctant as it has been to provide troops on a large scale, without Cuba the USSR might never have been able to save the MPLA in Angola and the dergue in Ethiopia. Moreover, Cuba is far better qualified than the USSR to exert influence in Central America.

Cuba has also strengthened the Soviet hand in the international Communist movement, particularly by having sided with the USSR against China. Cuban moral support has been valued in crises in Soviet relations with neighboring states in Czechoslovakia (1968), Afghanistan (1979), and Poland (1981). The USSR has needed such support because its policy toward Latin America has produced in sixty years only one enduring success, Castro's Cuba. Most of those years have been filled with disappointments elsewhere in Latin America, including Allende's Chile.

In spite of Castro's glittering achievements in international politics, Cuba has not become a country to emulate. The realities of Castro's authoritarian, one-party state are well known in Latin America and command a narrowing base of support among Leftists. After twenty years the Cuban economy still is not viable, and living standards on the island are a source of continuing dismay and frustration. Most observers also realize that Cuba represents a special case, which probably could not and should not be duplicated. On the basis of his own hard-earned experience, Castro has advised other leaders against revolutionizing society too fast, antagonizing powerful neighbors unnecessarily, and cutting ties with the market economies of the West. Thus, while Castro has bolstered the Soviet position in the international arena, the impact of the Cuban model and experience has been to temper the most radical revolutionary movements. Realities have therefore had the effect of bringing Castro closer to Soviet pragmatism in international politics.

If Soviet policy toward Cuba has been a smashing success in political terms, it has been a resounding failure economically. Castro and Cuban socialism very likely would not survive without Soviet economic assistance. Cuba does not export enough to buy the vital machinery, equipment, fuel, and other necessities it must import. Part of the reason is that Cuba is not a resource-rich country; also, its ties with its natural economic partner, the United States, were abruptly severed over twenty years ago. The Soviet Union has been picking up the difference, first a few hundred million dollars a year, then a billion, and now several billion. The small circle of Soviet leaders appropriate this aid, largely on their own, much more easily than could leaders in a Western democracy. Yet Soviet society, living on an austere and sometimes painful living standard, can probably afford it less. Were Cuba not so exceptionally useful politically, the USSR would not continue to subsidize the Cuban economy so generously. Even now, there are inconclusive signs that growth in aid has slowed.

The USSR has invested a great deal of time, patience, money, and prestige in Cuba. That investment is terribly exposed strategically— almost as much as West Berlin in East Germany. One reason is that Cuba is far less important strategically to the USSR than such neighboring states as Afghanistan, Iran, and Poland. Each side knows that and knows the other side knows it. If the United States were to attack Cuba, the Soviet Union would probably find it impossible at that distance to repel the attack with conventional arms.

Moscow would be faced with a terrible dilemma: to defend Cuba and risk a nuclear war with the United States or to refuse to act, lose its investment in Cuba, and face political humiliation. Soviet leaders hope never to have to make that choice. That is one reason they have not opposed normalization of relations between Cuba and the United States. Although such normalization would have political costs for them, it would strengthen Cuba's security and reduce Soviet strategic risks. Such normalization might also strengthen the Cuban economy and reduce, if only slightly, Cuba's need for Soviet economic assistance.

VI | Central America: Coping with Radical Nationalists

From the Soviet perspective, the Nicaraguan Revolution and the civil war in El Salvador have been the most important events in Latin America since Allende's election as president of Chile.

Several generalizations may be made about the revolutionary movements in those two countries. First, the paramilitary operations launched against both incumbent governments were planned, organized, and carried out by local leaders. Second, the local pro-Soviet Communists in both countries played a relatively small role in the two revolutions and did not control the central organizations in either. Third, the Cubans had early and friendly relations with a wide spectrum of revolutionaries in both countries and provided them with moral and material support. Fourth, the Soviet Union had ties with the tiny Communist parties in each country and little initial contact with the revolutionary mainstream. Soviet contacts with the Sandinistas became, however, increasingly significant after Somoza's fall.

In fact, the Soviet Union became more deeply involved in Nicaragua than it has ever been in any other country in the Americas, except Cuba. The Soviet, or more accurately, East bloc presence has attracted so much public attention that many observers assume that Soviet and Communist activities in the region are quite new. In fact, many of the issues and problems so prominent since the 1970s are a replay of political conflict in the 1920s and 1930s. Knowledge of the earlier period helps us understand Soviet objectives and strategies today. Some of the same questions about Soviet capabilities and influence arose then as now. Does the Soviet Union seek to Communize Central America? Are revolutionary movements there under Soviet control? Did the USSR have an important impact on local politics and society?

Moscow dabbled in Central American politics in the years before the Great Depression, operating mainly out of Mexico City. There were scarcely any Soviet citizens in the region except at the Soviet Embassy, which itself had a short life (1926–1930). Local Communists, not necessarily even nationals of the countries where they were working, were few in number, having been recruited to the cause through their association with radical trade unions and front groups administered from Moscow and selected Western capitals. Most of the revolutionary activity which was the source of political turmoil was the work of the local populace, which had virtually no contact with Moscow and only casual interest in Communism.

Thus, the political or revolutionary oppositions, which existed before the Communists came to the region, were not a product of Communist activity but had their independent origins, national causes, and particular objectives. Since the United States was the hegemonic power in the region and was blamed for supporting local dictators, most of these movements were hostile to Washington. The Soviet Union was one alternative power to which these radical nationalists could turn.

The pro-Soviet Communists tried to harness these organizations to their own purposes. Not infrequently Washington's bungling produced the anti-Americanism that provided them with the opening they needed. The Communist international organizations were about the only external forces from which the Latin American revolutionaries could expect help. Much of that support, incidentally, was moral and political and was expressed in the columns of Comintern publications. There was also some material support from the Soviet Embassy in Mexico City and from Comintern organizations like the International Red Aid. Although small, the amounts were a precious supplement to the revolutionaries' minimal resources. Outsiders, the Communists sought to use their political skills, small material resources, and the prevailing anti-Americanism to gain influence in these local movements.

The Soviet presence in these years in Mexico City was made possible by a fortuitous juncture of events. Mexico's relations with the United States were strained, partly because of prior U.S. interventions and current disputes over properties of American companies in Mexico. Establishing a Soviet tie was one way Mexico could counter what was perceived as U.S. domination. Mexico sought to become the dominant power in Central America and jockeyed with the United States in this respect too. The Mexican government also found collaboration with the Communists useful for domestic political purposes. When Mexican internal politics shifted in the opposite direction in 1930, however, ties with the USSR and the Comintern ended abruptly, a development that had repercussions in Central America.

After 1930 Soviet relations with the Central American countries were exclusively extraofficial, that is through the Comintern and its organizations. There were no diplomatic relations with any of the Central American states before World War II.

• Early Comintern Activities

Today's revolutionaries in Central America are the successors of Augusto César Sandino in Nicaragua and Agustín Farabundo Martí in El Salvador, the martyrs of the 1930s for whom the revolutionary movements in these two countries are named. Then, as now, armed rebels from the left sought to unseat right-wing governments and eliminate U.S. influence from their countries. Then, as now, the United States feared that local rebellions were backed by extrahemispheric powers— especially the Soviet Union—acting through proxies within the hemisphere (in the 1920s and 1930s it was the new revolutionary government in Mexico rather than Cuba that Washington regarded as Moscow's proxy). Then, as now, Washington worried that its inability to defeat the rebellions would open the hemisphere to foreign penetration, thereby endangering vital U.S. interests.

When the U.S. marines landed in Nicaragua in 1927 to resolve a conflict between Nicaraguan liberals and conservatives by installing a conservative president, one liberal general, Augusto César Sandino, refused to accept the U.S.-imposed settlement. Instead, he withdrew his forces to the interior and launched a guerrilla war against the marines that lasted for nearly six years. In his first manifesto on 1 July 1927, Sandino spoke as one of the "oppressed" who opposed the Yankees who had come "to murder us in our own land."[1] The general's romantic guerrilla operations and his defiance of the Colossus of the North aroused sympathy in Latin America and elsewhere in the world.

Sandino's rebellion took place amidst a complex political rivalry over

Central America involving the United States, Mexico, and the Soviet Union. The United States was intent upon maintaining its naval supremacy in the Caribbean, preserving its control over the only canal across the isthmus, and protecting the business interests of U.S. citizens. In the aftermath of the Mexican Revolution, Mexico considered Central America a zone of special interest and an area of potential conflict with the United States. The Soviet Union was interested both in advancing the world revolution and in stirring up difficulties for the United States in its "own backyard" as part of its long-term campaign against U.S. imperialism.

The Mexican government supported Sandino's guerrilla war, giving the general a headquarters in Mexico City and 2,000 pesos a month. The executive committee of the Communist International, attracted by the political turmoil in Central America, urged anti-imperialists everywhere to help Sandino in his fight against "American imperialism" and established the Hands Off Nicaragua committee to oppose U.S. policy.[2]

Agustín Farabundo Martí, a Salvadoran Communist, was detached from the International Red Aid, a Comintern-affiliated legal aid society, to serve on Sandino's general staff as his personal secretary. Martí appears to have tried to pressure Sandino in the direction of a more radical social revolution, but the latter insisted the "neither the extreme right nor the extreme left, but a united front is our slogan."[3]

Before 1929, Soviet relations with the Mexican government were cordial. At the end of that year, however, General Ortiz Rubio was chosen president of Mexico. A committed anticommunist, he immediately launched a wave of repression against the Mexican Communist Party and in 1930 broke relations with the Soviet Union. Torn between his Mexican patrons and Communist International supporters, Sandino opted to maintain his close ties with Mexico. He dismissed Farabundo Martí from his staff and shortly thereafter the Comintern denounced him as a traitor.[4]

Martí said Sandino had "betrayed the world anti-imperialist movement and converted himself into a petit bourgeois liberal caudillo." Sandino maintained that "an effort was made to twist a movement for national defense . . . into a struggle of a social character. I opposed that."[5] A 1972 Soviet book on Central America reaffirmed Martí's charge that Sandino had refused to accept a Communist program, arguing that Sandino's coming to terms with internal "reaction" was a profound mistake leading to the defeat of his movement and his own assassination by Somoza. After the Sandinistas' victory, however, an authoritative Soviet study characterized Sandino as a "revolutionary democrat" and "patriot," an obviously positive assessment of a noncommunist.[6]

After Martí failed to win Sandino to Communism, he returned to El Salvador as the Salvadoran representative of the International Red Aid. With a few followers, he traveled the country organizing the peasants. In 1930 and 1931, the Communists were committed to electoral participation as a means of gaining political power. They supported the successful campaign of Labor candidate Arturo Araujo in 1931, only to have him jail several of the party's top leaders, including Farabundo Martí. When Araujo was ousted by General Maximiliano Hernández Martínez in 1931, the Communists at first sought to resume electoral activity. They participated in the municipal and congressional election of January 1932, but subsequently denounced the results as fraudulent. This led the party to abandon its electoral strategy and resort to arms. Led by Martí, the Central Committee decided on 7 January 1932 to organize an insurrection.[7]

Before the uprising could be mounted, Martí and two of his followers were captured and shot. When the insurrection was finally underway, the Communists, whose experience was primarily in political rather than paramilitary mobilization, proved no match for the army. Some soviets were established briefly in a few communities, but soon the insurrection was brutally suppressed, with deaths estimated at between twenty thousand and thirty thousand persons.[8] It was a disaster for the Salvadoran Communist Party. Most of its leaders were liquidated and its political base, the Indian peasants, was decimated and dispersed. The party was not reorganized until 1936 and did not recover for another thirty years.

The role of the Communist International in Sandino's guerrilla resistance to the United States and the Salvadoran insurrection illustrates the long-established willingness of the Soviet Union to back national liberation movements against old regimes in the shadow of hegemonic powers. But it also demonstrates the difficulty of trying to affect events in distant and unfamiliar areas.

Washington's view that outsiders who meddle in Central America constitute a challenge to U.S. hegemony has changed little from the early decades of the century, and the Soviet Union's readiness to try to take advantage of political instability there has not changed much either.

• Communists and Radical Nationalists

After the suppression of popular revolts in Nicaragua and El Salvador in the early 1930s, Moscow had little contact with Central America. The Soviet government had no formal diplomatic dies with any governments in the region until after World War II when Guatemala and Costa Rica, along with many other Latin American countries, recognized the Soviet Union. Consequently, its primary contact with regional events was through the Communist Party in each country.

In the 1950s, Soviet policy stressed the peaceful road to political change in Latin America. In part this reflected Moscow's view that Latin America was not yet ripe for socialist revolution, and in part it reflected doubts—based upon the experience of the Guatemalan revolution—that the United States would allow the survival of a revolutionary regime in its sphere of influence.[9]

The Communist parties in Central America generally followed this strategy, preferring peaceful political competition to armed struggle wherever possible. Even in countries where the Communist Party was outlawed, such as in Nicaragua and El Salvador, it continued to seek whatever marginal political gains it could from quasi-legal activity. As a result, dissident members in several countries left the party to form more aggressive armed movements of their own. It proved to be these movements that grasped the opportunity provided by the social and economic changes that had swept the region after World War II. The 1970s witnessed the rapid growth of guerrilla organizations and radicalized mass political movements in Nicaragua, El Salvador, and Guatemala. By the end of the decade, the military regimes of all three nations seemed on the brink of collapse. But as in Cuba twenty years earlier, it was not Communists but "petty bourgeois adventurers" who led the revolutionary wave, with the orthodox Communist parties in their wake, frantically trying to catch up.

In Nicaragua the revolution was led not by the Communists, but by the Sandinista National Liberation Front, founded in 1961 by Carlos Fonseca Amador. Born in 1936, Fonseca grew up as a radical youth, tutored in Marxism by a friend who was familiar with the Guatemalan revolution.[10] Fonseca became a Communist in 1955, joining the youth movement of the Nicaraguan Socialist party (PSN), the Moscow-aligned Communist Party in Nicaragua.[11]

Founded in 1937, the PSN was outlawed almost immediately and remained illegal throughout the Somoza period. Although it never ruled out the possibility of insurrection, the party's leaders did not believe conditions in Nicaragua were suitable for the use of violence. Instead, they sought to build a mass base of popular support through peaceful political organizing, despite the party's illegal status.

In 1957, Fonseca went as a delegate from the PSN to the Sixth World Youth and Student Festival in Moscow. He was greatly impressed by the USSR and wrote a paean to Soviet Communism entitled *A Nicaraguan in Moscow*—an uncritical account of Soviet life and a refutation of Western criticisms of Soviet Communism. On returning to Nicaragua, Fonseca was arrested, jailed, tortured, and eventually exiled. In June 1959, he joined a guerrilla column of some fifty Nicaraguans and Cubans who planned to invade Nicaragua from Honduras. The Honduran army surprised the group, wiping it out. Wounded, Fonseca escaped to Havana.

After this experience, Fonseca split definitively with the PSN, rejecting its adherence to the line of peaceful political work. He believed that the Communists showed "insufficient interest in integrating the tactic of armed struggle in the context of the struggle against the dictatorship."[12] Only "armed popular insurrection" could remove the Somoza dictatorship.[13] The PSN, which in December 1959 reiterated its view that military action against Somoza was premature, was not tolerant of Fonseca's heresy. When he tried to return to Nicaragua clandestinely in July 1960, the PSN publicly announced his arrival, which in turn led to his arrest and deportation.[14] The following year, Fonseca, Tomas Borge, and Silvio Mayorga founded the Sandinista National Liberation Front, dedicated to overthrowing the Somoza dynasty by force.

The PSN's adherence to the peaceful road did not change even when popular opposition to Somoza grew rapidly in the late 1970s. The gulf dividing the Sandinistas from the PSN was clearly evident in an interview with PSN First Secretary Luis Sánchez Sancho published in Moscow in 1976. There were "deep strategic and tactical divergences" between the two parties, he said, and the masses did not support the Sandinistas. He expressed willingness to collaborate with the Sandinistas but rejected their "messianic avant-gardism."[15]

As these analyses suggest, the PSN played almost no role in the Nicaraguan Revolution. Moscow, which presumably got most of its information from the PSN, paid little attention to Nicaragua even after the insurrection gained momentum in 1978. As one Soviet analyst later observed "the small Nicaraguan Socialist Party, which was largely cut off from the masses and which was weakened by a factional struggle, was unable to lead the antidictatorial popular movement."[16] Shafik Jorge Handal, leader of the Salvadoran Communists, was more blunt: "Latin America has had two great revolutions, those of Cuba and Nicaragua, in neither of which did Communists take the lead. In Nicaragua the experience of our brother party was disastrous, except for the segment that joined the armed struggle after 1978."[17]

Neither the Soviet Union nor its local ally, the Nicaraguan Socialist party, played any significant role in the Nicaraguan Revolution. The insurrection was led by others whose ideology was radical and nationalistic, and who stood at the front of a broad and ideologically heterogeneous coalition of anti-Somoza political and economic groups.[18] The Soviets and the local Communists were certainly happy to see Somoza's demise, but they made no real contribution to attaining it.[19] After Somoza fell, the Sandinistas, not the Communists, took over the leading governmental and political positions in Nicaragua.

In early 1979 the Nicaraguan rebellion was reaching a climax, and there was much pessimism when I was living Moscow about the future of revolution in Latin America. Soviet leaders were following events in Central America, but did not give it a high priority on their research agenda.[20] So the Sandinista victory came as a surprise.[21]

In the first three issues of *Latinskaia Amerika* in 1980, Soviet Latin Americanists discussed the Nicaraguan Revolution at great length. Most of their attention focused on the Sandinistas as the revolutionary vanguard. Descriptions of the formation of the Sandinista movement made it perfectly clear that the Nicaraguan Socialist party (the Nicaraguan Communists) was only one small group of many that joined forces to overthrow Somoza.[22] The various authors agreed that unity among the forces of the left had been the key to victory.[23] In Nicaragua, as initially in Cuba, a broad national movement had seized the leadership of the revolution with the Communist Party on the sidelines. As Sergo Mikoyan has pointed out, ''the title [*revolutionary*] *vanguard* is not bestowed forever, but must be continually justified in the course of the class struggle—it may be forfeited, and it may be acquired.''[24]

Like their Nicaraguan comrades, the Salvadoran Communists also joined the revolutionary armed opposition late. The historical burden of the repression of the Communist-led insurrection of 1932 was so severe, and its effects on the party so crippling, that the spirit of armed resistance lay dormant for many decades. In fact, the Communists did not become fully involved in the armed opposition until 1979, when they founded the Armed Forces of Liberation (FAL). The main armed forces of the Salvadoran resistance had already been assembled during the previous decade.

One of the strongest revolutionary organizations in El Salvador was the Popular Forces of Liberation (FPL), founded in 1970 by Salvador Cayetano Carpio, former secretary general of the Salvadoran Communist Party. Carpio broke with the party in 1970 because it refused to abandon its electoral strategy. ''I did it when it was evident that the party would not recognize the need for a politico-military strategy, for an intregral revolutionary strategy, and it was necessary to demonstrate this in practice to our people.''[25] Fighting under the nom de guerre of Marcial, Carpio continued to consider himself a Marxist-Leninist, directing the struggle against U.S. imperialism and the Salvadoran oligarchy. He began with only a few close comrades, many from the Communist Party, lacking arms, training, and money. By 1980, the FPL had become the largest of the political-military organizations.

In 1972, the Revolutionary Army of the People (ERP) was formed by young members of the Communist and Christian Democratic parties and radicalized members of the middle class. Two factions developed, one a Maoist group that insisted on a heavy military emphasis, and a second group that called for mixing military and political methods. Roque

Dalton, the Salvadoran Communist and a well-known poet, was a leader of the latter group.[26] The promilitary faction of the ERP charged him with betrayal, condemned him to death, and executed him. Dalton's group broke off from the ERP and formed its own organization, called the National Resistance (RN), and its own armed wing, the Armed Forces of National Resistance (FARN). A fourth armed group, composed mainly of trade union members, was formed as the Revolutionary Workers Party of Central America (PRTC), which was organized selectively on a regional basis in 1976.

The Communist Party of El Salvador (PCES) was thus the last group to take up arms. Of the five politico-military organizations fighting against the Salvadoran armed forces in the early 1980s, it was one of the smallest, having at most a few hundred combatants in the field, compared to thousands fighting with the FPL, ERP, and FARN.

The armed organizations included ex-members of the Communist Party, Castroites, Maoists, socialists, and radicals from various parties. Carpio and certain others, especially in the FPL, considered themselves Marxist-Leninists. But they rebelled from or rejected Moscow-sponsored strategies. While the members of these armed revolutionary movements were risking their lives, the Communist Party spent the 1970s taking part in local and national elections and working closely with reformist parties.

During most of the 1970s, the Communist Party functioned quasi-legally in the National Opposition Union (UNO), collaborating with Christian and Social Democrats. As one Soviet scholar commented, the UNO recognized "the possibilities of the peaceful road of revolution, tried to achieve the unity of the people and the army by means of propaganda. With the aim of mobilizing the masses, these opposition forces developed a broad parliamentary struggle.[27] When the army rigged the results of the 1977 elections (as it had in 1972), the Communist Party concluded that another route to power would have to be found. The decision to give up the peaceful road was taken in 1977, but was not formalized until the party's Seventh Congress in 1979. General Secretary Handal explained why it took two years to implement the decision: "Our Party never had gotten to the point of condemning armed struggle . . . but other ideas and styles . . . influenced us against the development of military work." The party, he concluded in another article, had "suffered more in those forty years from reformist than from leftist illnesses."[28]

By early 1981, the various revolutionary political and military organizations, including the Communists, were edging toward unity. Together they formed the Farabundo Martí Front for National Liberation (FMLN), named for the Communist Party leader of the 1920s and 1930s. Meanwhile, the popular organizations, including the Communist Party, created a political body, the Democratic Revolutionary Front (FDR). Finally, these two groups joined together to form one broad revolutionary coalition (FDR-FMLN) which included everyone from dissident Christian Democrats to Maoists. The Communists joined the FDR-FMLN as a minority, and not a large minority at that.[29]

Since the Salvadoran Communists' decision to take up arms, Soviet spokesmen have never concealed their strong political and moral support for the armed opposition in El Salvador. Nor is there any reason to believe that they would hesitate to provide material support if they deemed it in their interest to do so. But whether the Soviet Union has actually provided material support to the FMLN is another question. In early 1981 the U.S. Department of State published a much criticized White Paper describing the travels of the Salvadoran Communist Shafik Jorge Handal to various Communist countries in search of arms. The Soviet Union was prominently featured in the report, but the documents upon which the White Paper was based actually showed Soviet reluctance to become involved in aiding the Salvadorans. In one, Handal expressed frustration at his inability to get the Soviets to finally agree to ship weapons provided by other East bloc countries. None of the documents indicated that Moscow ever did help, and there was no other indication in the documents of a Soviet role in providing material support for the FDR-FMLN.[30] No convincing evidence has been uncovered since, suggesting that there was probably little or no *direct* assistance from the Soviet Union.[31]

The other Central American nation that the Soviets came to see as ripe for armed revolution was Guatemala. Guatemala has intermittently been the scene of fierce civil conflict and guerrilla war since the fall of the Arbenz regime in 1954. The Communist Party, known as the Guatemalan Labor party (PGT), has been illegal, active, and vocal during much of this time. In fact, however, the main guerrilla and revolutionary forces have been composed of other groups, many of whose members are ex-Communists. The PGT, like its fraternal parties in Nicaragua and El Salvador, tended to focus on political rather than guerrilla activities. Over the years, many members left the party to take up arms in the mountains, and there have been many internal disputes and factions over the tactics of armed struggle. Although the PGT approved the use of force in 1969, it did not actually commit itself fully to armed struggle until 1981.[32]

Many of the revolutionary organizations in Guatemala are now united in the Guatemala National Revolutionary Unity (URNG), which includes the Rebel Armed Forces (FAR), the Guerrilla Army of the Poor (EGP), and the Revolutionary Organizations of the People in Arms (ORPA). These are anti-imperialist, Marxist organizations that are independent of the PGT. The Communists, still not in the front in 1984, spoke positively about the URNG, adding, however, that it should be made "complete, without any exception," that is, the PGT should be admitted as well.[33] Subsequently, one group of Communists went with the guerrillas in the mountains, another was working for political mobilization, and the party was seriously disunited.[34]

• The Sandinistas in Power

The overthrow of Somoza and the seizure of power in Nicaragua by the Sandinistas in July 1979 was a sharp political defeat for the Soviet Union. The Sandinistas not only seized the leadership of the anti-Somoza movement and pushed aside the Communists in doing so, but they also showed how wrong the Moscow-sponsored strategy of the peaceful road had been. Experience, however, had taught Moscow to swallow its pride and collaborate with leftist parties it could not defeat. A strategy designed to influence the newly victorious Sandinistas required, at a minimum, prompt and continuing political, and the possibility of material, support.

Soviet leaders moved more rapidly to establish ties with the Sandinistas than they had with Castro in Cuba. Within hours of the Sandinista victory, General Secretary Leonid Brezhnev's message congratulating the Nicaraguan people was broadcast in Managua. *Kommunist* quoted

Brezhnev as reaffirming the "sacred right of each nation and of each country to select its own development path," and expressed the Soviet Union's readiness to normalize relations with Nicaragua.[35]

In March 1980, Moscow warmly welcomed a delegation of Sandinista leaders and concluded a wide range of agreements on economic and technical cooperation with them.[36] Several aspects of the talks appeared significant. In the first place, although Nicaragua was not a socialist country and the Nicaraguan Communists were not influential in the government, the talks were conducted through party as well as government channels. This suggested that Soviet leaders believed that the FSLN might eventually evolve into a Marxist-Leninist party as did the 26 of July Movement in Cuba. Second, the two sides reached wide agreement on a broad range of issues in Africa, the Middle East, and Asia (including Afghanistan). Finally, they signed an agreement on economic planning that opened up the possibility for closer economic relations than is typically the case between the Soviet Union and a non-communist country.

Over the next few years, a fairly large number of high level Sandinista delegations traveled to Moscow. The Sandinista leader, Daniel Ortega, seemed to make at least one major visit annually, meeting with Brezhnev in May 1982, Andropov in March 1983, Chernenko in February 1984, and Gorbachev in May 1985.[37] By 1985, Soviet relations with Nicaragua were closer than with most other nonsocialist countries. There was a conformity of views on many international issues, and economic cooperation was greater, too. Yet Sandinista leaders have not hesitated in private conversations to criticize the Soviet Communists for being unresponsive to popular needs and shackled by dogma.[38]

As table 20 indicates, Soviet trade with Nicaragua was minimal in the first two years of the revolution, less than 6 million rubles altogether. The USSR provided granulated urea in exchange for coffee beans. Trade picked up rapidly in 1982 and rose to over 200 million rubles by 1985. In that latter year the principal Soviet exports were petroleum, machinery, equipment, and vehicles.

There are two important aspects to recent Soviet trade with Nicaragua. First, almost all of it was Soviet, not Nicaraguan exports. Soviet imports dropped to less than half a million rubles by 1985. One explanation may

Table 20
Soviet Trade with Nicaragua
(millions of rubles)

Year	Exports	Imports
1980	0.1	5.5
1981	4.7	5.7
1982	36.6	5.9
1983	42.4	9.5
1984	138.0	0.5
1985	212.6	0.3
1986	276.4	7.7

Sources: USSR, Ministerstvo, Vneshnei Torgovli, Vneshniaia Torgovlia SSSR v 1981g. Statisticheskii sbornik (Moscow, 1982). Also volumes for 1983 and 1985. For 1986 see supplement to the journal Vneshniaia Torgovlia, no. 3, 1987.

be that the Soviets sought to help the Sandinistas by permitting them to sell as much as possible in hard currency markets, while providing generous credit for almost everything the Sandinistas bought. Second, Soviet petroleum exports rose sharply in 1983 and came to one-half of exports to Nicaragua in 1985.[39]

Soviet exports to Nicaragua grew rapidly to 276 million in rubles in 1986, while Nicaraguan exports to the USSR were only 8 million rubles.[40] Several hundred million rubles of an import surplus from the Soviet Union constitutes a huge sum for a country like Nicaragua. Soviet deliveries of oil have made it possible for the Sandinistas to survive.

On the other hand, Soviet exports to Nicaragua in 1986 were still only a fraction of what they were to Cuba. Nicaragua's population is one-fourth Cuba's, but that same year Soviet exports to Nicaragua were about one-eighteenth of those to Cuba. In the first half of 1987 Soviet exports fell by about 15 percent, possibly reflecting a hardening in Soviet policy.

Soviet support has spurred aid from other socialist countries, chiefly Bulgaria and the German Democratic Republic. The Soviet Union, however, was probably persuaded by Cuba to aid Nicaragua rather than the reverse. In spite of her own urgent needs, Cuba was making a

Table 21
Structure of Nicaraguan Foreign Trade

	% of Total Trade		
	1980	*1984*	*1985*
Central America	28.1	9.2	7.2
Latin America	13.5	12.8	9.2
U.S.A.	30.4	14.9	5.4
Western Europe	17.6	25.2	28.8
Eastern Europe	**1.0**	**15.4**	**27.1**
Japan	3.0	9.9	9.9
Canada	2.6	2.9	2.9
Cuba	—	4.0	4.3
Others	3.8	5.7	5.3
Total	100.0	100.0	100.0

Source: Ministry of Foreign Trade, Nicaragua.

substantial contribution by supplying 5.1 percent of Nicaragua's imports and taking only 2.3 percent of its exports in 1985.

Tables 21 to 23 show that many countries, both East and West, have sprung to Nicaragua's assistance. Its trade has shifted from countries in the Americas to Eastern Europe in particular, but there are also some increases to Japan and Western Europe. Note, too, that in 1985 almost three-quarters of Nicaraguan exports were to Western Europe and Japan and all but a fraction of trade with Eastern Europe was imports.

Economic aid from the Soviet Union and other Comecon countries has been mostly in the form of concessionary trade credits, technical assistance, and development project aid. The Soviet foreign aid program rarely includes hard currency grants since Moscow itself faces a shortage of hard currency, and since such grants are used only for purchases outside the East bloc. The data on Soviet economic aid clearly indicate the limits of Soviet largesse. From 1979 to 1981, economic aid totaled about $125 million. It jumped sharply in 1982 to a peak of about $253 million and subsequently fell to about $146 million in 1983 and $170 million in 1984, even though Nicaragua's economic situation has deteriorated substantially, making its need all the greater.[41] Since the U.S. trade embargo of

1985 one would expect Soviet aid to increase, but the source of the earlier figures, the Central Intelligence Agency, has not made figures since then public.

The socialist countries began carrying the burden of Nicaraguan external financing in 1984 and 1985 (see table 23). Note that these countries accounted for 84 percent of contracted financing in that year, and Western Europe provided most of the rest. How much of the Eastern European portion was Soviet financing is not known. For the period 1979 to June 1984, the socialist countries provided 24.2 percent of contracted loans and lines of credit.[42] The USSR extended about 43 percent of the socialist countries' share. The latter included Cuba, Korea, and Yugoslavia as well as other Comecon countries.

Since economic pressures on Nicaragua have escalated since 1984, it is quite likely that the Soviet burden and share have both gone up. In December 1986, for example, there were reports that a Nicaraguan mission to Moscow, headed by Henry Ruiz, a Sandinista leader who studied in the USSR, raised $300 million in Soviet assistance.[43] In any

Table 22
Structure of Nicaraguan Exports and Imports
(percentages)

	1984		1985	
	Exports	*Imports*	*Exports*	*Imports*
Central America	9.6	9.0	8.1	6.8
Latin American				
Integration Association	1.8	17.9	—	12.4
U.S.A.	12.3	16.1	3.1	7.7
Western Europe	36.3	20.0	48.6	21.9
Eastern Europe	**3.0**	**21.3**	**4.7**	**35.8**
Japan	24.8	2.9	22.52	3.5
Canada	3.0	2.9	4.7	1.1
Cuba	3.1	4.5	2.3	5.7
Others	6.1	5.4	6.0	5.7
Total	100.0	100.0	100.0	100.0
Absolute figures				
(thousands of US$)	384.803	826.236	293.969	835.970

Source: Ministry of Foreign Trade, Nicaragua.

case, other socialist countries are participating in a significant way. They had similarly helped Cuba with Soviet encouragement in the 1960s. After some years Cuba paid off much of its debt to the Eastern Europeans and the USSR now carries most of Cuba's economic burden.[44]

In September 1983, Nicaragua was granted observer status in Comecon. Whether it is admitted to full membership at some future date will depend on a variety of factors, not the least of which are the efforts of the United States to cut the Nicaraguan economy off from the West. So far the Sandinistas do not appear to prefer heavy reliance on the Soviet bloc, but Nicaragua's economy remains underdeveloped and deeply dependent upon foreign trade. If U.S. policy aimed at cutting Nicaragua off from Western market economies succeeds, Nicaragua will have no choice but to reorient its economy further toward the East—just as Cuba did twenty-five years ago.

It is not at all clear, however, that the Soviet Union is interested in

Table 23
Nicaraguan Official External Financing[a] *Contracted: Distribution by Source, 1979–1985* (percentage)

	1979	1980	1981	1982	1983	1984	1985[b]	1979–85
Multilateral	78.4	36.4	11.4	18.9	16.3	0.0	0.0	18.0
Bilateral	21.6	63.6	88.6	81.1	83.7	100.0	100.0	82.0
Capitalist Countries	21.6	54.0	65.5	36.4	50.8	39.6	15.9	41.4
Socialist Countries	**0.0**	**9.5**	**23.1**	**44.8**	**32.9**	**60.4**	**84.1**	**40.5**
Total	100.0	100.0	100.0	100.0	100.0	100.0	100.0	100.0
Total (millions of US$)	271.7	472.0	757.3	495.7	401.9	341.7	756.3	3496.6

Source: Ministry of External Cooperation, Nicaragua. Table quoted in part from Richard Stahler-Sholk, "Foreign Debt and Economic Stabilization Policies in Revolutionary Nicaragua," in *The Political Economy of Revolutionary Nicaragua,* ed. Rose J. Spalding (Winchester, Mass, 1987), table 4, p. 162. Michael E. Conroy's assistance for this section is also gratefully acknowledged.

a. Loans and credit lines. Excludes donations. Columns may not add up exactly due to rounding. In addition to the loans and credit lines, foreign donations from 1979 to 1984 amounted to a total of perhaps $450 million. This figure is only a rough approximation because Nicaragua received some donations in the form of goods of undetermined value as well as donations that were not channeled through the Ministry of External Cooperation.

b. Preliminary figures.

payiug the price necessary to acquire another client state in Latin America as dependent as Cuba. Soviet burdens in Vietnam, Afghanistan, Poland, and elsewhere, not to mention a weak economy at home, do not encourage it. Moreover, Nicaragua's security is particularly tenuous. surrounded by hostile neighbors, facing an army of some fifteen thousand contras, and the target of a concerted destabilization effort by the United States, Nicaragua is not an attractive place for the Soviet Union to invest large resources.

As the war between the Nicaraguan government and the counter-revolutionary forces aided by the United States escalated, the Sandinistas undertook a major military buildup. Pressure from the United States hampered Nicaragua's efforts to purchase arms in the West, except in a few countries like France, so most of the Sandinistas' military supplies have come from either the East bloc or other Third World countries. Although the Sandinistas have acquired arms that are mostly of Soviet manufacture, they avoided obtaining arms directly from the Soviet Union until 1983. Algeria was a primary supplier.[45]

However, as the civil war intensified and the Nicaraguans' ability to purchase arms decreased because of the shortage of hard currency, Nicaragua has relied more and more on direct military aid from the USSR and other East bloc nations. Equipment provided thus far includes tanks, armed transport vehicles, rocket launchers, and armed helicopters.[46] Although U.S. officials have repeatedly charged that Nicaragua is preparing to receive advanced MIG fighter aircraft from the Soviet Union by way of Cuba, no such planes had appeared by early 1987.

Neither the Soviet Union nor Nicaragua make public data on military aid. Most of what is public comes from the U.S. Department of Defense. According to this source, East bloc military aid to Nicaragua grew from very limited amounts in the years just after the fall of Somoza ($5 million in 1979 and $7 million in 1980) to ever greater quantities as relations between Nicaragua and the United States deteriorated. In 1981, President Reagan's first year in office, Soviet military aid jumped to $45 million. The following year, when the United States launched the covert war, Soviet military aid doubled to approximately $100 million. It totaled $110 million in 1983 and more than doubled to $250 million in 1984.[47] The Defense Department also makes tonnage figures available: arms shipments totaled 20,570 tons in 1984, the high point until 1986 when tonnage was estimated at 25,300.[48]

Nevertheless, Moscow has been very careful not to offer any security guarantees to the Sandinistas. When Yuri Fokin, general secretary of the Soviet Foreign Ministry, was asked how the Soviet Union would react to a U.S. invasion of Nicaragua, he replied, "We will support Nicaragua politically in every way." In general, Soviet media coverage of Nicaragua's war with the contras has stressed the Sandinistas' ability to defend themselves.[49]

• Understanding the Soviet Role

The Soviet presence in Nicaragua should not be confused with Soviet influence. The former is not so great. Cuba's presence has long been greater, as has the aggregate of other East bloc nations. There have been some Soviet advisors, important new Soviet military equipment, and some visitors. Evidence of direct Soviet aid to Nicaragua before the fall of Somoza and in El Salvador at any time is sparse, but it indicates that the Cubans were playing the leading role; Cuba's major activities inside Nicaragua did not begin until after the outbreak of the Nicaraguan Revolution. Moscow has apparently deliberately kept a relatively low profile. That has the advantage of minimizing friction with the United States while not having major disadvantages for the USSR. It also makes Moscow less vulnerable politically should the Sandinistas lose control of the country.

Meanwhile, the USSR continues to nurture and increase what counts for more, Soviet influence. That is firmly based on the Sandinistas' debt to the Soviet government for having made possible its survival in the face of U.S. military and economic sanctions. Dependence on Moscow is partly a product of U.S. hostility, which forces Managua to seek a patron and protector against Washington.

The Nicaraguan revolution made the pro-Soviet Communists in Central America face up to two unpleasant facts: their strategy of peaceful political organizing was a failure, and, as a result of that failure, other revolutionary movements willing to engage in armed struggle had taken over leadership of the revolution. In order to play any role whatever in the revolutionary process, the Communists were forced to seek unity with the broad and ideologically heterogeneous radical movements that became the political vanguard. In Nicaragua, this meant supporting the Sandinista regime, despite the fact that the Communists (PSN) had virtually no role in it. In El Salvador, it meant subordinating the Communist Party (PCES) to the joint command of the FDR-FMLN, led in the political domain by Christian and Social Democrats and on the battlefield by a renegade Communist.

The Cubans, of course, have had a much greater role in Central America than the Soviets. The Sandinistas, and several of the revolutionary organizations in El Salvador and Guatemala, have had Cuban support for a decade or more. But Cuba's leverage in the region is not equivalent to the USSR's. Certainly the Cubans and Soviets share many interests and objectives—including a desire to weaken the position of the United States in Latin America. But as the controversies of the 1960s demonstrated, Latin America is a much higher priority for Cuba than it is for the USSR, and that difference can lead to sharp policy disagreements. In recent years, Moscow seems inclined to follow Havana's lead in Central America, but cautiously.

The Soviet Union's restrained involvement in Central America does not mean that Moscow is indifferent to the region. On the contrary, the Soviets would be delighted to see socialism wax and capitalism wane. Moscow backs the emergence of Marxist-Leninist regimes in Central America, so long as it is not called upon to keep their economies solvent with large infusions of aid. While the United States doesn't want "another Cuba" for strategic reasons, the Soviet Union doesn't want one for economic reasons.

In any event, the Soviets may now be gathering confidence that Marxist-Leninist regimes can survive in Central America, in spite of the overwhelming power of the United States, traditionally unwilling to tolerate such regimes in its sphere of influence. Cuba is regarded by both sides as an exceptional case because of the accord reached with Washington at the time of the 1962 missile crisis. The Soviets would probably settle for revolutions in Central America that produced radical nationalist regimes independent of, and perhaps hostile to, the United States. Since such regimes would not be Marxist-Leninist, Moscow would feel less obligated to meet their economic and security claims.

Soviet objectives in Central America are, therefore, more political than strategic or military. While military planners in the United States may worry about the possibility that some government in the Caribbean Basin might allow the creation of a military outpost that could endanger vital sea lines of communications and supply, the Soviets do not have a great need of such an outpost. The Soviet navy can send ships out on the high seas just about wherever it wishes, including the Caribbean, but it remains at a tremendous conventional military disadvantage in the area compared to the United States. It is unlikely that the USSR would deploy any significant forces into such a vulnerable area far from their home bases. The acquisition of basing facilities in the Caribbean would not prevent this balance from continuing to be unfavorable.

Sanctions imposed by the United States in Central America have not intimidated the Soviets; their economic and military assistance to Nicaragua have grown along with sanctions. The escalation of tensions in the area has resulted in growing Sandinista dependence on the Soviet Union and therefore growing Soviet influence.

Ultimately, Soviet leaders have little to fear from U.S. military intervention in Central America. Defeat of the Sandinistas would probably be interpreted in the United States as a great victory over the USSR, but not elsewhere. The Soviets have made no commitment to the security of any Central American regime, so the demise of the Sandinistas and other revolutionary movements in the area, while unwelcome, would threaten no vital Soviet interest. So far the USSR has had little to lose in Central America and continues to make important political gains there.

VII The Strands of Soviet Policy

The USSR acts on the world stage through two channels: the Soviet state apparatus and the Soviet-sponsored international Communist movement. Western observers have often focused mainly on the revolutionary activities of the latter, regarding it as a subversive force creating political disorder and instability. There are, of course, grounds for this concern, since Communist parties related to Moscow in almost every country in Latin America have the long-term objectives of eliminating capitalism and establishing socialism. Many do not advocate the use of force now, but a few are employing it and none rule it out completely. Communists have been operating in the region for nearly seventy years, so it is possible to judge the extent to which Western fears about subversion were justified.

Political ferment has afflicted many countries in which the Communists are not politically influential. In such countries the native revolutionary forces are local, not linked to Moscow. The Communists' revolutionary role should be judged more by their actions than their aims.

In fact, pro-Moscow Communists have not yet led a rebel movement that has seized power by force of arms in the Western Hemisphere. Such movements have ordinarily been led by radical nationalists like the Castristas or the Sandinistas, sometimes with the Communists in opposition. In a few cases in the 1930s the Communists led armed insurrections unsuccessfully (El Salvador and Brazil), but Moscow tended to oppose them until 1979. (After the Sandinistas' victory in 1979, Moscow came out more firmly in favor of the armed road in selected cases, such as El Salvador, Guatemala, and Chile.) In that it has never seized power by force anywhere in the region, the international Communist movement as a revolutionary organization has been a failure in Latin America.

With the other channel, government-to-government relations, however, the USSR made great progress. When the United States imposed severe economic and military sanctions on Cuba, and twenty years later on Nicaragua, the Soviet Union provided first Castro and later the Sandinistas with the oil, arms, and markets they needed to survive. That association became the basis of Soviet influence in both countries. The USSR had better success extending its influence into the Americas as a great power than as the leader of the international Communist movement. Its most important governmental activities were legal transactions with recognized governments. In these cases the political threat the USSR posed to the United States was not subversion, but the means to help the radical Castro and Sandinista regimes survive U.S. sanctions.

Some observers are critical of the distinction that is drawn between pro-Soviet Communists on the one hand and the wide assortment of Marxists, ex-Communists, socialists, and anti-imperialists on the other. They are uncomfortable because the latter hold many views in common with the Soviets. But these observers err by equating pro-Soviet Communists with radical nationalists. The pro-Soviet Communists, whose leaders constitute a kind of foreign service for Moscow, are much more closely tied to Moscow than the radical nationalists. The latter have distinct national interests of their own, and voice them. The Yugoslav and the Chinese Communists have many similarities with the Soviet Communists, but world history has shown what different paths various varieties of Communism can follow in both domestic and foreign policy. It is a serious analytical error to lump all these different brands of revolutionaries together.

Soviet relations with certain military governments in Latin America have also shown that Soviet strategies do not promote revolution or subversion always and everywhere. In fact, the USSR has maintained traditional relations with most of the governments of Latin America. For years its main trading partners in the region were the military regimes of Argentina and Brazil. It has also long maintained relatively cordial relations with centrist governments such as Colombia, Mexico, and Venezuela, not to mention military governments that have been redemocratized lately.

The USSR works under a serious commercial handicap in Latin America in comparison with most Western governments and Japan. It has had great difficulty selling its exports in Latin America (except in Cuba and Nicaragua). That has been made painfully apparent in Argentina, which has sold huge quantities of grain to the USSR but has bought scarcely anything in return. Soviet technology simply cannot compete with Western. Nor can the USSR afford to buy in volume what the West buys in Latin America. Most governments in the region are reluctant to risk access to Western markets in order to trade with the USSR. About the only governments who have thrown in their lot with the Comecon countries are those who really had no other choice. In order to supplant U.S. hegemony in many countries, Moscow would require a much stronger economy than it in fact has.

For its part, the Soviet Union has paid a huge price for its dominant role in Cuba. Its subsidies are enormous, but Cuba will probably have to continue to depend on Soviet assistance for the indefinite future. Given the continuing need for assistance in such countries as Poland, Vietnam, and Afghanistan, Cuba is a heavy long-term burden. That is one of the reasons for Soviet caution about Nicaragua's growing dependence on the East.

The USSR has a mixed record in military affairs in Latin America. Perhaps its biggest achievement has been the growth of the Cuban military and its cooperation with the USSR. Cuba's forces, generously equipped by the USSR, are the largest in Latin America after Brazil. With Cuban cooperation the Soviet Union has established a military presence in the Caribbean Basin through its naval and air patrols, a presence it never had before Castro.

Soviet behavior in Latin America cannot be understood simply in the framework of bilateral relations. Global factors are often decisive. For example, Soviet-American strategic competition made contemporary Soviet-Cuban relations possible and placed limits on Soviet military collaboration in the area. Soviet-Chinese competition in the international Communist movement has shaped Moscow's relations with the Latin American Communist parties. Soviet and Cuban intervention in Africa have had repercussions on Soviet and Cuban relations in the Americas.

Nor can Soviet behavior be understood only in terms of one particular Soviet interest. All of them come into play. Soviet trade with South American countries has occasionally been described as an effort to buy political influence. But with respect to Argentina, the USSR needs the grain it buys. Political influence is a by-product. Nor can the USSR afford flamboyant military initiatives in areas outside its vital interests. The missile crisis brought that point home. Moscow's behavior has to be understood in terms of changing interests in the USSR and elsewhere in the world as well as Latin America.

Soviet domestic concerns—for example, internal security, economic growth, and energy—have played the dominant role in Soviet policy. In the Politburo there are usually only three or four members who have extensive foreign affairs experience or responsibilities. The other members, about eighteen, are concerned primarily or wholly with domestic matters. The ratio between members with responsibilities for foreign affairs and those in charge of domestic affairs is even higher in the Central Committee, the body of political appeal. As a result the men who control the Soviet party and ultimately the international Communist movement have strong vested interests in Soviet internal problems. It is inconceivable that the CPSU would consciously sacrifice vital interests of the Soviet state in support of a particular Communist party in Latin America.

Given the realities, many of the time-encrusted goals of the international Communist movement, voiced generations ago, are no longer reliable guides to contemporary Soviet behavior. It is not that these goals have been repudiated or that Soviet leaders do not pay them lip service from time to time. Rather, it is that goals such as the establishment of world Communism, the spread of socialism everywhere, and the like are simply not viable in today's world and probably not in tomorrow's.

The USSR has come to terms with the romantic goals of its early revolutionary period just as has the United States. Making little progress on their own in Central America and elsewhere, many pro-Soviet Communists are joining national fronts in a subordinate role, and Moscow is supporting those fronts. Whereas the USSR stands for destroying capitalism and spreading socialism, the United States insists on democracy and free enterprise. Yet both superpowers are faced with an intractable world, the many parts of which insist on going their own way, neither Soviet nor American. When they find that their goals are unattainable, each seeks to promote its interests in other, less ambitious ways.

Moscow's evolving policies have been an expression of Soviet state interests with respect to the area. In later sections of this chapter, I discuss the major strands of those policies and then show in the concluding section how they are woven together. But Soviet policies are only half the story, and often not the decisive half. It has been the Latin American governments which have usually placed the limits on bilateral relationships. Therefore, it is important to explain first some of the interests that the Latin American governments have at stake in their relationships with the USSR.

• Latin America's Interests

Many Latin American leaders are not necessarily admirers of the Soviet system, its foreign policies, nor of the local Communist parties whose programs many believe are contrary to their country's interests. Even so, they welcome ties with the Soviet Union, first and foremost as the right of an independent state. Second, such ties give them room for maneuver and bargaining leverage in disputes with the United States. Finally, relations with the USSR can bring material benefits.

Mexico was the first Latin American country to seize the opportunity of such diversification. In the 1920s, as during World War I, Mexico's relations with the United States were intermittently tense, partly due to disputes over U.S. nationals' investments in Mexico. Mexico was consolidating its own revolution, and ties with the new Bolshevik state seemed right and proper. But by 1930 the vocal involvement of Mexican Communists in politics, or so the Mexican government charged, led to a break in diplomatic relations. The breach was not healed even when Mexico swung sharply left under Lázaro Cárdenas. Mexico reestablished relations early in World War II. After that its relations with the USSR were a symbol of Mexican independence of the United States. During the postwar years Mexico maintained correct relations with the Soviet Union. Those ties have been a card, which Mexico has seen fit not to play.

Venezuela has also used its ties with the USSR as a form of diplomatic diversification. Since Venezuela is more distant from and less entangled with the United States than Mexico, Soviet connections have helped it, as an oil-rich nation, assume leadership in the hemisphere. In addition, Venezuela's ambitions to play a leading role in the Third World generally require open channels to the USSR. President Carlos Andrés Perez visited Moscow in 1976, and Venezuela has maintained an active embassy there.

More than other leader except Castro, Allende needed to diversify his foreign relations in the face of the hostile political and economic pressures of the United States. He learned that Moscow, whatever its political sympathies, was not prepared to move rapidly or commit large resources to save him as it had Castro. Not only was Chile far from Moscow, but Allende's prospects were dimmed by the fact that he was a potential prisoner of the Chilean armed forces from the day of his coming to office.

Argentina and Brazil were primarily interested in the USSR as a means of increasing and diversifying their exports. Since the early 1920s, Argentina has been a valued source of consumer goods for the Soviet market and frequently sold more to the USSR than any other Latin American country. Brazil, too, has sold large quantities of coffee, cocoa, and other products to the USSR and has on occasion purchased petroleum in exchange. When the military government seized power in 1964, the new leaders were quick to reaffirm their interest in maintaining Soviet markets and thus diplomatic relations. Yet the military governments which have been in power during most of these years have been explicitly anticommunist and often anti-Soviet. Their ideological and political differences with Soviet Communists have been so great as to rule out political collaboration. That pattern persisted in Argentina until after the Soviet invasion of Afghanistan, when the U.S. grain embargo caused the USSR to make huge purchases of grain and meat in Argentina. Both partners then also began to make political accommodations to one another.

The Peruvian and Bolivian military governments of recent years have been concerned not only with trade but also with economic development. The USSR provided facilities for a variety of projects, civilian and military, in Peru and tin smelters in Bolivia.

Many of the smaller Latin American countries such as Uruguay, Colombia, and Ecuador, have looked to the USSR to diversify their export markets. Others, like Jamaica and Guyana, tried without great success to attract Soviet investment in the form of development projects. Grenada under Bishop moved toward socialism in an effort to attract economic support from socialist countries for its needy economy.

Almost none of these governments look kindly on the local Communist party. Such parties were at best a nuisance and at worst a potential threat. Argentina and Brazil have occasionally placed legal restrictions on their operations, and Mexico only recently relaxed such restrictions. Some of the left-wing governments, like Michael Manley's in Jamaica, regarded the local Communists as competitors. The parties are and have long been a liability in Soviet relations with most of these governments. In one case when they were not, Allende's government, the Soviet response in material terms was limited.

Most of the governments mentioned in the foregoing discussion have been controlled by the armed forces or by entrenched industrial, commercial, or agricultural interests. Only a few, like Allende's government in Chile, the Peruvian military governments, and Manley's government in Jamaica, were change-oriented. It is interesting that even Manley's regime never became strongly pro-Soviet, partly because the USSR lacked the material means to help Jamaica.

Since Afghanistan, Soviet demands for agricultural imports have had a great impact on a medium-sized country like Argentina. But it is also clear that Soviet resources are not available to stretch much further. Barring some sharp turn in hemispheric affairs, such as more U.S. military interventions, Soviet ties with Latin American governments are likely to remain limited until the USSR sharply increases its capacity to buy in Latin America and to sell Latin America what it needs. As 1986 trade figures show, the prospects are not very bright.

Cuba is the only country in Latin America that is unreservedly pro-Soviet and whose interests are closely linked to those of the USSR. Since 1960, when the United States began to levy heavy economic and political sanctions, the Cuban government has depended on the USSR and its client states to survive. What Castro fears most is a Soviet-American deal over Cuba. If Soviet support were to falter, Castro might have to turn to the United States. Castro's survival under any such arrangement would be problematical. Such scenarios seem pure fantasy since the Soviet Union is not likely to sacrifice its huge investment on the island. Castro's

Soviet tie has thus been essential to his maintenance of control over the island as well as his independence of the United States. The Soviet armed forces, though formally uncommitted to defend Cuba, give any potential attacker pause and serve to reinforce Castro's control.

• Diplomatic Relations

Although the Soviet Union has almost always wanted to maintain diplomatic relations with most Latin American countries, it only began to do so on a broad scale in the 1970s. Most Latin American governments, fearful of Communist subversion, unwilling to put their relations with the United States at risk, or seeing insufficient accompanying benefits, had delayed recognizing the new Soviet state until 1968 or later. The Soviet position has usually been to maintain relations with states irrespective of ideological and political differences.

Although Latin American states have broken relations time and again with the USSR, beginning with Mexico in the 1930s and through a rash of such breaks early in the cold war, Moscow itself has seldom initiated a break. It did "suspend" relations with the military junta that overthrew Allende in Chile. The dictatorships in Paraguay, Guatemala, and Honduras apparently have no interest in establishing relations with Moscow, a sentiment the latter shares. The Soviet Union probably would like relations with Panama and the Dominican Republic, whose dependence on the United States has made the latter cautious about establishing ties with Moscow.

For the USSR recognition and the exchange of diplomatic representatives are the sine qua non of most other interstate ties. It ordinarily requires rather elaborate commercial, financial, and other economic agreements to begin and expand normal economic relationships. A commitment from the Latin American government is essential, and the bilateral agreements provide the authority for putting the large Soviet foreign relations bureaucracies into motion. The exclusive participation of state agencies at the Soviet end is quite different from the private deals which in capitalist states often proliferate with or without the blessing of the governments concerned. One exception to the rule was the activity of Iuzhamtorg, the Soviet South American trading agency, in Argentina in the 1920s when no formal relations existed. A contemporary exception is Panama, where the USSR has sold many watches, cameras, and television sets with only commercial representation.

Another reason the Soviet Union, a pariah for many years in the society of nations, sought recognition from Latin American governments was to take what it regarded as its rightful place in the world. Since most of these governments have now recognized the USSR, the stigma of nonrecognition is a thing of the past. The USSR hopes to reach deeper into these societies not only through trade but through economic development projects, technological and scientific cooperation, and educational and cultural exchanges. Formal relations not only make possible bilateral ties but also bolster Moscow's position in international organizations like the United Nations and its specialized agencies, in the nonaligned movement, and in regional organizations. A central Soviet purpose, like that of other great powers, is to extend its political and economic influence globally.

Cuba, of course, is the bastion of Soviet influence in the Americas. Its strategic location in the Caribbean, Castro's dynamic foreign policies, its large armed forces, Cuba's economic dependence on the USSR, and the commonality of the two governments' foreign interests all recommend Cuba to Soviet purposes.

Cuba's primary utility to the Soviet Union is political; its strategic advantages are offset by its exposed and not easily defensible location near Florida. Cuba has been politically useful, particularly outside the hemisphere. Castro has been a loyal supporter of the USSR in its conflicts with the socialist countries, such as the Soviet invasions of Czechoslovakia and Afghanistan and the Polish upheaval of the early 1980s. He has supported Soviet actions because he would like Soviet help himself should he be faced with an uprising of his own in Cuba. As in the other cases, Soviet actions would be justified as a means of protection from imperialist intervention. The USSR has been economically much more generous to Cuba than has China, and Castro has swung over almost completely into the Soviet camp. Similarly, Castro has become the champion of the USSR in the Third World, most particularly in the nonaligned movement. Soviet intervention in Angola and Ethiopia would have been difficult or impossible without Cuban troops.

In the Western Hemisphere, Castro has been a firm ally in the ideological and political struggle with the United States. His various military adventures in the Caribbean, Central America, and the Andes in the 1960s, however, made the Soviet Union uncomfortable. Soviet leaders believed correctly that Cuban-sponsored revolutionary movements had little chance of success and would waste precious human and material resources. In the early 1980s, Castro played a prominent role in dealing with the revolutionary movements of Central America, a role that permitted the USSR to maintain a low profile in the region. The ultimate assessment of Cuba's utility to the USSR there will depend on how the United States reacts, Castro's own effectiveness, and his responsiveness to Soviet wishes.

As Soviet economic and military aid to Nicaragua has grown, so have Soviet ties with the Sandinistas. While its influence is necessarily great, it has kept its profile low, encouraging other socialist and left-wing governments to expand their relations with Nicaragua.

Next to Cuba and Nicaragua, Soviet attention is riveted on the strongest and most influential Latin American countries. Three such countries are preeminent for their large area, population, economies, and influence: Argentina, Brazil, and Mexico.

Whereas Mexico had long been the center of Soviet interest in noncommunist Latin America, American and British actions propelled Argentina to the forefront in the 1980s. The U.S. embargo on grain shipments to the Soviet Union after the invasion of Afghanistan forced the USSR to buy large quantities of grain in Argentina. Waiving U.S. objections aside, the Argentines were delighted to accept the attractive Soviet terms. Reciprocal economic interests became a firm basis for collaboration, often tacit, on Argentine Communist Party matters, human rights, military exchanges, nuclear power, and other foreign policy issues. American support for British military reoccupation of the Falkland Islands and Soviet sympathies for the Argentine claim further strengthened Argentine-Soviet ties.

The Soviet government probably regards Brazil, demographically and economically the largest nation in the region, as the political prize in Latin America. In spite of Soviet efforts, the Brazilian government has also been among the most elusive. After Goulart fell, the new military government was swift to reaffirm its ties with the socialist countries, but strictly as a business matter. Anticommunist prejudices among the military and civilian elites persist.

Next to Cuba and possibly Nicaragua, the Mexican government has been most open to dialogue. Its revolutionary traditions, disillusioning experiences with the United States, and general sophistication set a scene conducive to cordial talks. Mexico's need for counterweights for its huge neighbor and Soviet interest in establishing strong ties near the United States have created an enduring commonality of interest. Neither government, however, has been able to match its domestic needs and interests with ties to the other in the economic field.

The Andean countries are at an abruptly lower level of Soviet interest. Peru, Bolivia, and Ecuador are perhaps politically more unpredictable than Argentina and Brazil and certainly more vulnerable to foreign influence from whatever source. They offer the Soviet Union better opportunities for local involvement with accompanying benefits and costs. The close Soviet relationship with the Peruvian military regime after 1968 shows how broad Soviet collaboration can become, and, after 1980, how transient.

The Soviet Union has exercised caution in dealing with the Central American and Caribbean countries, lying as they do within the sphere of U.S. vital interests. Moreover, they could become immensely dependent and costly clients. These small countries on the American doorstep could offer certain strategic opportunities. Initially, the USSR has let Castro take the lead in dealing with them.

Since détente the Soviet Union has demonstrated its capacity to work closely worldwide with its Caribbean client state, Cuba. And during the Falklands crisis, it shored up its ties with Argentina. Similarly, the Soviet government has demonstrated its flexibility in maintaining substantial trade with a right-wing military government in Brazil and participating in a broad range of economic development projects with a left-wing military government in Peru. Its cordial relations continue with Mexico. Beyond that, the USSR has gained access to countries like Bolivia, Ecuador, Colombia, Venezuela, and Costa Rica. Most particularly, it has welcomed revolutionary-style governments in Chile, Jamaica, Grenada, and

Nicaragua while maintaining its reserve with respect to significant foreign aid. Twenty years ago most of these developments would have been unthinkable.

• Military-Strategic Issues

The Soviet Union's close relations with Cuba has permitted the USSR to counter, at least symbolically, U.S. bases near Soviet borders. The optimum method of capitalizing on its Cuban tie would have been to establish nuclear rockets on the island. President Kennedy's successful quarantine forced Khrushchev to withdraw Soviet missiles before they became operational, and the USSR also agreed not to establish offensive forces on Cuba in exchange for Kennedy's no-invasion pledge. Soviet submarines, surface vessels, and aircraft, however, visit Cuba as necessary for fuel, supplies, and rest for their crews, all of which has given the USSR a military capability in the Western Hemisphere it did not enjoy before Castro. The United States has continued to insist successfully that no Soviet bases be established on the island.

Cuba has also provided Soviet specialists with an opportunity to collect electronic and other intelligence and become well acquainted with Caribbean and adjacent waters. Cuban facilities have been especially useful in permitting Soviet vessels to increase their station time in the Atlantic, for they can refuel at nearby Cuba rather than in distant Soviet ports. Access to the South Atlantic is also much easier from Cuba than from the USSR.

Cuba is like Berlin in that it constitutes a strategic asset and a liability at the same time. Cuba and Berlin are both penetrations and listening posts within the rival power's sphere of influence. The Soviet position in Cuba, like the U.S. position in Berlin, is not really defensible against a full-scale surface attack by the rival great power. If the United States were to attack Cuba, the USSR would be faced with a horrible dilemma: either to defend Cuba and face almost certain nuclear devastation or to permit Cuba to be overrun and face political humiliation. The record so far suggests that the second is the most likely if not certain choice. In order to prevent such a choice, Moscow's most important strategic objective in Latin America may be to contain tensions over Cuba.

The USSR has been providing many of the new arms that the Sandinistas have needed to turn back the contras. Military aid appears to be in the hundreds of millions of rubles but still a fraction of that given Cuba. The USSR has not yet shown a large military presence in the region.

Cuba, Nicaragua and other Latin American countries do not rank high among Soviet strategic priorities. The first concern of Soviet leaders is their own and their country's security. That means that their strategic and military priorities lie along their own borders—Poland, the Germanies, the Middle East, and China—and not in the Americas. The great distance from the USSR to Latin America means that military operations there would be difficult to support and conduct.

Strategically, the USSR has sought to minimize the risks of its political support for Cuba and Nicaragua, and briefly Grenada. The symbols of this caution are the absence of any formal Soviet military guarantee of Cuba and a low profile in Nicaragua. Cuba wooed and won Moscow when the USSR was inexperienced in such matters. Moscow has since become more cautious, seeking to follow the tried and true strategic rule that one's commitments should not exceed one's capabilities. The U.S. armed forces clearly have the upper hand in the Americas. As a result the Western Hemisphere seems an unlikely place for the USSR to initiate a conventional military engagement with the United States. Soviet military progress in the hemisphere is important mainly for symbolic political purposes or possibly for harassment in the unlikely event of hostilities.

The Soviet Union has maintained military relations with Argentina, Mexico, and Peru as well as with Cuba. Military attachés have been exchanged, and there have been exchange visits of military officers. Argentina particularly has been interested in military ties because of an established commitment to the study of global strategies. The Soviet Union's close economic relations with the Peruvian military governments of the late 1960s and 1970s spilled over into the military field when Peru bought tanks, helicopters, and other military equipment on vary favorable terms. According to unconfirmed reports, the Soviet Union has also sought to sell arms to Argentina and Mexico, partly to offset the huge trade deficit with the region. Although the arms embargo on Argentina during the Falklands-Malvinas crisis made clear the desirability of diversifying arms sources, Argentina and other countries apparently have not bought Soviet military equipment. Also of strategic interest were Soviet deliveries of heavy water to Argentina in 1981 and acceptance of Argentine uranium for enrichment in 1982.

• Economic Relations

Soviet economic relations with Latin America are not shaped primarily by the goals of the international Communist movement, the needs of member parties, nor the strategies of the Soviet armed forces. They are formed by the economic and, in the case of Cuba and Nicaragua, political interests of the Soviet state. The USSR has two economic problems in Latin America: the large trade deficit with the region (except Cuba and Nicaragua) and the annual subsidies required to keep these two countries afloat.

Certain Latin American nations, especially Argentina, Brazil, and Uruguay, produce consumer goods the USSR needs badly, such as grain, meat, hides, coffee, and cocoa. The quality and price are right for Soviet markets. Soviet buyers prefer to buy these products for hard currency in cash in Latin America rather than from other exporters. Latin Americans buy very little in return, in some years only one-fifth or even one-tenth as much as they sell. As noted earlier, the USSR has long run a big deficit with the area, sometimes constituting a substantial fraction of the total Soviet deficit.

In order to increase exports to the area and lessen the deficit, Soviet officials have attempted to sell the region large projects in irrigation, hydro and thermal power, and transport. One purpose of the sales is to have a demonstration effect and boost exports not only to the country where the project is located but to neighboring countries as well. Projects have been sold to Argentina, Uruguay, Brazil, Peru, Bolivia, and other countries, but none of these projects has had the dramatic effect the sale of a Soviet steel mill to India had on Soviet trade there.

Whereas the trade balance of many Latin American countries vis-à-vis the USSR is strong, Cuba's is weak. Cuba lacks mineral resources, except for nickel, and has almost no oil. Its exports consist of tropical products: sugar, fish, citrus, tobacco. It must import most of its chemicals, machinery, and equipment, as well as oil. The Soviet Union subsidizes some of its exports and imports, covers balance-of-payments deficits, postpones interest and amortization payments, and has given Cuba most of its military equipment free. This assistance has been estimated in the early 1980s at US $3 billion a year, or almost as much as one-fifth of the Cuban gross national product. The Soviet Union cannot really afford this much aid to Cuba but probably has little choice, having already made such a large investment on the island.

Since the USSR shoulders the Cuban economic burden, it has been cautious about taking on any new obligations elsewhere. Most of the leftist governments who have since approached Moscow with high hopes have had them dashed. Soviet "aid" to Chile in the early 1970s was mainly credits for buying Soviet exports, not the hard currency Allende needed. The Jamaicans and the Guyanese were disappointed in the 1970s, and the Nicaraguans have found the Soviet Union cordial but cautious in the 1980s.

The Soviet government has good reasons to be careful about taking on costly new client states. Economic growth in the USSR has slowed in recent years. Although housing has dramatically improved since the immediate postwar period, it still is insufficient. Soviet agriculture is intermittently unable to supply sufficient quantities of basic food items for its own population. Moscow, a showplace, still offers a narrow choice of indifferent quality consumer goods, and shortages are chronic. Although distribution is evener than in many Western societies, the general standard is lower than that of the middle classes in many Latin American countries. As a result Soviet leaders are on firm ground in their caution about Latin America. Resources that might be sent abroad are needed to boost civil and military investment at home.

• Party Relations

At the summit of the Communist world, the Politburo of the CPSU coordinates the work of the Soviet state and the pro-Soviet international Communist movement. From 1919 to 1943, Soviet control of the international Communist movement was exercised formally through the Executive Committee of the Comintern or Third International. Since 1945 representatives of the Soviet party, men such as the late Mikhail Suslov and Boris Ponomarev, exercised Soviet influence through regional groupings, the *World Marxist Review* (edited in Prague), reciprocal visits, party congresses, and the like. The *World Marxist Review* identifies itself as "a theoretical and information journal of Communist and Workers' Parties." The policies of the international movements are coordinated through the speeches, reports, and articles of the leaders of national parties, some of which surely are cleared, and presented at party meetings or in party journals.

The Soviet government has no juridical relationship with the ruling Communist prties in Eastern Europe and Asia, nor with the nonruling parties, such as those in Latin America. Yet both are, as a practical matter, accountable to the Soviet Politburo. While the Soviet leaders cannot control foreign Communist parties as they control internal Soviet institutions, their dominance of the pro-Soviet international Communist movement is a widely recognized reality.

The Communist parties in Latin America almost always take positions on international issues identical with those of the Soviet Union. The critique of the Soviet invasion of Czechoslovakia made by Mexican Communists in 1968 was among the rare exceptions. The conformity of Latin American Communists with Soviet policy is partly the result of their methods of political recruitment. Local recruits who join the Communists are aware of the ground rules and usually agree with Soviet positions. In fact, that conformity is often what distinguishes the Communists from other leftist parties in Latin America. Because the parties there are usually rather small and with limited local resources, their financial and political base does not encourage them to cut loose from Moscow's sponsorship.

Soviet leaders deny any conflict between the interests of the Soviet state and of the international movement. The rationale for the primacy of Soviet interests is that the fatherland of world revolution, the USSR, must be kept safe and strong to help revolutions elsewhere. Such a defense need not be considered pure sophistry because Soviet leaders and lower-rank citizens appear convinced that revolutions all over the world will need Soviet help to succeed. Doctrine holds that these revolutions are inevitable. Because of the rule of inevitability, there is no need to endanger the Soviet state here and now. Such doctrine, plus the policy of state-to-state relations in spite of ideological differences, has made possible Soviet ties with a wide spectrum of Latin American governments.

These relationships would not be possible if the Latin American governments felt seriously threatened by Soviet-sponsored subversion or revolution.

Some observers in the West interpret many social revolutions in Latin America, and elsewhere, as part of a conspiracy whose main purpose is to weaken the United States. While the USSR is often motivated by anti-imperialist objectives, it is misleading to interpret Soviet policy solely in terms of the United States. For example, Soviet support for revolutions in Latin America is politically and ideologically motivated and part of a long-range strategy to encourage the development of socialism in the world.

The Communist parties in Latin America are an asset for the USSR in that they propagate Soviet ideology, support Soviet foreign policies, and keep Moscow informed about local developments in their individual countries. The Soviet Union has an entree to the local politics of these countries not available to any Western power. Originally the main purpose of these parties was to promote social revolution within their own societies in order to abolish capitalism and imperialism and establish a socialist state. Yet the Communists in Latin America have never led a revolution; not the Mexican Revolution against Díaz, which antedated the Bolshevik Revolution; nor the Guatemalan Revolution against Ubico; nor the Cuban Revolution against Batista; nor the Dominican revolt against Trujillo and his successors; nor the Nicaraguan Revolution against Somoza. Nor have they abolished "capitalism" or defeated "imperialism" in any Latin American country. Castro and his radical nationalist 26th of July Movement revolutionized Cuba, inviting the Communists on his bandwagon after the fact. In Chile, Allende and the Chilean socialists, with the Communists in a supporting role, led the social revolution.

The Communist parties pose a dilemma for the Soviet state. The pursuit of revolutionary goals by organizations linked to Moscow would make Soviet official relations with the countries difficult or impossible. The parties have made no satisfactory progress—they have not taken over any Latin American state—but have at the same time the potential for preventing the USSR from pursuing its political and economic interests with local governments. Under these circumstances Moscow made the pragmatic choice. The USSR emphasized its political and economic relations with incumbent military and civilian dictatorships, such as those in Argentina, Brazil, and Peru, and the local Communist parties abstained from subversive efforts and often gave helpful support to the local governments. Such policies worked well in Peru in the 1970s and in Argentina in the early 1980s. Lingering suspicion of Communist revolutionary goals cloud Soviet relations with Brazil.

• Soviet Strategies

Compared to other governments, the Soviet Union has had a remarkable continuity of leadership and policies toward Latin America since the 1917 Revolution. Soviet leaders have pursued multifaceted strategies involving government, military-strategic, economic, and party objectives. Some progress has been made on each of these strands of strategy.

Overall, the most important Soviet achievement in Latin America in the last twenty years has been to establish and strengthen ties with most governments in the region. Cuba and Nicaragua are the most prominent examples, but the USSR has in fact established and/or consolidated relations with more center and right-wing governments. Many were Andean governments, such as Peru, Colombia, and Venezuela, as well as Caribbean states. Most important were Argentina, Mexico, and Brazil. The USSR has long hoped to make Argentina the centerpiece of Soviet economic operations in South America.

The United States succeeded in imposing limits on Soviet military-strategic ambitions in the Americas during the missile crisis of 1962. As a result Soviet military operations in the hemisphere have been limited primarily to showing the flag, naval and air provisioning, patrols, and intelligence-gathering missions.

The Soviet Union has made less progress in economic relations, always chronically troubled. The Soviet trade deficit with the area has continued to mount, most steeply after the U.S. grain embargo. Soviet exports keep falling behind Soviet imports. Another and more serious problem is the faltering Cuban economy, whose long-term need for Soviet subsidies grows.

As noted above, pro-Soviet Communists have not led successful revolutions, have had little success at the polls except in Chile, and have the support of only a small fraction of the population in these countries. Most of the parties are, relative to other political parties, small and weak. It was the Soviet government which provided the markets, oil, and arms that Castro needed, not the Cuban Communists. It was the Soviet government to which the Sandinistas looked for aid, not the Nicaraguan Communists.

Each strand of strategy tends to have a limiting effect on another strand. For example, Communist-sponsored revolutionary activity in a country can damage Soviet relations with that government, and conversely, the ties of Soviet officials can place limits on the local Communists' tactics. Soviet economic difficulties have limited the capacity to strengthen political relations with particular governments, such as Mexico and Manley's Jamaica. Expansionist military operations in the Caribbean could raise fears and anti-Soviet feelings threatening other Soviet political interests.

Future Soviet strategies in Latin America will most likely be determined by developments outside rather than inside the narrow framework of bilateral relationships. Will efforts to revitalize the Soviet economy and society begun in 1987 focus Soviet attentions inward and away from distracting and costly ties with revolutionary movements? Will Soviet aims to achieve arms control cause the USSR to avoid actions perceived as threatening in Washington? Answers to these questions as well as the future of the Soviet economy will have a bearing on the Soviet capacity to influence changing societies in the region.

In the future as in the past, Soviet-American relations will also cast their shadow on the Americas. If détente is revived and continued, the prospects for strengthened and nonthreatening Soviet economic and political relations in the area are good. If there should be a sharp deterioration in Soviet-American relations, there could be a parallel polarization in Latin America with a potential for confrontation and violence greater than during the Cold War, partly because the potential for violence in such countries as El Salvador, Guatemala, and Chile is greater than in the 1950s. If U.S. policies retreat to the hegemonic patterns of earlier years, there could also be sharp divisions between the United States and many Latin American governments. These conflicts would provide fresh opportunities for Soviet manipulation.

If current Soviet policies are projected into the future, the USSR may concentrate on conserving existing gains and avoiding new risks and obligations in the Americas. The pressing need in Cuba is how to cut back the heavy economic burden without undue damage to the Cuban economy and relations with Castro. Developments in the world economy, including the price of sugar, may make that difficult. Since the Soviet population's knowledge of their Cuban burden is controlled and the party leadership makes such decisions largely alone, the Soviet government probably can continue resource transfers in the future. The present Soviet government may not oppose a resumption of Cuban trade with the United States partly because such trade could ease, though not resolve, Cuba's economic problems.

The test in Nicaragua is how to check rapidly growing economic assistance while at the same time preventing the fall of the Sandinista regime in the face of external pressure. The USSR will probably continue to encourage socialist, Third World, and even Western states to support the Sandinista government.

Meanwhile, the Soviet government has conducted a flexible policy of intergovernmental relations across the political spectrum. When Argentina, Brazil, and Bolivia were military dictatorships, Moscow mounted diplomatic and commercial relations, stimulating the latter. The USSR treats Argentina and Brazil delicately because of their political and economic potential, and its vested interest of years of cultivation. The Soviet investment of time, money, and technology in the Bolivian tin smelters needed to be protected and the Soviet presence sustained for the day when domestic or foreign developments might provide the local Communists better political opportunities. Now that all three countries have democratic governments, Moscow continues its limited cooperative relationships.

In the center there are countries such as Mexico, Venezuela, and Peru, in each of which the USSR has some kind of political, diplomatic, or economic stake. Prospects for stable relationships over the long term are rather good because the prospects of the local Communists in the near term are limited, and these governments want normal relations with the USSR.

The Soviet leadership can be counted on to check the revolutionary enthusiasms of Communists in countries with whose governments Soviet relations are good and whose prospects for revolution are bad. Soviet diplomatic ties and trade with Latin American countries have tended to dampen Communist opposition in countries like Argentina and Brazil. On the other hand, recent developments in Central America have given Soviet leaders a new sensitivity to political opportunities in societies experiencing deep-set political upheaval. In such societies the Soviet Politburo will continue to give the local Communists the green light for armed opposition. For example, Soviet-sponsored leaders called for the formation of broad national fronts to overthrow ruling tyrants and military juntas, not only as they already have done in El Salvador and Guatemala, but in other countries ripe for revolutionary takeovers. In the revolutionary movements of some of these countries, the Communists are weak and small and will have to subordinate themselves to noncommunist leadership. The Communists' prospects for leading an armed revolt are better in Chile than in many other countries.

The Soviet leadership is not likely to emphasize the military-strategic strand of Soviet policy toward the area, at least not as long as Washington is adamant with respect to Soviet bases. Soviet resources are limited and can be used most effectively nearer home. Moreover, stepped-up Soviet military activities in the Americas are counterproductive in a strategic sense so long as arms control agreements with the United States constitute an important Soviet objective. Expanded military activities in the Western Hemisphere do not seem a promising way to achieve Moscow's ultimate security objective of avoiding a nuclear war.

Soviet leaders and officials are acutely aware of the huge comparative advantage the United States and the West have over the Soviet Union in Latin America. Western markets are the largest and most desirable places for Latin America to sell its exports and to buy what it needs. The West controls the largest aggregation of capital, the most advanced technology, and the most sophisticated laboratories. Western Europe and the United States also have a geographic advantage of being closer to Latin America than the USSR. For many generations there has been a large network of individual and group relationships among North Americans, Europeans, and Latin Americans that leaves the USSR out.

As a result Soviet strategy is based on recognition of those U.S. advantages. Soviet leaders appear to have no intention of investing heavily in Latin America beyond the huge amounts now sustaining Cuba, nor of assuming new strategic risks in the area. Soviet leaders don't want to pay for the luxury of another Cuba, nor have they forgotten the lessons of the 1962 missile crisis.

In any confrontation with the United States in Latin America, the Soviet Union is handicapped by the fact that the region has a relatively high priority for the United States and a relatively low one for the USSR. The United States is prepared to go to great lengths to have its way there, but the USSR is not ready to go very far. The reverse is the case in regions peripheral to the USSR.

Under circumstances of relative disadvantage, the USSR has been following a strategy of the martial arts: turn the weight of a more powerful opponent against him. With an occasional exception, Soviet leaders have avoided the initiative and kept a low profile, waiting for Washington to make errors that might ultimately seal its fate. As Communists, they believe, or say they believe, that capitalism contains the seeds of its own destruction and will eventually collapse of its own weight.

In fact, Soviet expectations proved right in the cases of two important partners in Latin America, Cuba and Nicaragua. American economic and military sanctions against Cuba in 1960 and thereafter were the pretext and rationale for developing close relations with the USSR. Castro probably believed that a sharp break with the United States was necessary to achieve his domestic and foreign political objectives, and U.S. sanctions facilitated the break he wanted. Those sanctions also gave Castro no alternative to dependence on the USSR and all that came to mean.

Similarly, as U.S. economic and military sanctions against the Sandinistas have grown, Nicaragua has become increasingly dependent on Soviet oil, arms, and markets. That growing dependence, and growing Soviet aid, have meant sharply increased Soviet influence.

VIII Afterword on U.S. Policies

Previous chapters have discussed Soviet relations with Latin America, but this chapter evaluates U.S. official responses to Soviet actions and revolutionary change in the area. It also proposes how the United States should respond to such challenges in order to protect U.S. national interests in the region. By national interests I mean protecting the physical security and material welfare of the American people as a whole. These recommendations are a product not only of this book but of my earlier studies of the United States, the Soviet Union, and revolutionary change in Latin America.[1]

Most of the major crises in U.S. policy toward Latin America since 1945 have been the result of perceptions of Soviet interference. In some cases, as in Cuba beginning in 1960, the perception was very real; in others, as in the Dominican Republic in 1965, largely illusory. More important, these crises were a test of U.S. ability to deal effectively with social revolutions in its sphere of influence.

The U.S. record is mixed. Sometimes U.S. leaders have been able to adjust to new social orders. Woodrow Wilson's and Franklin Roosevelt's policies toward the Mexican Revolution are good examples of compromise and accommodation that served the interests of both countries. Those accommodations were vital to U.S. security in World War I and II, when, despite tensions, Mexico did not join Germany. Mexico's relations with the United States, for example, have been much healthier and mutually beneficial than Poland's relations with the USSR. Another example of U.S. adaptability was the Eisenhower administration's coming to terms with the Bolivian Revolution in the 1950s.

In most other cases U.S. leaders have been unable to settle their differences peacefully with the leaders of the other Latin American revolutions. United States administrations took paramilitary action against revolutionary governments in Guatemala and Cuba, military action against the revolt in the Dominican Republic, and covert political action against the Allende government in Chile. All these crises involved U.S fears of Soviet or Communist involvement, and all resulted in some kind of U.S. interference. There were at least two aspects to U.S. action in each of these cases. First, American leaders misperceived the local political situation and the revolutionaries' ties with international communism. Second, they reached a decision to interfere on the basis of this misperception. Decisions based on misperceptions proved defective.

In the rest of this chapter, I will show how and why U.S. leaders misperceived these revolutions and explain how their armed interventions or political interference hurt U.S. interests. I will conclude with recommendations for protecting and advancing U.S. interests when revolutionary situations arise in the future.

• Perceptions

American leaders have not understood the fundamental causes of the revolutions, the political weakness of incumbent governments, the strengths of the revolutionary opposition, nor the consequences of their actions for U.S. interests. Their most serious misperception has been that the USSR, acting throughout the Communist parties or conspiratorial activities, actually caused social revolutions in Latin America.

Central to commonly held misperceptions about the USSR as an instigator of revolutions in Latin America is the concept of the export of revolution. The world knows that as the leader of the international Communist movement, the Soviet Union sends people, money, propaganda, and arms abroad from time to time. Observers also have noted that the USSR has often done those things in countries where revolutions have not taken place. The Soviet Union did not supply arms for the Guatemalan, Cuban, Dominican, Chilean, or Nicaraguan seizures of power. Nor did any other great power. That suggests that the key elements were not arms (or foreign money, for that matter) but something else. Governments cannot export revolution.

The official U.S. belief that the USSR exports revolution because it has exported arms and money was the source of other mischief. American officials seem to have concluded that if, like the USSR, they exported arms, they could also export counterrevolution.

The acquisition of arms or foreign aid in general was not the main issue in the Latin American revolutions. The main issue was which side could mobilize the most dedicated fighters and command the most popular support. With men and political support guaranteed, political movements could acquire arms from many sources. This was true in Cuba, the Dominican Republic, and most recently in Nicaragua and El Salvador.

In the sale or transfer of arms, a distinction needs to be made between revolutionary oppositions and revolutionary governments. As indicated above, the Soviet Union has sent few or no arms to revolutionary *oppositions* in this hemisphere. That may even apply to El Salvador, where the opposition's arms appear to have come from other governments, including Soviet-supplied Cuba. The USSR and other socialist countries, however, have sent arms to various Latin American *governments* recognized by the United States. One shipment of Czech arms was sent to the Arbenz government in Guatemala in 1954. The Soviet Union sent massive shipments of arms to Cuba, made sales to Peru in the 1970s, and may have encouraged shipment of arms to Nicaragua in the 1980s. These shipments were made to buck up new elites already in power, not to overthrow incumbent regimes.

Domestic circumstances have created social revolutions in Latin America. Arms shipments, propaganda, and agitators from the Soviet Union have not. In fact, the Latin American Parties have played only a peripheral role, if any, in the coming to power of revolutionary movements in Guatemala (1944), Cuba (1959), and Nicaragua (1979). As already noted, in Cuba, Castro did not convert his 26th of July movement into communism until several years after overthrowing Batista. The Soviet Union does not claim to have caused these revolutions. Instead, Soviet doctrine holds that these social revolutions reflect global trends, most particularly of workers in industry and agriculture seeking to eliminate exploitation and foreign domination by overthrowing capitalism and establishing socialism. The Soviet Union seeks to assist and capitalize on these forces in the interests of international communism.

A second and related misperception is that the CPSU controlled revolutionary governments such as those in Guatemala, Cuba, and Nicaragua. None of the top leaders of these governments were Communists when they came to power. Castro turned Communist two years later. The Chilean Communists who gained their posts in elections in 1970 were the second party in a multiparty coalition.

Confusion arises when U.S. leaders assume that non-Communist leaders are pro-Moscow because they happen to be Leftists or socialists. Such a view overlooks a fundamental distinction, namely that non-Communists are rarely beholden to a foreign power and are dedicated to national causes whereas the pro-Moscow Communists have strong loyalties and obligations to Moscow.

The fact that U.S. leaders have had these misperceptions about Latin America should come as no surprise. Top U.S. policymakers have had little or no first hand knowledge of these small countries nor of their leaders. Few men who have risen to the top of the political ladder in the United States have had the time to immerse themselves in the affairs of any world area, much less Latin America. Getting and staying elected, keeping on top of the economy, and staying informed on global issues have been more important for them than knowledge of that region. They have cared a great deal about American politics, especially their place in it, and about their nation's most powerful rival, the Soviet Union—and not so much about Latin America. As a result, the reactions of U.S. leaders to revolutions are more comprehensible in terms of domestic American politics and Soviet-American rivalry than in terms of the problems of Latin America itself.

Theoretically, subordinate political and career appointees are supposed to provide the expertise presidents and secretaries of state lack. Yet such appointees are selected because their perceptions of events and policy orientations conform to the preconceptions of their superiors. Officials lower in the hierarchy tend to fall in line because that is their job and it suits their career interests. Critics of the incumbents' policies are shuttled into obscure jobs or retired.

Latin American dictators and other incumbents have skillfully played on American official and public ignorance to sustain themselves in power. Often they have succeeded in pinning the Communist label on their opposition, whatever its political complexion and have sought to hide their own repressive measures. They form links with powerful business or other interests which promote their cause in the United States. The tactics of revolutionaries, involving kidnapping, sabotage, and other violent measures shock Americans who come from a relatively orderly society. The Americans may never become aware that these tactics are in response to equally or more violent suppression by an incumbent authoritarian regime. Most American leaders, like the public, are not equipped by temperament or historical experience to understand social revolutions.

• United States Interference

On the basis of these misperceptions, U.S. leaders have attempted to impose their choice of leadership on four Latin American countries. They used covert paramilitary means to try to overthrow Arbenz in Guatemala and Castro in Cuba. They sent troops to the Dominican Republic to prevent Juan Bosch from regaining the presidency and used a variety of nonmilitary means to prevent Allende from becoming president of Chile and then to unseat him after he took office.

At the root of U.S. interference has been the assumption, widely held in the United States, that a government, particularly the U.S. government, has the capacity to influence constructively the political development of another country by direct interference. Such an assumption implies that the U.S. government knows what is best for other countries and how to achieve it. Since the assumption is so widely held, the domestic pressures on the U.S. president to intervene, and his fear of the political consequences of not doing so, are immense.

A major theoretical question is why the United States and other great powers intervene in small countries. The Soviet Union explains U.S. intervention as one logical outcome of capitalism and imperialism. The Soviet solution for ending imperialism and intervention is abolishing capitalism and establishing socialism. I find that solution unpersuasive because the Soviet Union itself, long after establishing socialism, has intervened with armed forces in Hungary, Czechoslovakia, and Afghanistan. My own view is that intervention comes about partly because of the huge power disparities between large and small countries.

As long as these disparities exist, temptations to intervene may prove irresistible. Since 1945 the United States has been cautious about acting directly against the USSR as has the USSR against the United States. Both fear the possible result of such hostile actions. Both, however, have been unable to resist moving against small neighbors, the United States in the name of democracy, the USSR in the name of socialism.

In Guatemala, after CIA-sponsored forces entered the country, the Guatemalan army, not CIA forces, overthrew Arbenz. Although the immediate objective, the ouster of Arbenz, was achieved, the long-term objective of supporting democracy failed. That nation has since had a string of tyrannical military leaders and thousands of political assassinations suffered by all political parties. Few countries are now more polarized between extremists of the Right and Left and more vulnerable to revolution.

Cuba represents a classic case of the failure of intervention. Not only did the immediate objectives of overthrowing Castro fail at the Bay of Pigs in 1961, but the effect of U.S. sanctions was to accelerate the formation of Cuban ties with the USSR, the outcome they were designed to prevent.

Although I believe that domestic rather than foreign forces were primarily responsible for Allende's fall, the consequences were contrary to the stated U.S. objectives of strengthening democracy in Chile. The military government that followed Allende was one of the most authoritarian and repressive in Chilean history.

A good argument can be made that the Dominican intervention did not serve the long-term interests of the United States. Since this case is too complex for treatment here, I do not cite it as having been against U.S. interests.

The U.S. democratic system is peculiarly unfitted to shape the internal affairs of other nations. Political change in Latin America requires years to mature and administrations in Washington average little more than four years. Rarely does a single leader, seized of a problem in mid-term, have more than two or three years to see it through, and successors often take contrary positions on the same problem. Compare, for example, the contrasting policies of the following pairs of U.S. policymakers: John Foster Dulles and John F. Kennedy; Lyndon Johnson and Henry Kissinger; Cyrus Vance and Alexander Haig. How would an activist program to influence the political development of a country survive the succession of two or more of these leaders?

• Three Rules

The Latin American policies of the United States should not be a by-product of U.S.-Soviet relations. In the past these policies have been too often shaped by U.S.-Soviet global rivalry and by misperceptions of Soviet actions in the region. Washington should deal with Latin American governments on their own merits. If U.S. ties with particular Latin American nations are healthy, strong, and mutually beneficial, the USSR will not be able to threaten Washington's interests there.

In order to protect and advance U.S. political and strategic interests, and establish a climate for profitable economic relations, I suggest three rules for the United States to follow during political upheavals south of the border:

1. American authorities should prevent the USSR from acquiring any military bases in the Western Hemisphere.
2. The United States should not intervene unilaterally with armed forces in any Latin American country.
3. The United States should not attempt to determine the political leadership of Latin American countries, whether by economic or military assistance or political interference.

Critics of U.S. policies and Latin Americans will resent rule 1 on the grounds that the United States has no right to control their governments' military relations with the USSR. Perhaps not, but such a position does not take into account realities. The two superpowers have the means to destroy each other, and neither is going to stand idly by while the other acquires new means of doing so. Nor would any Latin American government with the power to prevent it permit a hostile government to install nuclear weapons next door.

Moreover, U.S. presidents must act within the limits of public opinion. The American public would not accept the installation of Soviet nuclear weapons in the hemisphere. The prohibition of Soviet bases in the hemisphere is the sine qua non of any enlightened U.S. policy toward the region.

Rule 1 involves simply the continuation and extension of the de facto arrangements made during the missile crisis of 1962. At present the Soviet Union does not appear to require or to intend to establish military bases in the hemisphere. The temporary arrangements it already has in Cuba appear sufficient to support its forces. Some day, however, the enforcement of this rule may involve grave risks. In that event, and to the extent possible, the U.S. response should be made multilaterally through the inter-American system. In any case, the action would be only against Soviet, not Latin American, forces.

Rules 1 and 2 do not exclude military action against an extrahemispheric power. The model is provided by the missile crisis when U.S. actions were directed against Soviet rocket shipments, not against Cuba per se. Nor do they rule out other military action under inter-American agreements.

The expansion of Soviet military involvement in Latin America is more likely through the increased provision of arms in the area than through the establishment of a Soviet base. The USSR has already showered arms on Cuba, giving Castro one of the most powerful armed forces in the area; it has also sold Peru aircraft, tanks, and other weapons on generous terms. Washington appears to have decided that the political costs of preventing Peru from buying Soviet arms exceeded the costs of allowing them. Peru did not become dependent on Soviet arms, and the outcome has confirmed Washington's handling of the case.

From a strategic point of view, Washington's main objective should be to prevent any Latin American country, such as Nicaragua, from becoming dependent on the USSR for arms. But there seem to be so many governments in the East and West sympathetic to Nicaragua that excessive dependency on a single government seems unlikely. Most Latin American governments, including the Sandinistas, prefer to avoid dependency no matter who the patron state is. Since the U.S. embargo on arms transfers to Argentina in the Malvinas crisis, Latin American governments may seek to diversify their sources of arms, buying more from the Soviet Union.

Rule 2 against armed intervention is especially important when U.S.

leaders insist on preventing rival great powers from establishing military bases in the hemisphere. Latin Americans believe that if the United States claims the right to prevent foreign intervention, the least it can do is *not* intervene itself.

The main argument against armed intervention is that it does not work. Military control, if it can be established over hostile populations, creates more problems that it solves. The United States sent troops into Nicaragua under President Taft and into Mexico, the Dominican Republic, and Haiti under President Wilson. In the 1920s the Republican presidents soon found remaining occupations a nuisance, costly in human life, and a fiscal burden. The withdrawal of troops begun earlier was completed under Franklin Roosevelt. United States admirals and generals are not effective rulers of foreign countries. President Kennedy did not pursue the intervention after the Bay of Pigs because victory would have been bloody, and occupation a nightmare. Nor is it possible to overlook Vietnam as the most persuasive example of the futility of armed intervention in small countries.

Another reason armed intervention does not work is that it places the opposition in a desperate situation. Under such circumstances it has little choice but to seek help against the intervening government's rivals. When the United States enforced an arms embargo in Europe and elsewhere against Arbenz and armed a guerrilla force to overthrow him, Arbenz sought arms in the East, his only remaining source of supply. When the United States threatened intervention, Castro asked the USSR to buy sugar and provide him with arms and petroleum. Intervention has had the effect of achieving what it sought to avoid.

Rule 3 prohibits U.S. efforts to determine the political leadership of a Latin American country. Specifically, this means attempts to remove, install, or sustain particular leaders or groups in power. Economic and military assistance are standard means for bucking up the status quo. The Alliance for Progress, the best-known example, sought to head off revolutions by reforming the status quo. The consensus is that the alliance did not work. Covert political action, including the financing of politicians, labor leaders, and journalists, is another form of political interference.

United States officials working on behalf of the alliance and other such bilateral aid programs became deeply involved with Latin American political leaders, governments, and political parties. Sometimes U.S.

ambassadors become active for or against particular Latin American presidents. In 1963 the American ambassador to the Dominican Republic gave the green light to the military officers who overthrew Juan Bosch. In 1964 the American ambassador to Bolivia joined the campaign travels of the incumbent president, symbolizing the collaborative effort of the candidates and the U.S. government. That same year the American ambassador to Brazil, who was critical of President Goulart, called in the U.S. fleet on the eve of the military coup that overthrew Goulart. Latin American presidents attempt to mobilize U.S. power to stay in office while opposition groups attempt to mobilize U.S. power to get rid of an incumbent. In both categories U.S. resources become pawns of competing political factions.

The burden of proof for any proposal for U.S. interference should fall on the person who makes the proposal. Up to 1982, charges of Soviet interference were generally unfounded or flimsy at best in Guatemala, the Dominican Republic, Nicaragua, and El Salvador. In Cuba there was no evidence of Soviet interference in early 1960, only the fear that the USSR would intervene. American sanctions had the effect of ensuring that the prophecy came true.

Some U.S. leaders have used charges about Soviet interference for political purposes. John Foster Dulles, who criticized the previous administration for not liberating Eastern Europe, had to make good with a country he could liberate, and that was Guatemala. Lyndon Johnson feared the Dominican revolt might lead to another Cuba and jeopardize his chances in 1968. The Reagan administration needed a victory over the Soviet Union and decided to draw the line in Central America. The effect of these maneuvers was to exaggerate Soviet influence and denigrate that of the Latin Americans. Washington's actions, if any, should be taken against an offending state, not against the latter's supposed victims.

Probably the most effective argument in favor of U.S. interference is that failure to counter Soviet interference yields the field to Communism. Thus, this argument requires U.S. leaders to counter Soviet involvement in Latin America where they find it. Among the difficulties of applying this strategy is that it has often been difficult in particular cases to determine whether or how the USSR has been interfering. In the cases examined above Soviet interference proved slight or nonexistent.

More important, countering Soviet interference wherever it is believed to have occurred turns over the initiative for U.S. policy to Moscow. The usual result has been U.S. alignment with whomever Moscow opposes, thereby permitting Moscow to choose U.S. allies. Such alignments do not necessarily suit U.S. interests, sometimes associating the United States with the losing side.

The argument that in revolutionary situations the United States should counter Soviet interference by interference of its own is based on two false assumptions: first, that Moscow can create and control revolutions, and second, that the United States has the power and knowhow to prevent them. The historical record does not support the validity of either assumption as a sound basis for policy. Fear of extrahemispheric interference has lured the United States in the past into traps from which it has extracted itself only with great difficulty.

U.S. interference has often served Soviet rather than U.S. causes. That is because interference by the United States in Latin America has often had the effect of uniting a wide spectrum of Latin Americans against the United States, creating anti-American political alignments on which the Soviet Union has been able to capitalize.

United States officials, whether in Washington or Latin America, are not equipped to decide who should lead other countries. They endanger long term U.S. interests by getting involved in domestic political struggles. American ambassadors remain in a country for only a few years and go home. Each new set of officials wants to put its stamp on policy, changing the emphasis. One administration tries to aid democratic regimes while the next tilts toward dictators, nullifying the efforts of the predecessor. Both might better have minded U.S. business. Washington has spent billions of dollars in economic and military assistance to get Latin Americans to conform to a particular prescription. Meanwhile, U.S. taxpayers footed the bill: loans and grants to Latin America from 1946 to 1981, less repayments, totaled more than $11 billion. The United States does not have much to show for this huge expenditure. Which of these aid programs would you and I have supported out of our own pockets?

Rule 3 against aid as an instrument to promote political development is not directed against aid for certain other purposes. Humanitarian bilateral assistance in the case of floods, earthquakes, famine, and the like is a moral obligation, now as always, and should be continued. In its long term economic and political interests, the United States should support economic development in Latin America as elsewhere in the Third World. Such aid should be provided through public international organizations like the Inter-American Development Bank and the World Bank. Some bilateral assistance, such as technical assistance, may be necessary, but not huge transfers sought and justified as a way to shape political outcomes in the country concerned. The United States no longer has the surplus resources that it once thought it had. It can no longer afford to foot the bill for U.S. officials' misadventures in Latin American politics.

If these three rules seem extreme, look again. All three are officially sanctioned U.S. policy. Rule 1 against Soviet bases in the Americas was reaffirmed by President Kennedy and supported by all presidents since. Rule 2 on nonintervention has been official U.S. policy ever since Franklin Roosevelt and enshrined in inter-American agreements, the OAS and UN charters, and in implementing legislation. As to rule 3 forbidding political interference, U.S. commitments to respect independence, sovereignty, and territorial integrity mean nothing unless they prevent U.S. efforts to determine who rules a particular Latin American country. My three rules simply propose that U.S. officials respect and carry out existing U.S. policies.

Rule 1 will probably not be difficult to implement, at least in the near future. Adhering to rules 2 and 3 will not be easy. Washington's hostility to the guerrilla opposition in El Salvador and the Sandinista regime in Nicaragua involved political interference (El Salvador) and paramilitary actions in neighboring Honduras. Feeling threatened, the Reagan administration has taken a belligerent position toward Nicaragua, and its military assistance to the incumbents in El Salvador guarantees the vulnerability of the Left to Soviet blandishments in both countries.

My three rules may seem negative to some readers, but the most constructive step in U.S. policy would be to eliminate errors of commission. In the past, U.S. policies designed to meet inevitable problems have too often made matters worse. The original problem remained and was further complicated by U.S. responses. What is needed is a simple, workable, long-term framework which these rules are designed to provide. Within that framework policymakers can negotiate a variety of mutually beneficial relationships with Latin Americans. Policies for U.S.–Latin American relations generally is appropriate for other studies; my subject here has been Soviet relations with Latin America.

Except for the Cubans and probably now the Sandinistas, most Latin American governments are not pro-Soviet. But they also believe that U.S. armed intervention in the hemisphere is more likely than Soviet intervention—not an unreasonable conclusion given the historical antecedents. For that reason many feel that the ultimate protection against U.S. intervention is countervailing Latin American power. This is not a Utopian prospect because Latin American power need not be equal to U.S. power, only sufficient to prevent intervention. In recent years the Latin American nations have been increasing their bargaining power with the United States, particularly in regional economic organizations. A Latin America that is truly independent of the United States will be most capable of remaining independent of the Soviet Union.

Just as a stronger Western Europe has served U.S. interests well, so too will a stronger Latin America. That strength should be reflected in greater political responsiveness to popular needs and, therefore, in more stable governments and economies capable of resisting extrahemispheric interference. Greater stability also means better trade and investment opportunities for the United States. A stronger Latin America will help prevent the United States from doing what it shouldn't do anyway. And a United States which stands free and clear of domestic strife in the region will best be able to protect and promote its interests.

Appendices

Notes

Index

Appendix 1.
A Note on Sources

Acknowledging one's debt to other scholars is an intimidating business, and one is tempted not to do it at all for fear of omitting a significant name. Many works are cited in the notes, but my debt to the works of the following authors was incurred over a period of years: Luis E. Aguilar, Robert J. Alexander, Philip Bonsal, Stephen Clissold, Jorge Domínguez, Boris Goldenberg, Edward Gonzalez, Bruce Jackson, William Leogrande, Jacques Lévesque, Carmelo Mesa-Lago, William E. Ratliff, David Ronfeldt, A. I. Sizonenko, Wayne S. Smith, Andrés Suárez, Lawrence H. Theriot, and Blanca Torres Ramirez. I thank them and hope for the understanding of those mistakenly omitted.

In order to comply with the terms of the grant from the National Council for Soviet and East European Research, which financed most of my research, I prepared and copywrited in 1980 a mimeographed study entitled "Soviet Relations with Latin America in the 1970's." It contains the core of chapters 2, 3, and 4 of this work and was widely distributed to specialists at that time.

The literature on Soviet relations with Latin America and the Communist parties is vast; my purpose here is to provide only a short introduction, enough to get analysts started.

Studies are listed mainly according to language. To keep the list manageable, I have excluded almost all works on individual Communist parties and on bilateral diplomatic relations. An exception is made for Soviet-Cuban relations where the studies in various languages are grouped together.

Herbert S. Dinerstein's "Soviet Policy in Latin America," a pathbreaking article, was published in the *American Political Science Review*, March 1967. A fundamental volume is Stephen Clissold's collection of documents and a long authoritative introduction entitled *Soviet Relations with Latin America 1918–1968, a Documentary Survey* (London, 1970). Other early studies include T. S. Cheston and B. Loeffke, *Aspects of Soviet Policy Toward Latin America* (New York, 1974); Roger Hamburg, *The Soviet Union and Latin America, 1953–1963* (Ann Arbor, Mich.: University Microfilms, 1965); James D. Theberge, *The Soviet Presence in Latin America* (New York, 1974) and *Russia in the Caribbean* (Washington, D.C., 1973); Leon Gouré and Morris Rothenberg, *Soviet Penetration of Latin America* (Miami, 1975); and J. Gregory Oswald and Anthony J. Strover, eds., *The Soviet Union and Latin America* (New York, 1974). For an earlier period see Russell H. Bartley, *Imperial Russia and the Struggle for Latin American Independence, 1808–1828* (Austin, 1978). Raymond Duncan, Roger Kanet, and Alvin Rubinstein have included Latin America in their books on Soviet policies toward the developing countries.

The Yearbook on International Communist Affairs of the Hoover Institution, ed. Richard F. Staar et al., is fundamental for following the local Communist parties. Robert J. Alexander, *Communism in Latin America* (New Brunswick, 1957) was a base line study in English, as were Luis E. Aguilar, *Marxism in Latin America* (Philadelphia, 1978), and D. Bruce Jackson, *Castro, the Kremlin, and Communism in Latin America* (Baltimore, 1969). William E. Ratliff, *Castroism and Communism in Latin America 1959–1976* (Washington, DC., 1976) is also very useful. Other early studies include Rollie Poppino, *International Communism in Latin America, 1917–1963* (New York, 1964), and Harry H. Ransom, *The Communist Tide in Latin America* (Austin, 1972). Studies of Communist parties in individual countries are too numerous to mention here. Robert Leiken's *Soviet Strategy in Latin America,* Washington Papers 93 (Washington, D.C., 1982), was published just as this study was going to press.

Fundamental to the study of Soviet sources on Latin America is the bibliographic tool, *Latinskaia Amerika v sovetskoi pechati.* The first volume, published in 1964, covers the period 1946–1962. The Institute of Latin America publishes a volume every two years, covering books and periodical literature listed topically and by country. The volume for 1976–1978 contained over eleven hundred entries. The two-volume Soviet encyclopedia *Latinskaia Amerika,* published in 1979 and 1982 is a handy quick reference. The Soviet Foreign trade annual *Vneshniaia*

Torgovlia SSR provides trade statistics and has statistical updates published as supplements to the monthly *Vneshniaia Torgovlia*. The richest single source of Soviet scholarship on the area is the monthly journal *Latinskaia Amerika*, published in Russian and Spanish editions, which contains scholarly articles, articles on literature and art, and policy studies. Historical studies also appear in *Novaia i noveishaia istoria*. A. I. Sizonenko is the principal specialist on Soviet diplomatic relations with Latin America; his works include studies such as *Ocherki istorii sovetsko-latinamerikanskikh otnoshenii* (Moscow, 1971) and *Sovetskii Soiuz i Latinskaia Amerika segodnia* (Moscow, 1978). Bilateral relations are discussed in the commemorative series, SSSR-Argentina, SSSR-Brasil, and SSSR-Meksika. Economic relations are described in works edited by V. V. Volskii and L. L. Klochkovskii, including *Strany SEV i Latinskaia Amerika* (Moscow, 1976).

The best sources on the Communist parties are the journals *Kommunist, Rabochii class i sovremennyi mir*, and *Latinskaia Amerika*. The minutes of the Soviet party congresses and of meetings of Communist and workers' parties at global and regional levels are essential. Textbooks of the Party schools, such as *Istoriia mezhdunarodnogo rabochego i natsional' no-osvoboditel' nogo dvizheniia*, Vol. IV (Moscow, 1978) give helpful summaries. A recent authoritative survey is M. F. Kudachkin, ed., *Velikii Oktiabr' i kommunisticheskii partii Latinskoi Ameriki* (Moscow, 1978). See also B. I. Koval', S. I. Semenov, and A. F. Shul'govskii, *Revoliutsionnye protsesy v Latinskoi Amerike* (Moscow, 1974).

Many of the works in Spanish and Portuguese deal with Soviet relations with, or with the Communist party in, a particular Latin American country, subjects not covered here except for Cuba. Carlos Muñiz Ortega published *URSS y América Latina* in Lima in 1968. Among the early books was *The Yenan Way* by Eudocio Ravines, published in both Spanish and English, and Pedro de Basaldua, *La Garra Comunista en América Latina* (Buenos Aires, 1962). See also Juan A. Ortega y Medina, *Historiográfica Soviética Iberoamericanista*, 1945–1960 (Mexico, 1961).

Sources in German include an exhaustive study of Communist activities in Latin America by Boris Goldenberg, *Komunismus in Latein*

Amerika (Stuttgart, 1971). A comprehensive short survey of Soviet policy is Wolfgang Berner, *Die Sowjetische Lateinamerika Politik 1919–1973* (Cologne, 1973).

A rich literature exists on Cuba and Soviet-Cuban relations and I will list only a few titles here: Andrés Suárez, *Cuba: Castroism and Communism, 1959–1966* (Cambridge, Mass., 1967); Jacques Lévesque, *L'URSS et la revolution Cubaine* (Montreal, 1976), published in English as *The USSR and the Cuban Revolution: Soviet Ideological and Strategic Perspectives, 1959–77*, trans. Deanna Drendel Leboeuf (New York, 1978); Blanca Torres Ramirez, *Las Relaciones Cubano-Soviéticas, 1959–1968* (Mexico, 1971); and Angel García and Piotr Mironchuk, *Esbozo Histórico de las relaciones entre Cuba-Rusia Cuba-URSS* (Havana, 1976). The unclassified studies of the Central Intelligence Agency and of Lawrence Theriot of the U.S. Commerce Department on the Cuban economy are important to an understanding of Soviet trade and aid. See also my two chapters in Cole Blasier and Carmelo Mesa-Lago, eds., *Cuba in the World* (Pittsburgh, 1979); Robert K. Furtak, *Kuba und der Weltkomunismus* (Cologne, 1967); and the works of Lynn Darrell Bender on U.S.-Cuban relations.

For Soviet sources see L. Iu. Sleskin, *Istoriia kubinskoi respubliki* (Moscow, 1966); A. D. Bekarevich and N. M. Kukharev, *Sovetskii soiuz i Kuba, ekonomicheskoe sotrudnichestvo* (Moscow, 1973); A. D. Bekarevich, ed., *Rossiisko-Kubinskie i Sovetsko-Kubinskie sviazi XVIII–XX vekov* (Moscow, 1975); A. D. Bekarevich and V. V. Volskii, eds., *Velikii Oktiabr' i kubinskinskaia revoliutsiia* (Moscow, 1977); and I. D. Statsenko et al., *Muzhestvo i bratstvo* (Moscow, 1982).

Appendix 2.
The Soviet Latin Americanists

The Soviet Union has established what has become the largest, and probably the most prolific, research center devoted exclusively to Latin America. Soviet progress has been especially dramatic because the USSR was so weak in this field in 1961, when the Institute of Latin America was established in Moscow. The Institute now has one hundred full-time researchers and supports the activities of many other Latin Americanists there and in other Soviet cities. It also has maintained ties with new Latin Americanist groups in Eastern Europe, particularly in East Germany and Poland.

Soviet ambitions in Latin American studies have been apparent now for nearly a decade, but Soviet work has failed to attract much attention in the United States, partly because few western Latin Americanists know Russian and they have been understandably skeptical about access to Soviet scholars and sources. My training as a Soviet specialist at the Russian Institute, Columbia University, and nine years as a career foreign service officer working in and observing Eastern Europe and the USSR caused me to share this skepticism. Then, in 1975, Allen Kassof, the director of the International Research and Exchanges Board (IREX), told me that serious research in the USSR on contemporary problems, though still difficult, was possible. As a result, I paid a brief visit to Moscow that summer, which revived the fascination Russia has always held for me but provided little evidence to support Kassof's view. However, my acquaintance with the leaders of the Institute of Latin America became more firmly established, and we arranged later to have the Institute send representatives to the national meetings of the Latin American Studies Association (LASA) in Atlanta in 1976 and in Houston in 1977.

A year later I received an IREX grant for senior scholars, under an agreement between the American Council of Learned Societies and the USSR Academy of Sciences, which provided for four months of research in Moscow, the first such grant for work at the Institute of Latin America. As late as Christmas 1978, when I left for Moscow, I feared that access to Soviet sources might be denied. My experience in the USSR was a pleasant surprise: I met many Soviet scholars and officials and was able to consult many Soviet books, articles, and other published works on Latin America.

• The Institute of Latin America

Prior to the Cuban Revolution, which gave the decisive impetus to the formal establishment of Latin American studies in the Soviet Union (just as it did to the expansion of such studies in the United States), there were some Soviet Latin Americanists scattered about the country, particularly at the Institute of Universal History and the Institute of World Economy and International Relations in Moscow. When Anastas Mikoyan, the first high Soviet official to visit Cuba, returned home from his trip to the Americas in 1960, he recommended the foundation of an institute for the study of Latin America. In the spring of 1961 the Presidium of the Academy of Sciences authorized the establishment of the Institute of Latin America as part of its Social Science Department. Sergei Sergeyevich Mikhailov transferred from the Soviet Foreign Service to become its first director. After four years at the Institute he was appointed ambassador to Brazil and was succeeded by the current director, Viktor Vaslavovich Vol'skii, then chairman of the Department of Geography at Moscow State University. A doctor of economic sciences, he is best known as a scholar for his book, *Latin America: Oil and Independence*. M. I. Lazarev, a legal specialist, was recently named deputy director.

The Institute of Latin America, referred to here as the Institute, is located on Bolshaia Ordynka Street, a main artery leading to Red Square. It is just a fifteen minute walk to the Kremlin, and two subway stations are conveniently nearby. The offices are located in a yellow and white nineteenth-century Greek Revival mansion, once the home of a rich merchant. Cars and pedestrians enter the courtyard through wrought iron gates. Several older women, who request credentials from strangers, are usually in attendance inside the main entrance. The foyer is decorated with idealized figures of American Indians, other Latin Americans, and what appears to be their oppressors, including the U.S. Army. The library of the Institute has about 54,000 books and journals. Catalogs in the Russian and Latin alphabets contain subject as well as author and title cards. The reading room proper houses a collection of reference works and most relevant Soviet and foreign periodicals. The collection on Soviet relations with Latin America and on the Communist parties for the period after 1961, when the Institute was founded, is the best I have used anywhere. Working conditions in the reading room are comfortable; the librarians are alert, attentive, and helpful. Although attached to the Institute of Latin America, the library is actually a branch of the Institute of Scientific Information in the Social Sciences (INION).

Like the director, department and several sector heads have private offices. Staff researchers are usually grouped together, one sector to a room, with perhaps as many as eight desks crowded into small space. Such crowding is not as serious as it may seem because researchers do much of their work at home or in Moscow's libraries. More office space will become available in the next few years when the Institute takes over an adjoining building.

Most of the Institute's staff of one hundred full-time researchers have advanced degrees in historical or economic sciences. The *candidat* degree is roughly equivalent to the American Ph.D., the doctor's degree representing a higher level of achievement. Nine have doctor's degrees, five in historical sciences, four in economic sciences. About seventy of the remainder have candidat degrees. Researchers who work on politics, international relations, or social topics usually have degrees in historical sciences. The staff of the Institute, whose academic work is drawn up as a part of the Five Year Plans, are divided among three departments: country studies and international relations; sociopolitical problems; and economics.

Anotolii Nikolayevich Glinkin heads the department for country studies and international relations. A doctor of historical sciences, Glinkin wrote his candidat's and doctor's dissertations on U.S. imperialist expansion in Brazil (1945–52) and on Brazilian history (1939–61). He has published on other themes, such as Latin America and UNESCO, in whose Paris office he worked for four years, and he was an exchange scholar at Columbia University for six months several years ago. The country sectors include Cuba, under the direction of A. D. Bekarevich, an economist. This group has probably published more scholarly work on Cuba than any other group in the USSR. Other sectors work on the Andean countries, the La Plata Basin and Brazil, and Meso-America. Much of the ethnographic work is under the direction of Iu. A. Zubritskii, a Quechua specialist, and leader of the Andean sector. Multidisciplinary surveys have been published on most of the leading Latin American countries. Soviet relations with Latin America also are in this department, A. I. Sizonenko is the responsible specialist and one of the Institute's most prolific scholars.

Anatolii Fedorovich Shul'govskii heads the department for research on sociopolitical questions. A doctor of historical sciences, he is another prolific writer specializing in Marxist-Leninist theory as it relates to Latin America. Sectors in his department deal with general social problems, the Communist and worker movements, ideology, and culture. This department's books have been about such subjects as the revolutionary process in Latin America, national liberation movements, the ruling classes, agrarian questions, the role of the army, political parties, and the church. Lev Levovich Klochkovskii, a doctor in economic sciences, heads up the Institute's economic work. At one time he worked at the research institute of the Ministry of Foreign Trade specializing on Asia. His department has sectors dealing with general economic relations, Soviet–Latin American economic relations, territorial and regional problems, and geography. Among the department's recent projects is a study of Comecon economic relations with Latin America to which Latin Americanists from various Comecon countries contributed.

Between 1961 and 1978, scholars associated with the Institute have published more than two hundred books and countless articles, reports, conference papers, and so forth. Many of the most important and authoritative books appear under the imprint of Nauka, the publisher of the Soviet Academy of Sciences. The Institute itself publishes, usually in inexpensive and limited editions, short specialized studies and reports which are useful to foreign scholars. These are sold from a small office in the wing directly across the court from the library. However, the work of the Institute staff receives its widest and most frequent diffusion in the

Institute's journal, *Latinskaia Amerika,* founded in 1969. The offices of the journal used to be located at the Institute; now they have moved to more comfortable and freshly decorated quarters off Kropotkinskaia Street.

Although attached to the Institute and depending heavily on its scholars to fill its pages, the journal is also expected to reflect the work of, and be responsible to, a larger scholarly community, since the Institute is part of the economics section of the social science department of the Soviet Academy of Sciences. With other scholarly journals, *Latinskaia Amerika* reports through the Academy's publications' hierarchy, thereby gaining latitude vis-à-vis the Institute.

Some of the more innovative and unconventional Latin Americanists work outside the Institute, since, by Soviet standards, the leaders of the Institute tend to hold predominantly orthodox and conservative views. Opposing opinion with the Institute, especially among the junior staff, tends to be muted. Thus, *Latinskaia Amerika* provides a forum for the spectrum of scholarship approved by Soviet authorities, although it is livelier, more colorful, and more innovative than most other Soviet scholarly journals. Emphasis is on contemporary economic and sociopolitical topics; there are also articles on historical and cultural themes, and the journal reproduces Latin American art in full color and frequently publishes photographs of authors. Round-table discussions among Soviet Latin Americanists are a standard feature (I had the unique opportunity to contribute several pages of commentary to one such round table on President Carter's Latin American policy, which was carried in number 4 [1979]). Interviews with leading Latin American political and intellectual leaders, most particularly from the Communist parties and the labor movement, are also frequent features. The editor of *Latinskaia Amerika* is Sergo Anastasovich Mikoyan. The journal has a circulation of about eight thousand, and *América Latina,* the Spanish edition, about fifteen thousand. Both editions began monthly publication in 1980.

The Institute has no "undergraduate" students; the training of Soviet Latin Americanists at the undergraduate level takes place at the universities—Moscow State and Leningrad State are the main feeder institutions, but other universities participate too. The Institute's primary mission is research, but it does train students in historical and economic sciences for the candidat and doctoral degrees. In 1979, the Institute had eighteen graduate students *(aspiranti)*, the majority from Moscow State University. Aspiranti normally train at the Institute for three years under renewable annual stipends of 100 rubles a month from the Ministry of Higher Education, which, together with a Committee of the Council of Ministers, supervises the awarding of advanced degrees. Soviet aspiranti usually have completed five years of university preparation and must pass a series of qualifying oral examinations in special fields. One is in foreign languages; most prepare in Spanish, some in English, and a very few in Portuguese, often in addition to Spanish. Another qualifying examination is in Marxist philosophy, a requirement common to study for all advanced degrees. Finally, aspiranti must pass an oral examination in their special field, such as the history of the international relations of Latin America. While they can take courses at other universities or institutes in preparation for that and other examinations, the Institute does not offer formal "courses" itself. Instead, members of the staff offer seminars, attended by clusters of graduate students, on themes directly related to such special fields.

The aspiranti spend most of their time doing research for and writing their dissertations, which are defended formally in oral examinations. There is also an unwritten rule that they publish the equivalent of about three articles before the award of the degree, which are apt to be drawn from the dissertation. Abstracts are published individually and widely distributed, and the dissertations themselves are ordinarily available to be read at the home institution. Aspiranti are assigned to advisors at the Institute whose interests correspond to the students' dissertation topics. The aspiranti are not responsible for helping complete the Institute's obligations under the Five Year Plan, but they do participate in the regular activities of their particular sector: they attend meetings and seminars, contribute to discussion, and the staff makes use of their findings. From time to time, the Institute publishes collections of students' work on particular themes. Many of the aspiranti have remained at the Institute as full-time researchers *(sotrudniki)* after completing their three-year training period.

The Doctor's degree is not ordinarily achieved until mid-career, late thirties or older. Successful candidates for this degree have at least the equivalent of one book beyond the candidat's degree; the criteria relate, not surprisingly, more to the quality of the scholar's work and his professional stature.

• Other Soviet Latin Americanists

Many of the first Soviet Latin Americanists were on the staff of the Institute of Universal History in Moscow, which still has one of the largest contingents outside the Institute of Latin America. The group of about ten specialists there, under the leadership of N. M. Lavrov, confines itself mainly to the pre-1945 period. The most influential institute in contemporary international relations is the Institute of World Economy and International Relations (from which came many of the original staff of the Institute of Latin America); Latin Americanists there include K. L. Maidanik and I. N. Zorina. The staff of the Institute of the International Workers' Movement, which deals with labor and political parties, includes Boris Iosifovich Koval', and I. V. Danilevich, daughter of the pioneering Soviet Latin Americanist, M. V. Danilevich; its yearbook frequently carries chapters on Latin America. The Institute of Economics of the World Socialist System and the Institute of the U.S.A. and Canada have only recently begun to build up their expertise on Latin America. The former studies the Comecon countries and their relations with one another. Although it has several trained Latin Americanists and publishes works on Cuba, the main center of Cuban studies is still the Institute of Latin America. The Institute of the U.S.A. has added young Latin Americanists to its staff to interpret U.S. policy toward the region. Other Soviet institutions with several Latin American specialists are the institutes for geography, ethnology, and literature and the arts.

The universities, and particularly those outside Moscow, tend to offer more courses in literature, history, geography, and anthropology than in economics and politics, which depend more on access to current sources. Most Soviet training in economics is technical, without an area focus, and training in government and politics often has a legal or administrative orientation, or is part of Marxist-Leninist indoctrination. As a result, undergraduate students may never take broad introductory courses on Latin American politics or economics of the sort now common in the

United States and the United Kingdom. Part of the explanation also lies in the Soviet and European organization and philosophy of higher education as mainly professional in character; for instance, Patrice Lumumba University has over a thousand Latin American students, almost all in programs of professional study. Cities in other republics with nascent programs in Latin American studies include Minsk, Kishinev, and Kiev. Latin American specialists from other Soviet cities come to Moscow for brief periods of research.

Several of the most influential Soviet Latin Americanists are not employed directly by the Institute of Latin America. No doubt the most politically powerful is Mikhail Fedorovich Kudachkin, the chief of the Latin American section of the Central Committee of the Communist Party of the Soviet Union. Kudachkin heads a staff of about thirty professionals concerned mainly with Soviet party relations with the Communist parties of Latin America and general oversight of Soviet policies toward the area. Kudachkin, who appears to have minimal contact with representatives of the capitalist West in Moscow, recently edited an authoritative, discursive study of the contemporary history, organization, and policies of the Latin American Communist parties.

K. A. Khachaturov, who has published extensively on U.S. propaganda operations in Latin America, is deputy director of the Soviet press agency, *Novosti,* the major agency for foreign propaganda. Iosif R. Grigulevich of the Institute of Ethnography was recently elected as a corresponding member of the Soviet Academy of Sciences, one of the few Latin Americanists ever to be so honored. Great prestige is attached to such election as well as extra compensation; 500 rubles a month for full members and 300 rubles for corresponding members. Since the vast majority of Academy members are from the natural sciences and the remaining seats for the social sciences and humanities are few, prospects for additional memberships for Latin Americanists are not promising. Grigulevich has written on indigenous populations in Latin America and, under his pen name, I. R. Lavretskii, has published popular biographies of many Latin American heroes from Bolívar to Ché Guevara. He is also the editor of the Academy's Spanish-language journal, *Ciencias Sociales.* Another of the Academy's corresponding members is Georgii

Vladimirovich Stepanov, director of the Institute of Linguistics and author of a book about the Spanish language in Latin America.

• Foreign Ties

The Institute of Latin America has also been active in organizing conferences and research projects with Latin Americanists from other socialist countries. Formal gatherings of Latin Americanists from socialist countries usually take place at least once a year. Among the principal collaborators are the Latin American section of the Wilhelm Pieck University, Rostock, the German Democratic Republic; the Latin American section of the Institute of History of the Polish Academy of Sciences, Warsaw; and the Institute of World Economies of the Hungarian Academy of Science, Budapest. The Czechs often participate, and occasionally the Rumanians; Bulgaria has been the least active of the European socialist countries. The Institute of Latin America has developed close ties with Cuban specialists through the Cuban Academy of Sciences. The European socialist countries emphasize their particular strengths: the Poles, history and anthropology; the East Germans, revolutionary movements and literature; the Hungarians, economics. The Comecon Latin Americanists recently published a book on their economic relations with Latin America (mentioned above), and a book on their political relations was published in 1979.

Leaders of Latin American Communist parties routinely visit the Institute during their periodic stays in Moscow and give lectures to the staff; leading Latin American intellectuals and artists also visit the Institute and contribute articles or give interviews to *Latinskaia Amerika;* and students from Latin America frequently work at the library. There were no Latin American scholars (other than Cubans and students) in residence at the Institute during my stay. Latin Americanists from Western countries occasionally come to the Institute, but these visits have a largely formal and social character. Contacts between U.S. and Soviet Latin Americanists have not been extensive. Since 1968 several Latin Americanists from each country, usually academic administrators, have made brief visits to the other's country, devoted primarily to getting acquainted, establishing professional ties, and participating in conferences, such as the national meetings of LASA or international congresses of historians or geographers; few scholars have engaged in field research in the other's country. Russell H. Bartley, a historian from the University of Wisconsin-Milwaukee and the first U.S. Latin Americanist to conduct fieldwork in the USSR, was in Moscow during the academic year 1967–68. To my knowledge, the only Soviet Latin Americanists to complete research assignments in the United States are A. N. Glinkin and E. E. Litavrina. As far as I know, neither U.S. nor Soviet students in Latin American studies have completed a term or more of graduate work in the country of the other.

The Institute's exchanges of persons and publications are managed by the Department for International Liaison. Its head is A. D. Maevskii, a former Soviet government official who served in Latin America; his deputy is A. N. Borovkov, whose dissertation for the candidat's degree dealt with Bolivia's contemporary foreign relations. The department receives foreign visitors and helps selected visitors with personal travel, interviews, and other arrangements that do not fall within the scope of the Soviet tourist agency, Intourist. Such matters in the Soviet Union are far more complicated and time consuming than in the United States, or so they seem to foreign visitors. The rules and procedures tend to be detailed and inflexible, causing a variety of complications not experienced in the West. They impose a heavy burden on Maevskii's department, which ordinarily does its best to satisfy the visitor within the existing norms. Its services, often welcome and sometimes indispensable, obviously also help insure close supervision and control over visitors.

One of the most sensitive aspects are interviews between foreign visitors and Soviet scholars and officials. The latter ordinarily make available data that is generally understood to be suitable for release and give interpretations of developments that are in accord with party and government policies. Well-informed foreigners soon learn the rules and can predict Soviet responses; most Soviet scholars and officials, but significantly not all, follow those rules. Established controls over foreigners' appointments and interview situations reenforce existing Soviet procedures governing the transmission of information and opinion. Some foreigners hastily conclude that this restraint applies only to Western visitors. However, Soviet specialists are believed to be only somewhat less restrained with visitors from other socialist countries. Even with respect to their own colleagues, especially in public situations, Soviet specialists are more cautious in expressing themselves than most of their counterparts in the West. One suspects that control over information are more a matter of domestic than of foreign policy.

Soviet Latin Americanists' ties with their counterparts abroad are limited. Not surprisingly, contacts with scholars from the socialist countries are most frequent, but even these are probably more reserved and formal than in the West. Soviet acquaintance with scholars in the West is limited mainly to that of a few senior men who have been authorized to travel abroad in the past. Soviet Latin Americanists are hungry for books and contacts with the West but many seem reluctant to initiate contact or to press on with contacts once made. Senior staff of the Institute are frequently invited to receptions at Latin American embassies, and, although Latin American diplomats usually are warmly welcomed at the Institute, personal contacts are rather formal and limited. This pattern is not unusual and corresponds to that of Soviet contacts with foreign embassies generally; there may be slightly more personal contact with the large staff of the Cuban embassy.

Trips to Latin America, and even more to Western Europe and the United States, are dreams of many Soviet researchers. Such trips last usually from two to four weeks so the objectives are as much personal as professional, serving as an exhilarating break with the daily routine.

• Fieldwork

A glaring handicap of Soviet scholarship related to Latin America is insufficient field experience in the area, outside of Cuba. Graduate students rarely have an opportunity to visit the area before the completion of their dissertations, much less engage in sustained field research. Those who have shown exceptional scholarly promise, or tactical cleverness, are able to arrange short trips as tourists, interpreters, delegates, and the like. Few senior men have been able to complete field investigations of an academic year or more. The Institute's academic administrators make frequent trips to the area, but these are usually limited to a few weeks and are largely of an administrative character. Cuba constitutes a happy exception in that there are institutional opportunities for field experience at almost all levels; Mexico and Peru are the two other countries to which trips are easiest to arrange. When prospects for visits to the area come up in conversation with some researchers, they exhibit a depressing pessimism and resignation, a personal version of "geographic fatalism."

Shortage of hard currency is frequently, and correctly, cited as a deterrent to fieldwork. The Soviet authorities could allocate the necessary foreign exchange but do not assign the area a high priority. The fact that Aeroflot, which has had weekly service to Mexico City and Lima and daily service to Havana, can provide space payable in rubles greatly facilitates travel. Such flights are vital to the maintenance and expansion of Soviet scholarly relations with the area. Foreign exchange to cover expenses in Latin American countries must also be raised; more Soviet scholars are dependent on host country institutions to pick up these expenses, in exchange for which they can usually arrange to cover reciprocal expenses in the USSR. But scholars in Latin America have difficulty raising locally funds for visitors from Europe and the United States, much less the Soviet Union. As a result, Soviet Latin Americanists face an uphill struggle in building exchange relationships in the area. Soviet scholars sometimes also cite political discrimination: visas are refused or, more likely, delayed many months. Latin Americans may prefer not to be closely associated with Soviet exchanges. Certain governments, such as the traditional military dictatorships, may be hostile. Two countries with military regimes where trade has been relatively large, Brazil and Argentina, are frequently charged with spotty and sporadic discrimination. Foreign currency problems and Latin American disinterest are enough in themselves to minimize fieldwork opportunities. But the Soviets may not want to expand such exchanges too rapidly for domestic political reasons. Soviet society is so effectively insulated and protected from influences from the outside world that the authorities may not want a sudden increase in the number of Soviet scholars in foreign areas, including Latin America.

Insufficient field experience has had its impact on the Soviet scholars' concept of research: most seem to view it as something that takes place exclusively in a library. The younger people work with what they find there (which, incidentally, is considerable), and a few of the resourceful will request missing materials, too. Many do not seem to be motivated to seek the reports and documents, that is, the memoranda, government publications, business reports, and other public and private publications, which can be so illuminating. One reason may be that such materials are so hard to come by in the USSR that they are not in the habit of using them, much less requesting them from abroad. The younger scholars, particularly, may not be fully aware of, or are pessimistic about, the possibilities for capitalizing on interviews and informal personal contacts. Even if opportunities for such contact in Latin America are limited or absent, some opportunities do exist in Moscow (few Soviet scholars approached me for data or ideas about their research; most contacts were initiated by me). They also do not seem to have much contact for specific research purposes with the Latin Americans who come to Moscow.

• Professional Life

Most scholars at the Institute of Latin America are full-time researchers. A few who love teaching, or want a following of younger scholars, teach at local universities in their "spare" time. For this they receive extra pay (as much as 200 rubles a month) and an academic title, the latter carrying prestige. Teaching in addition to research responsibilities, however, imposes a strain that many scholars prefer to avoid.

The entire staff is required to be at the Institute on Wednesdays, when many administrative meetings and lectures take place. Researchers must also be present on a second day each week, with different departments coming in on different days. Much of the socializing and casual plotting, so common to scholars everywhere, takes place in a low-ceilinged, white-tiled cafeteria in the basement. On week days, the concessionaire, a sturdy, no-nonsense matron, dispenses soups, meats, cheese, cabbage, sour cream, tea, and other beverages to a chatty queue of staff members. Fridays she sells sausage and fowl to take home to families for the weekend. During the three days of the week the staff are not required to be at the Institute, they work at home or in various libraries in the city; among the most popular is the Institute of Scientific Information in the Social Sciences, whose glass and steel structure is a showplace located in the rapidly developing southwest section of Moscow; other collections used by the staff are the Lenin Library and the Library for Foreign Literature.

Salaries at the Institute vary from 100 rubles a month for graduate students to 600 rubles for the director. Scholars' other earned income is from sources similar to that of their counterparts in the West. Payment for articles and books is made by the *list* (a unit of printed text, equivalent to about twenty-four legal-size pages typed double spaced); as a result, there is no economic incentive to keep articles short, a partial explanation why so many Soviet articles are wordy. Royalties range from one hundred or more rubles for articles to several thousand rubles for books, the latter mainly for books in mass circulation, rare in the Latin American field. Scholars also take commissions for various kinds of propaganda work, such as publications distributed abroad or radio broadcasts. Selected books have been translated into Spanish and distributed in Latin America by the Soviet publishing house, Editorial Progreso.

Some members of the Institute staff are also active in binational friendship societies whose Soviet headquarters are located only a few minutes by subway from the Institute. These societies appear to serve primarily public relations and social purposes.

Vacations are more generous for the scholarly professions than in government and industry. Junior scholars have under a month and senior scholars, for example, doctors of sciences, approaching two months vacation annually. Some of the latter have cars, possibly a dacha. The director of the Institute is assigned a car and driver.

The Scholar's Club (Dom Uchenii) is among the most prestigous of the clubs for intellectuals. The Writers' Club and the Journalists' Club are also frequented by employees of the Academy of Sciences. Most of these Clubs emphasize their dining and bar facilities. Some have athletic or other recreational facilities and arrange programs for families. Membership in such clubs may not prove easy to obtain, requiring letters of recommendation and screening through a committee.

All members of the Institute staff, as far as I could determine, are Soviet citizens. There are no permanent staff who are Latin Americans, as is frequently the case in U.S. universities and research centers. There were two Cuban researchers in residence during my stay, but long visits of Latin American scholars from other countries are rare. Usually, there are several Latin American graduate students in residence, and Latin American students from local universities frequently use the Institute's library and participate in Institute activities.

The collegial body ruling the Institute is the Scholars' Council (Uchenii Soviet). I attended one meeting of the Council, which reminded me of the meetings of professional societies in the United States. While there were comments and suggestions from the floor, all the important business appeared to have been prepared and decided earlier, and the members present quietly ratified committee and administrative action.

The Institute has its own Communist party and Komsomol (Youth) committees; their meetings appear devoted primarily to political education and follow-up on party directives. Lectures and discussions elucidate the decisions of higher party bodies, examine prominent political documents, such as Brezhnev's autobiography, and celebrate anniversaries important in party life. The leadership of the party committee appears to correspond to the leadership of the Institute: the higher administrative posts in the Institute are occupied by party members; membership may be desirable but not necessarily essential for scholarly advancement.

Difficult to verify is the question whether, on balance, the private life of Soviet scholars cuts more or less deeply into professional time than in the United States. On the one hand, shopping for food and other consumer items is far more time consuming and frustrating than in the West. Paperwork and red tape seems everywhere more burdensome, if such could be possible. More Soviet scholars are members of families where both husband and wife work. (The burden on the Soviet wife is proportionately greater than in the United States, since Soviet husbands seem to take on fewer family chores.)

On the other hand, other housekeeping responsibilities are less time consuming. Small apartments require less care, maintenance is theoretically and sometimes actually provided by the building staff, and there are no lawn chores. ("Voluntary" labor is not taken very seriously.) The great majority do not have automobiles, nor the burden of keeping them operational. Families are slightly smaller, frequently only one child or less. The strain of getting children into the "right" university or institute (like the Institute of International Relations, Moscow) can be great, but the state pays most education bills. As a result, Soviet scholars seem more carefree in these respects. This is not to say that Soviet scholars would refuse the houses, gardens, cars, and their accompanying cares that are part of academic life in many Western countries.

• Scholarly Climate and Contributions

A place of intellectual discovery and excitement is rare enough in the West, and I did not expect that the Institute of Latin America would be one. The announcements, posters, and other visible signs confirmed my expectations and the discipline that tends to ensure politically approved behavior and findings. Some critics might term the atmosphere routinized and stale, but such a characterization seems harsh. My impressions of the Institute's intellectual climate, always such a subjective matter anyway, were of diligence and competence. There is evidence of tension and a respect for time, which often characterize purposeful institutions. The Institute also has its fair share of critics, particularly among the younger, energetic, and influential groups in the Academy of Sciences. Soviet Latin Americanists appear to be suffering from the same occupational hazards as their colleagues abroad, who get typecast as professionally parochial, committed as they are to an isolated and politically neglected area of the world.

The Soviet Latin Americanists of my acquaintance are dedicated to the study of the region, have a good reading knowledge of one of its languages (ordinarily Spanish), and seem broadly knowledgeable about the literature on the region. In general, they seem better informed about U.S. work on Latin America than U.S. scholars are about European work on the area. Assigning each researcher to a relatively narrowly defined topic for sustained investigation with limited or no teaching responsibilities permits greater specialization. Not surprisingly, their work, which is supposed to meet Soviet ideological and policy criteria, often seems stereotyped; such scholars are usually more interesting to talk to than to read.

Two decades ago, Soviet studies of Latin America were weaker and more rudimentary than in any other advanced industrialized society, except possibly Japan. Today, the Soviet Union has the largest centrally planned research program on the area in the world. I have listed below from the perspective of an international relations specialist some topics on which I believe the Soviets have made, and are likely to make, impressive contributions toward the advancement of scholarship in the field:

1. Russian and Soviet relations with Latin America: political, economic, and cultural. Russian and Soviet sources are indispensable for research on these topics.

2. Communist, revolutionary, and labor movements. Soviet sources are convenient and desirable for this subject, and indispensable for certain aspects: illegal Communist parties, historical episodes where primary sources have been lost or are inaccessible, and defining interaction between Soviet and Latin American party leaders. Such sources supplement Communist publications on international congresses and the like, which are usually available in western languages.

3. Highly specialized fields with a relatively low ideological, political, or policy content. Talented Soviet scholars may move ahead of their counterparts in the West on certain topics; archaeology, ethnology, and prerevolutionary history may have the greatest promise.

4. Data collection and collation. The Soviet scientific leadership has a great capacity to focus massive resources on sharply defined topics. The Institute of Latin America, for example, routinely assigns a half dozen or more scholars to work full time on a particular theme. As a result, Soviet scholars are able to bring together quickly vast information from widely dispersed sources on topics not always treated systematically in the West.

The Institute has prepared one-volume national studies of broad scope on almost all the important countries in the area, and a large, two-volume encyclopedia on Latin America is in press. Soviet scholars have also edited books that deal comprehensively with the literature and arts of a leading country and handbooks for statistics and political parties. Books on agrarian, religious, educational, and other topics assemble information from around the continent (I have found the book on foreign policy of Latin American countries since 1945 to be a handy reference). Although most Soviet works on Latin America will continue to appear only in Russian, the authors write articles on the same or similar subjects for *América Latina,* and their books are usually reviewed there.

• Public and Policy Impacts

Soviet specialists have had and will continue to have great opportunities to raise the level of public knowledge on Latin America, which has lagged behind many leading western countries. As in other fields, little information about Latin America from outside the Soviet Union is available to the Soviet citizenry. To help educate the public, Soviet Latin Americanists write popular articles and books for schools and institutions of higher learning, the media, and other bureaucracies. The All-Union Society for Knowledge, which popularizes advances in science and the arts, occasionally devotes one of the monthly issues of *Znanie (Knowledge)* to a Latin American topic in a format similar to that of the Headline Series of the Foreign Policy Association. Others who publish books on Latin America for the general public or for rank-and-file party members are Politizdat and Mysl'.

Soviet Latin Americanists exert some of the same kinds of influence on trade and diplomatic officials as do their counterparts in the United States. Soviet scholarship increasingly provides the basis for these officials' formal training about Latin America, a source of useful background and reference information. Except for training stints, however, government officials, there as here, often lack the time or the inclination to pursue such subjects systematically. Soviet scholarly materials on Latin America are also used to prepare the authoritative textbooks used in the schools of the Communist party.

Determining scholars' direct impact on Soviet policy is difficult. Western scholars may play their greatest role in policy decisions, such as it is, through criticism in letters to the editors of influential papers and through popular articles and books. Soviet scholars clearly have no such opportunity, at least after party decisions have been taken. Recently, there have been lively discussions in the pages of *Latinskaia Amerika* about the interpretation of developments *in* Latin America; the authors tend to avoid explicit discussion of Soviet policy, but their interpretations of "realities" have policy implications.

When asked how much impact his work has on policy, a Soviet scholar gives the same wry smile as would his U.S. counterpart. The various Soviet bureaucracies (party, government, scientific) may be even more insulated from one another than those in the United States. Lateral transfers occur more often *from* policy positions *to* the Academy of Sciences than the reverse, and if they take a turn in operations, scholars are more apt to do so in some international organization than in the Soviet diplomatic or commercial service. Thus, such lateral moves as those of Kissinger and Brzezinski, and their counterparts in the Latin American field, like Grunwald or Fishlow, seem rarer than in the United States. The Soviet Foreign Office consults scholars from the Institute of Latin America, but the instances described to me seemed insignificant. The Institute appears to have less political influence than certain other Soviet institutes, like those dealing with the United States or China. The latter two regions are much more important to Soviet interests and, correspondingly, their leaders are better placed in the party and government hierarchies.

• Conclusions

The isolation and insulation of Soviet Latin Americanists from Latin America and from their colleagues in the West is awesome; yet, in their own way and by their own rules, they are working steadily to break out. Soviet authorities have assembled a large, well-trained, and productive group of specialists on Latin America, and a rapidly growing literature on almost all aspects of life in the region is now widely available within the Soviet Union. Research on Soviet–Latin American relations, the Communist parties, and the labor movement, and handbooks for reference on many topics are among the products of Soviet scholarship that will be useful to the few Western scholars who know Russian. As in other fields, Soviet prospects for eventually meeting and surpassing Western scholarship in Latin American studies are probably best on topics farthest removed from politics and policy. The single most important handicap of the Soviet research effort that can ultimately be remedied within the existing Soviet context is insufficient opportunity for scholars and graduate students to have field experience in Latin America.

The Soviet Latin Americanists are doing a constructive job of informing the Soviet public and training Soviet officials, but their direct impact on policy appears slight. For Westerners, the most convenient, up-to-date source on Soviet scholarship in the field is the Spanish language monthly, *América Latina*.

• Note

Research for this article was supported by grants from the Kennan Institute of the Woodrow Wilson International Center for Scholars, the International Research and Exchanges Board, and the National Council for Soviet and East European Research. It is reprinted from *Latin American Research Review* 16 (1981): 107–23, by permission of the editor.

Appendix 3.
Soviet Magazines
and Communist Broadcasts

Soviet Magazines

Published in Portuguese

Tempos Novos
Ciências Sociais
Mulher Soviética
União Soviética

Revista Millitar Soviética
Socialismo: Princípios, Prática,
Perspectivas

Published in Spanish

Novedades de Moscú
El Teatro Soviético
El Siglo XX y la Paz
Comercio Exterior
El Libro y el Arte en la URSS
Cultura y Vida
América Latina
Tiempos Nuevos
Ciencias Sociales

Problemas del Extremo Oriente
La Mujer Soviética
Literatura Soviética
La Unión Soviética
Film Soviético
Revista Militar Soviética
Socialismo: Teoría y Práctica
Deporte en la URSS
Sputnik

Source: *Gazeti i zhurnali SSSR na 1982 god* (Moscow: Mezhdunarodnaia Kniga, 1981).

Communist Broadcasts to Latin America, December 1981
(hours per week)[a]

Language	Country of Origin			
	USSR[b]	Eastern Europe	Cuba	Total[c]
Armenian	7:00	—	—	7:00
Bulgarian	—	7:00	—	7:00
Creole/French	3:30	—	14:00	17:30
German	—	5:15	—	5:15
Hungarian	—	11:00	—	11:00
Guarani/Spanish	3:30	—	7:00	10:30
Portuguese	23:30	45:30	14:00	97:00
Quechua	1:00	—	12:50	13:50
Spanish	66:30	119:00	35:00	269:30
Total	105:00	187:45	47:50	438:35

Source: International Communication Agency of the United States of America, Washington, D.C., Research Memorandum dated 15 August 1982.

[a]Only programs beamed exclusively to Latin America are tabulated here. An additional 428 hours per week of global broadcasts could be heard in Latin America, including 7 hours per week in Spanish and 0 in Portuguese from the USSR, 166 in Spanish and 104 in English from Cuba.

[b]The USSR's broadcasts exclusively to Latin America in December 1982 were the same as in December 1981.

[c]The total figures include weekly broadcasts by Communist China (Portuguese 14, Spanish 35), North Korean (Spanish 38), and Vietnam (Spanish 10).

Appendix 4.
Eastern European Trade with Latin America

Soviet imports from Latin America averaged about 40 percent of the imports of the Council for Mutual Economic Assistance (Comecon) from the area between 1960 and 1978. After the Soviet Union, Poland and East Germany were the major importers. Although relatively low initially, socialist countries' imports of food, beverages, and tobacco rose in 1978 to about 75 percent of total imports from Latin America, far exceeding raw materials and manufactured goods.

Soviet exports to Latin America averaged about 40 percent of the Comecon total in the period 1960–1975, but had dropped by 1975 to about 10 percent. Poland and Czechoslovakia were both selling more to Latin America. Machinery and equipment, plus fuels in some years, accounted for 70 percent or more of Comecon exports to the region.

Because of its extensive aid programs, the Soviet Union has been Cuba's main trade partner, both for exports and imports, volumes being far greater than with other socialist countries.

• Note

The data in this appendix are from *Relaciones Económicas de América Latina con los Paises Miembros del Consejo de Asistencia Mútua Económica* (United Nations, Santiago Chile, 1982). The graphs are on page 14 and 25. For Cuban trade, see Cole Blasier and Carmelo Mesa-Lago, eds., *Cuba in the World* (Pittsburgh, 1979), chapter 9, 11.

Graph 1
Comecon Imports from Latin America, Excluding Cuba
(in percentage shares)

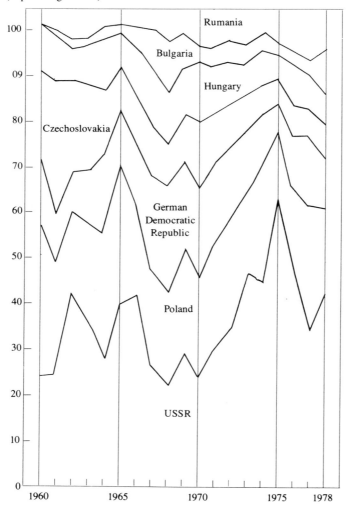

Source: Comisión Económica para América Latina, statistical annex to document E/CEPAL/G.1104.

Graph 2
Comecon Exports to Latin America, Excluding Cuba
(in percentage shares)

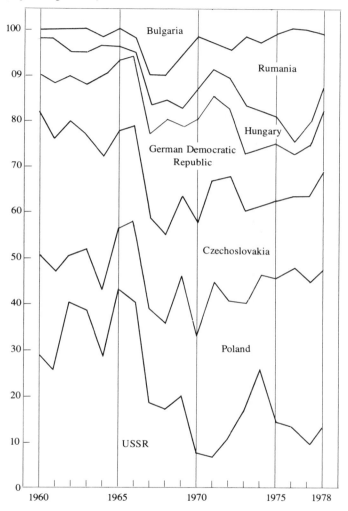

Source: Comisión Económica para América Latina, statistical annex to document E/CEPAL/G.1104.

Notes

• *Chapter I. The New Soviet Presence*

1. *Information Moscow* (Autumn/Winter 1978–1979): 125, 224. The Mexican attaché arrived after this issue went to press.

2. Stewart Cole Blasier, "Foundations of Comintern Policy Towards Latin America, 1919–1924" (Certificate Essay, Russian Institute, Columbia University, 1950).

3. *Latinskaia Amerika* 5 (1977): 128.

• *Chapter II. Building Diplomatic Networks: Political Relations*

1. Stephen Clissold, ed., *Soviet Relations with Latin America, 1918–1968: A Documentary Survey* (London, 1970). See pp. 95, 98, 118, 200, 207, and passim.

2. Interview with Soviet official, Moscow, April 1979. A trade accord was signed in 1980.

3. Robert D. Crassweller, *Trujillo: The Life and Times of a Caribbean Dictator* (New York, 1966), p. 425.

4. John Barron, *KGB: The Secret Work of Soviet Secret Agents* (New York, 1974), chapter 11; James D. Theberge, *The Soviet Presence in Latin America* (New York, 1974), p. 33.

5. See, for example, A. I. Sizonenko, *V strane atstekskogo orla: Pervye sovetskie polpredy v Meksike* (Moscow, 1969); also, his *Stanovlenye otnoshenii SSSR co stranami latinskoi ameriki* (Moscow, 1981).

6. *Vneshniaia torgovlia SSSR statisticheskii sbornik, 1977*, pp. 275–76, and ibid., 1978–1980.

7. A. I. Sizonenko, ed., *SSSR-Mexico 50 let* (Moscow, 1975), pp. 66–67.

8. *Vneshniaia torgovlia, 1918–1966* (Moscow, 1967).

9. Carl E. Solberg, *Oil and Nationalism in Argentina* (Stanford, Calif., 1979), pp. 136–37.

10. A. I. Sizonenko, ed., *SSSR-Argentina 30 let* (Moscow, 1976), p. 16.

11. Arturo Frondizi, *Petróleo y Política* (Buenos Aires, 1955), p. 250 ff.

12. A. I. Sizonenko, *Ocherki Istorii Sovetsko-Latinoamerikanskikh otnoshenii* (1924–1970 gg.), p. 117.

13. Aldo César Vacs, "Las relaciones equívocas: El nuevo carácter de las relaciones internacionales Argentino-Soviéticas en la década del 70" (unpublished manuscript, 1982).

Calculated from official figures. Mr. Vacs, a Tinker Fellow at the University of Pittsburgh, has been very helpful to me with regard to Argentine-Soviet relations.

14. *Washington Post,* 13 January 1981.

15. United Nations Economic and Social Council, Commission on Human Rights, 37th session, 2 February–13 March 1981, *Question of Human Rights of All Persons Subjected to Any Form of Detention or Imprisonment, in Particular: Question of Missing and Disappeared Persons,* p. 21.

16. Sizonenko, *Ocherki,* p. 132.

17. Ibid., p. 133.

18. A. I. Sizonenko and A. V. Bobrovnikov, *Sovetskii Soiuz i Latinskaia Amerika segodnia* (1978), p. 31.

19. Ibid., p. 34.

20. Sizonenko, *Ocherki,* p. 89.

21. Ibid., p. 144.

22. Paul E. Sigmund, *The Overthrow of Allende and the Politics of Chile, 1964–1976* (Pittsburgh, 1977), p. 194.

23. Sizonenko and Bobrovnikov, *Sovetskii Soiuz* (1976), p. 65.

24. Ibid., pp. 65–66.

25. Ibid., p. 70.

26. *Latin American Economic Report,* 3 March 1978, p. 71.

27. U.S. Central Intelligence Agency, *Communist Aid to Less Developed Countries of the Free World* (Washington, D.C., 1977), p. 26.

28. *Latin American Economic Report,* 3 November 1978, p. 71.

29. "Revolution in Grenada: An Interview with Maurice Bishop," *Black Scholar* (January/February 1980): 50–58.

30. Chris Searle, "Grenada's Revolution: An Interview with Bernard Coard," *Race and Class* (Autumn 1979): 178.

31. *Wall Street Journal,* 29 April 1981, p. 1.

32. *Political Affairs* (June 1981): 38; *New York Times,* 28 July 1982, p. A5.

33. See for example, Jiri Valenta and Herbert J. Ellison, eds., *Grenada and Soviet/Cuban Policy: Internal Crisis and U.S./OECS Intervention* Boulder Colo., 1986), documents 12 and 13, pp. 336, 348.

34. Ibid., documents 18 and 19, pp. 447–63.

• *Chapter III. The Stubborn Trade Deficit: Economic Relations*

1. For an authoritative general survey, see Gerard Fichet, "Tres decenios de relaciones entre América Latina y la Unión Soviética," *Comercio Exterior* 31 (February 1981): 160–69. See also the unpublished works on bilateral economic relations of Romuald G. Tomberg, E. Kossarev, and others from the UN Economic Commission for Latin America.

2. Annual supplements for 1980 and 1981 to *Vneshniaia torgovlia, SSSR statisticheskii sbornik, 1981.*

3. Aldo César Vacs, "Los socios discretos: El nuevo carácter de las relaciones internacionales entre Argentina y La Unión Soviética" (unpublished ms, 1982), p. 82.

4. *Strany SEV i Latinskaia Amerika: Problemy ekonomicheskogo sotrudnichestva* (Moscow, 1976), p. 24.

5. Although this study does not treat the relations of the countries of the Council for Mutual Economic Assistance (Comecon) other than the Soviet Union, a comparison of Soviet with other Comecon trade with Latin America is of interest. See Appendix 4.

6. The countries include Argentina (1971), Bolivia (1970), Brazil (1969), Colombia (1968), Costa Rica (1970), Ecuador (1969), El Salvador (1974), Grenada (1980), Guyana (1973), Jamaice (1978), Mexico (1973), Nicaragua (1980), Panama (1979), Peru (1969), and Uruguay (1969) (ibid., p. 29); also, *Vneshniaia torgovlia* nos. 6, 10 (1980).

7. U.S. Central Intelligence Agency, *Communist Aid to Less Developed Countries of the Free World, 1977* (Washington, D.C., 1978), pp. 6, 25.

8. U.S. Central Intelligence Agency, *Communist Aid Activities in Non-Communist Less Developed Countries 1978* (Washington, D.C., 1979), p. 30.

9. A. I. Sizonenko and A. V. Bobrovnikov, *Sovetskii Soiuz i Latinskaia Amerika segodnia* (1978), p. 31.

10. *Latin American Economic Report*, 17 November 1978, p. 1.

11. Sizonenko and Bobrovnikov, *Sovetskii Soiuz* (1978), p. 44.

• *Chapter IV. Many Roads to Power: Party Relations*

1. *Current Digest of the Soviet Press* 8 (7 March 1956): 12.

2. *XXV s'ezd kommunisticheskoi partii Sovetskogo Soiuza, 24 fevralia–5 marta 1976 goda, stenograficheskii otchet* (Moscow, 1976), p. 53.

3. *Dokumenty soveshchanii predstavitelei kommunisticheskikh i rabochikh partii, sostoiavshikhsia v Moskve v noiabre 1957 goda* (Moscow, 1957), pp. 18–20.

4. *Declaration of the Conference of Communist Parties of Latin America and the Caribbean* (Havana, 1975), p. 42.

5. *XXIV s'ezd kommunisticheskoi partii Sovetskogo Soiuza, stenograficheskii otchet* (Moscow, 1971), p. 45.

6. *XXV s'ezd kommunisticheskoi partii Sovetskogo Soiuza, stenograficheskii otchet* (Moscow, 1976), p. 56.

7. *Pravda*, 24 Feburary 1981, p. 2.

8. Stephen Clissold, ed., *Soviet Relations with Latin America, 1918–1968: A Documentary Survey* (London, 1970), p. 233.

9. Robert J. Alexander, *Communism in Latin America* (New Brunswick, N.J.: 1957), pp. 368–69.

10. Ibid., p. 111.

11. D. Bruce Jackson, *Castro, the Kremlin, and Communism in Latin America* (Baltimore, 1969), p. 49.

12. William E. Ratliff, *Castroism and Communism and Latin America, 1959–1976: The Varieties of Marxist-Leninist Experience* (Stanford, Calif., 1976), p. 196.

13. Jackson, *Castro*, p. 83.

14. Regis Debray, *¿Revolución en la Revolución?* (Havana, 1967), p. 119 ff.

15. *Istoriia mezhdunarodnogo rabochego i natsional'no-osvoboditel'nogo dvizheniia* vol. 4 (Moscow, 1978) p. 414.

16. Ratliff, *Castroism*, p. 116; Richard Gott, *Guerrilla Movements in Latin America* (Garden City, N.Y., 1971), p. 108.

17. *Istoria mezhdunarodnogo rabochego dvizheniia*, p. 415 ff.

18. Richard F. Staar, ed., *Yearbook of International Communist Affairs, 1979* (Stanford, Calif., 1979), p. 326 ff.

19. Gott, *Guerrilla Movements*, pp. 238, 256.

20. Boris Goldenberg, *Kommunismus in Lateinamerika* (Stuttgart, 1971), p. 462.

21. Gott, *Guerrilla Movements*, p. 381 ff.

22. Ibid., p. 429 ff.

23. Ratliff, *Castroism*, p. 140.

24. M. F. Kudachkin, ed., *Velikii oktiabr' i kommunisticheskii partii Latinskoi Ameriki* (Moscow, 1978), p. 175.

25. Ibid., p. 176.

26. Paul E. Sigmund, *The Overthrow of Allende and the Politics of Chile, 1964–1976* (Pittsburgh, 1977), p. 166. See also Luís Corvalán, "The Lessons of Chile," *World Marxist Review* (January 1978): 40.

27. *The World Marxist Review* carried a series of articles on the lessons of Chile in many different issues in 1977, and the concluding piece by Luís Corvalán appeared in January 1978. These articles have been collected and published in *1,000 dnei revoliutsii: Rukovoditeli KPCh ob urokakh sobytii v Chili* (Prague, 1978). There is probably a Spanish language edition.

28. Kudachkin, ed., *Velikii oktiabr'*, p. 181.

29. *World Marxist Review* (May 1977): 95.

30. Ibid., p. 94.

31. Ibid., p. 89 ff.

32. Kudachkin, ed., *Velikii oktiabr'*, p. 78.

33. Ibid., p. 80.

34. Ibid., p. 92.

35. Ibid., p. 94.

36. Ibid., p. 94.

37. Ibid., p. 97.

38. *Information Bulletin of the World Marxist Review*, no. 4 (1979): 39.

39. Kudachkin, ed., *Velikii oktiabr'*, p. 106; *New York Times*, 7 July 1982, p. 2.

40. Kudachkin, ed., *Velikii oktiabr'*, p. 107.

41. *World Marxist Review* (March 1978): 122.

42. Ibid., p. 123.

43. Quoted to author by Brazilian official in Moscow, April 1979.

44. Kudachkin, ed., *Velikii oktiabr'*, p. 108.

45. Mikoyan, "Ob osobonnostiakh," p. 36.

46. "Salvadorskii narod budet prodolzhat' bor'bu do pobedy," interview with Shafik Jorge Handal in *Latinskaia Amerika*, no. 6, (1981): 5–12.

47. "Armed Struggle Is the Only Road Left," *Information Bulletin* of the *World Marxist Review*, no. 14 (1980): 43–46.

• *Chapter V. Cuba: Political Asset, Economic Liability*

1. Cole Blasier, *The Chilean and Cuban Communist Parties: Instruments of Soviet Policy* (Ann Arbor, Mich., 1955).

2. L. Iu. Skeskin, *Istoriia kubinskoi respubliki* (Moscow, 1966), p. 333.

3. Andrés Suárez, *Cuba: Castroism and Communism, 1959–1966* (Cambridge, Mass., 1967), p. 26.

4. Sleskin, *Istoriia*, p. 337.

5. *Partinaia zhizn*, no. 20 (1958): 51.

6. Ibid., p. 53.

7. Fidel Castro and Janette Habel, *Proceso al sectarismo* (Buenos Aires, 1965), p. 49. Luis Aguilar drew my attention to this quote.

8. Cole Blasier, "The Elimination of U.S. Influence," in *Revolutionary Change in Cuba*, ed. Carmelo Mesa-Lago (Pittsburgh, 1971), pp. 63–73.

9. Sleskin, *Istoriia*, p. 381.

10. Suárez, *Cuba: Castroism*, pp. 92–94.

11. Carmelo Mesa-Lago, "The Economy and International Economic Relations," in *Cuba in the World*, ed. Cole Blasier and Carmelo Mesa-Lago (Pittsburgh, 1979), p. 170.

12. Jorge Domínguez, *Cuban Order and Revolution* (Cambridge, Mass., 1978), p. 211.

13. Blasier, "Elimination of U.S. Influence," p. 247.

14. Suárez, *Cuba: Castroism*, p. 93.

15. Ibid., p. 131.

16. Sleskin, *Istoriia*, p. 428.

17. Suárez, *Cuba: Castroism*, p. 162.

18. Ibid., pp. 162–63.

19. Cecil Johnson, *Communist China and Latin America, 1959–1967* (New York, 1970), p. 153.

20. Mesa-Lago, "The Economy," p. 184; U.S. Central Intelligence Agency, National Foreign Assessment Center, *The Cuban Economy: A Statistical Review* (Washington, D.C., 1981), pp. 25, 27.

21. *Granma Weekly Review*, 25 August 1968, p. 2 ff.

22. Carmelo Mesa-Lago, *Cuba in the 1970s* (Albuquerque, N.M., 1978), chapters 1–3; Edward Gonzalez, "Institutionalization, Political Elites, and Foreign Policies," in *Cuba in the World*, ed. Blasier and Mesa-Lago, pp. 3–36.

23. William M. LeoGrande, "Cuban-Soviet Relations and Cuban Policy in Africa," in *Cuba in Africa*, ed. Carmelo Mesa-Lago and June S. Belkin (Pittsburgh, 1982), p. 18 ff.

24. Ibid., p. 20.

25. Ibid., p. 26.

26. William M. LeoGrande, "Evolution of the Nonaligned Movement," *Problems of Communism* (January–February 1980): 50. K. F. Cviic, "The Nonaligned Summit in Havana," *The World Today* (October 1979): 389.

27. "Impact of Cuban-Soviet Ties in the Western Hemisphere, Spring 1980," Hearings before the Subcommittee on Inter-American Affairs of the Committee on Foreign Affairs, House of Representatives, 96th Congress, 2nd session, March 27, 1980, p. 28.

28. Ibid.

29. Ibid., p. 63.

30. *Granma Weekly Review*, 1 November 1982, p. 4.

31. The text was published by the *New York Times*, 24 February 1981, p. A8.

32. *Granma Weekly Review*, 1 November 1981, p. 4.

33. Much of the following discussion is based on Cole Blasier, "Comecon in Cuban Development," in *Cuba in the World*, ed. Blasier and Mesa-Lago, pp. 225–26. See also, ibid., chapter 2, Cole Blasier, "The Soviet Union in the Cuban-American Conflict."

34. V. G. Kolodkov, *"SSSR-Kuba: 20 let torgovo-ekonomicheskogo sotrudnichestva,"* *Latinskaia Amerika*, no. 5 (1980): 121. Carmelo Mesa-Lago, "The Economy: Caution, Frugality, and Resilient Ideology," in Jorge Domínguez, ed., *Cuba: Internal and International Affairs* (Beverly Hills, Calif., 1982), pp. 126–27.

35. Mesa-Lago, "The Economy: Caution," p. 127.

36. Comisión Económica para América Latina, "Notas para el estudio económico de América Latina" (Mexico, 1980), p. 14.

37. Kolodkov, "SSSR-Kuba," p. 131.

38. Mesa-Lago, "The Economy: Caution," pp. 150–51.

39. Lawrence H. Theriot, "Cuba Faces the Economic Realities of the 1980's," Joint Economic Committee, U.S. Congress, March 1982, p. 15.

40. *Granma Weekly Review*, 3 May 1970, p. 3.

41. For the forgoing, see International Institute for Strategic Studies, *The Military Balance 1981–1982* (London, 1981), p. 96.

42. *Granma Weekly Review*, 1 November 1981, p. 4.

• Chapter VI. *Central America: Coping with Radical Nationalists*

1. Neill Macaulay, *The Sandino Affair* (Chicago, 1967), p. 74.

2. Rodolfo Cerdas, *Sandino, el Apra y la Internacional Comunista* (San José, Costa Rica, 1979), pp. 70, 48.

3. Ibid., p. 69.

4. Ibid., pp. 77–80.

5. Ibid., pp. 76–77.

6. N. S. Leonov, *Nekotorye Problemy Politicheskoi Istorii Tsentral'noi Ameriki XX Stoletiia* (Moscow, 1972), p. 137, and chap. 4 passim; B. I. Koval', *Latinskaia Amerika: Revolutsiia i Sovremennost* (Moscow, 1981), p. 146.

7. Rodolfo Cerdas, *Farabundo Martí, la Internacional Comunista, y la Insurrección Salvadoreña de 1932* (San José, Costa Rica, 1982), pp. 56–67.

8. Ibid., pp. 65–67. The Communist International criticized the Salvadoran Party for acting irresponsibly, arguing that since the United States had the capability to crush the revolution, the insurrection had been an "adventure."

9. While the USSR provided political and moral support to the Guatemalan revolution of 1944 to 1954, Soviet leaders knew little about it, had little contact with it, and provided no known material assistance except possibly an arms shipment that arrived late. The Soviet leadership, of course, was otherwise engaged; the political struggle over the succession to Stalin was at a high pitch in 1954.

10. Jesús M. Blandón, *Entre Sandino y Fonseca* (Managua, Nicaragua, 1981), pp. 178–88.

11. Carlos Fonseca, *Un Nicaragüense en Moscú* (Managua, Nicaragua, 1981), p. 5; David Nolan, *The Ideology of the Sandinistas and the Nicaraguan Revolution* (Coral Gables, Fla., 1984), p. 144.

12. Blandón, *Entre Sandino*, p. 204.

13. Nolan, *Ideology of the Sandinistas*, p. 23.

14. Ibid.

15. "Beseda s Pervym sekretarem Tsk Nikaraguanskoi sotsialisticheskoi partii Luisom Sanchesom Sancho," *Latinskaia Amerika*, no. 4 (1979): 107–11.

16. Ibid.,p. 151.

17. Shafik Jorge Handal, "El poder, el carácter y la via de la revolución y la unidad de la izquierda," *Fundamentos y Perspectivas, Revista Teórica del Partido Comunista de El Salvador,"* No. 4 (January 1982): 27.

18. For a discussion of the role played by Cuba in the Nicaraguan insurrection, see *Confronting Revolution: Security Through Diplomacy in Central America,* ed. Morris Blachman, William Leogrande and Kenneth Sharpe. (New York, 1986), chap. 8.

19. As a senior Soviet official commented in June 1983: "We had no contacts with the Sandinistas when they started the revolution and it was not inspired by us; we are in favor of the Nicaraguan Revolution but we can only help here and there." Interview with the author, Moscow.

20. The Soviet Union does not have a large number of Central America researchers. Most work is in the Institute of Latin America and the Institute of the International Labor Movement in Moscow. In the two years before the Nicaraguan Revolution less than 10 percent of the 531 entries in the Soviet bibliography on Latin America (excluding Cuba) dealt with Central America. *Latinskaia Amerika v sovetskoi Pechati, Ukazatel Literatury 1977–1978 gg.* (Moscow, 1980).

21. S. A. Sergeev, "Latinskaia Amerika: God 1978," *Latinskaia Amerika*, no. 1 (1979): 24–25.

22. I. M. Bimov, "Sandinistskii front natsional'nogo osvobozhdeniia, reshaiushchaia sila v borbe," *Latinskaia Amerika*, no. 1 (1980): 47, n. 25.

23. K. L. Maidanik, "Kliuchevoi vopros—edinstvo," *Latinskaia Amerika*, no. 2 (1980): 41 ff; and S. A. Mikoyan, "Ob osobonnostiakh revoliustii v Nicaragua," *Latinskaia Amerika*, no. 3 (1980): 34 ff.

24. Mikoyan, "Ob osobonnostiakh," p. 37.

25. Mario Menéndez Rodríguez, *El Salvador: Una Auténtica guerra civil* (San José, Costa Rica, 1980), p. 29.

26. Roque Dalton, *Miguel Marmol* (San José, Costa Rica, 1972), p. 11.

27. Koval', *Latinskaia Amerika,* p. 157.

28. Shafik Jorge Handal, ''Consideraciones acerca del viraje del Partido hacia la lucha armada,'' *Fundamentos y Perspectivas, Revista Teórica del Partido Comunista de El Salvador,* no. 5 (April 1983): 23 and passim (the author wishes to thank Dr. Tommie Sue Montgomery for providing this material); Handal, ''El poder,'' pp. 37, 40, 41.

29. Handal, ''El poder,'' p. 42.

30. Robert G. Kaiser, ''White Paper on El Salvador Is Faulty,'' *Washington Post,* 9 June 1981.

31. Cuban leaders have admitted sending supplies to the Salvadoran guerrillas in 1980 and early 1981. It seems unlikely that the shipments could have been made over the opposition of the Soviet government, but in all likelihood the Cubans provided the aid on their own initiative.

32. Richard F. Starr, ed., *Yearbook of International Communist Affairs, 1984* (Stanford, 1984), p. 136. See also the yearbook for 1986, pp. 98–103.

33. Interview with Carlos González, general secretary of the Guatemalan Labor Party, *Latinskaia Amerika,* no. 2 (1984): 45.

34. *Information Bulletin* (Prague), February 1987', p. 29.

35. O. Ignat'ev, ''Pobeda naroda Nicaragua,'' *Kommunist,* no. 13 (September 1979): 101.

36. *Pravda,* 23 March 1984.

37. Morris Rothenberg, ''The Soviets and Central America,'' in *Central America: Anatomy of Conflict.* (New York: Pergamon Press, 1984), pp. 131–52.

38. Interview by the author with a staff member of the FSLN, Managua, April 1983.

39. *Vneshnaia Torgovlia SSSR v 1985 g.* (Moscow, 1986), p. 267.

40. Supplement to journal, *Vneshniaia Torgovlia,* no. 3, 1987.

41. ''The Jacobsen Report: Soviet Attitudes Towards Aid to and Contacts with Central American Revolutionaries,'' commissioned by the U.S. Department of State, 1 March, 1984 (mimeo), pp. 15–16; Clifford Krause and Robert S. Greenberger, ''Despite Fears of U.S., Soviet Aid to Nicaragua Appears to be Limited,'' *Wall Street Journal,* 3 April 1985.

42. See table 5 in Ruben Berrios and Marc Edelman, ''Los vinculos económicos de Nicaragua con los paises socialistas,'' *Commercio Exterior* (Mexico City) 35 (October 1985): 1005.

43. *Christian Science Monitor,* 23 December 1986.

44. A significant portion of aid from socialist countries to Nicaragua was given through technical cooperation, the full costs of which are probably not reflected in balance of payments figures. In early 1983, Soviet politicians and advisors in the country, including members of their families, numbered about 150. The East Germans had about 100 and the Bulgarians 50. All Eastern Europeans were estimated at something less than 500, although there were reportedly about 6,000 Cubans engaged in technical cooperation.

45. Jacobsen, *Soviet Attitudes,* pp. 15–16.

46. International Institute for Strategic Studies, *The Military Balance, 1983–1984* (London, 1983), p. 11.

47. Letter to Senator William Proxmire from Secretary of Defense Caspar Weinberger, 6 June 1984; Krause and Greenberger, "Despite Fears of U.S."

48. *Miami Herald,* 15 January, 1987.

49. Rothenberg, "The Soviets," pp. 140–41. The Soviets' reluctance to aid the Sandinistas in the face of U.S. threats reportedly caused some serious tensions between Moscow and Havana: Castro's refusal to attend the funeral of Chernenko was purportedly a protest against Chernenko's policy toward Nicaragua. It is worth noting that the Soviet Union has not offered Cuba any formal security agreement either, although the agreement ending the Cuban missile crisis of 1962 did involve a U.S. pledge not to attack Cuba in exchange for the withdrawal of Soviet missiles.

• Chapter VIII. Afterword on U.S. Policies

1. *The Hovering Giant: U.S. Responses to Revolutionary Change in Latin America* (Pittsburgh, 1976) describes U.S. responses in the Mexican, Bolivian, Guatemalan, and Cuban revolutions and to change-oriented regimes in the Dominican Republic, Peru, and Chile. That volume also examines actual or alleged Soviet involvement in each of these cases (see index, p. 314). Cole Blasier and Carmelo Mesa-Lago, eds., *Cuba in the World* (Pittsburgh, 1979) contains two chapers on Cuban-Soviet relations. See also various articles cited in these volumes as well as Victor Andrade, *My Missions for Revolutionary Bolivia* (Pittsburgh, 1976).

Index

About the Author

Cole Blasier is Professor of Political Science and Research Professor of Latin American Studies at the University of Pittsburgh. He was the founding director (1964–1974) of the Center for Latin American studies there, and a member of the founding committees of the Latin American Research Review and the Latin American Studies Association. He is now the chairman of the Advisory Board of the Handbook of Latin American Studies, the Library of Congress. He organized and is the U.S. representative of the US/USSR exchange in Latin American Studies.

In the 1950s Professor Blasier served as a foreign service officer in Belgrade, Bonn, Washington, and Moscow. In the 1960s he was secretary and executive assistant to the president at Colgate University, and visiting professor in Cali, Colombia, for the Rockefeller Foundation. He has lived and worked in three Eastern European and three Latin American countries, and is widely traveled elsewhere in these regions.

The Giant's Rival is a sequel to his earlier book, *The Hovering Giant: U.S. Responses to Revolutionary Change in Latin America*. With Carmelo Mesa-Lago, he edited *Cuba in the World,* and he is the author of numerous other works. These titles, together with several dozen others, constitute the Pitt Latin American Series which he organized and of which he is now general editor.

The Origins of the Peruvian Labor Movement, 1883–1919
Peter Blanchard

The Overthrow of Allende and the Politics of Chile, 1964–1976
Paul E. Sigmund

Panajachel: A Guatemalan Town in Thirty-Year Perspective
Robert E. Hinshaw

Peru and the International Monetary Fund
Thomas Scheetz

Primary Medical Care in Chile: Accessibility Under Military Rule
Joseph L. Scarpaci

Rebirth of the Paragayan Republic: The First Colorado Era, 1878–1904
Harris G. Warren

Social Security

The Politics of Social Security in Brazil
James M. Malloy

Social Security in Latin America: Pressure Groups, Stratification, and Inequality
Carmelo Mesa-Lago

Other Studies

Adventurers and Proletarians: The Story of Migrants in Latin America
Magnus Mörner, with the collaboration of Harold Sims

Authoritarianism and Corporatism in Latin America
James M. Malloy, Editor

Authoritarians and Democrats: Regime Transition in Latin America
James M. Malloy and Mitchell A. Seligson, Editors

Female and Male in Latin America: Essays
Ann Pescatello, Editor

Latin American Debt and the Adjustment Crisis
Rosemary Thorp and Laurence Whitehead, Editors

Public Policy in Latin America: A Comparative Survey
John W. Sloan

Selected Latin American One-Act Plays
Francesca Colecchia and Julio Matas, Editors and Translators

The State and Capital Accumulation in Latin America: Brazil, Chile, Mexico
Christian Anglade and Carlos Fortin, Editors

Transnational Corporations and the Latin American Automobile Industry
Rhys Jenkins